Children, Teachers and Learning Series
Series Editor: Cedric Cullingford

Children's Literature and its Effects

Titles in the *Children, Teachers and Learning* series

J. Anghilieri *Children's Mathematical Thinking in the Primary Years*

M. Bonnett *Children's Thinking*

T. Cairney *Pathways to Literacy*

C. Cullingford *Children and Society*

C. Cullingford *The Nature of Learning*

K. Gentle *Teaching Painting in the Primary School*

J. Glover and S. Ward *Teaching Music in the Primary School*

L. Haggarty *New Ideas for Teacher Education*

T. Jarvis *Children and Primary Science*

R. Johnsey *Exploring Primary Design and Technology*

R. Jones *The Child–School Interface*

A. Loveless *The Role of I.T.*

B. Mayall *Negotiating Health*

T. Maynard *An Introduction to Primary Mentoring*

L. Smart *Using I.T. in Primary School History*

P. Wiegand *Children and Primary Geography*

L. Winkley *Emotional Problems in Children and Young People*

Children's Literature and its Effects

The Formative Years

Cedric Cullingford

CASSELL

London and Washington

Cassell
Wellington House
125 Strand
London WC2R 0BB

PO Box 605
Herndon
Virginia 20172

First published 1998

British Library Cataloguing in Publication Data
A catalogue record for this book is available from the British Library.
ISBN 0 304 70092 4 (hardback)
0 304 70093 2 (paperback)

Library of Congress Cataloging-in-Publication Data
Cullingford, Cedric.
Children's Literature and its Effects: the formative years/Cedric Cullingford.
p. cm. – (Children, teachers, and learning)
Includes bibliographical references and index.
ISBN 0–304–70092–4. – ISBN 0–304–70093–2 (pbk.)
1. Children–United States–Books and reading. 2. Children's stories, English–History and criticism. 3. Popular literature–United States–History and criticism. I. Title. II. Series.
Z1037.A1C87 1997
028.5'5–dc21 97–11790
CIP

Typeset by York House Typographic Ltd, London
Printed and bound in Great Britain by Biddles Ltd, Guildford and King's Lynn

Contents

Foreword

Children's Literature and its Effects offers an intriguing insight into the worlds of children's literature. It is distinctive, and consequently richly repays reading for two significant reasons.

First, it focuses on the pleasures children get from their reading. Others have discussed popular children's literature and noted its limitations, both stylistic and referential; scholars have also undertaken ethnographic studies of young readers, often concluding that the reading of popular fiction is a conservative force in their lives. It is much rarer to find a work which examines in such detail the textual delights and gratifications on offer to young readers. Parents and teachers continue to be concerned (whether they have genuine grounds for those concerns is another matter) about children's perceived defection from reading, about the preponderance of other distractions, entertainments and opportunities. A book which concentrates our attentions, as this book does, on the delights and satisfactions available to children through reading has to offer a different perspective on these pressing questions. The focus elsewhere is so often on reluctant readers – on those who don't rather than those who do. By concentrating here on what it is that reading can offer children we come closer to seeing why some read compulsively. The focus is literary and textual rather than sociological, and attempts to understand the pleasures of reading in terms of the texts rather than in terms of the readers' lives and social experiences. Cullingford recognizes the importance of nurturing these early reading pleasures and offers intelligent advice on encouraging young readers to go further and tackle more challenging texts, without denigrating their current habits or expecting them to forgo their satisfaction in formula fiction. In this respect the work is practical as well as distinctive.

Secondly it is rare to find a survey of children's fiction with such breadth, covering such a range of genres and historical periods. Its compass ranges from the early 1900s to the current day; includes adventure stories, comics, school-fiction, romances and horror; touches on the almost forgotten and the perpetually popular; discusses work aimed at the under 10s through to the mid-teens;

books read primarily by boys; by girls, and those which appeal to both genders.

Some fascinating material emerges from this wide-ranging study. Of course there are huge differences between these texts, differences which reflect the different historical, cultural and social contexts in which they were written and read. For example, the contrast the book offers us between the delight taken in food by the Blyton children, the pleasurable disgust it affords in Roald Dahl's work and the straightforward disgust it engenders in the inhabitants of teen romances is most revealing. Nevertheless, the commonalities across these texts are at least as interesting as the differences. This book shows that a desire for security, the management of fear, comedic resolution, the need to categorize the world and its inhabitants, the narrative control of adults, to name but a few factors, seem to persist within much popular children's fiction.

The final point I want to make is that a book like this should be read for enjoyment. It is a book written by an enthusiast. The topic offers maximum scope for presenting the obscure and fascinating drawn from a long forgotten book, for humour and for reliving the pleasures of one's own childhood reading. The author makes the most of these opportunities and immerses us so well in the world of popular children's literature that we are able to get inside our childish minds again and re-experience some of those early reading pleasures.

Christine Jarvis
April 1997

Preface and Acknowledgements

This is a book about what children like to read. It is not about what they ought to read. Children's response to their favourite authors and the reasons for their success gives us an insight into the way in which the two worlds come together. We see why children prefer certain types of book and what this says about their lives.

This is a book about children's reading habits but it has an equal significance in the light of adult tastes. Popular literature is a particular genre with clear characteristics. There are substantial similarities in children's response to reading during their formative years and their subsequent habits.

There have been a number of books about classic children's literature and about the semiotics of the content, usually in terms either of psychoanalysis or stereotyping. There has been no such attention paid to children's own responses and thoughts. Whilst there is a literature, especially during the last few years, about the reader and his or her response, rather than the text, such analysis has been directed at sophisticated readers like the authors themselves. Here we gain an insight into the everyday reading habits of the substantial majority and the reason for them.

It is always easy to find satirical material in popular literature and whilst tempting to dwell on the rich absurdities, this needs to be as firmly avoided as taking the contents of the books too seriously. What we are after is an understanding of why readers are drawn to certain books and how certain authors recognize this need and in their turn respond to it. This does not mean that there ought to be an absence of humour. Many of the literary gestures are ludicrous and there is plenty of material quoted here that is wonderfully absurd. But it also reveals something serious about the children's response. Rather than quote from children – apart from the chapter on comics – attention is paid to the texts as they are far more accessible, and a way of communicating the reasons for children's tastes.

In surveys of children's favourite authors like those carried out most recently by the Children's Literature Research Centre, Enid Blyton and Roald Dahl dominate. There are clear reasons for this, if we think about their approach and their content and the intuitive reflection of the young person's styles of thought, experiences and needs. Whilst it is tempting for many to dismiss popular literature as purely ephemeral and vulgar, there is more to it than this. Not everyone can create the sustained popularity of Enid Blyton. There are particular factors about her work which explain the inner lives of children then and now. Popular literature, as in best seller lists, is a fact of life and adds another dimension to the understanding of the human condition. Whilst at one level the best sellers might seem like pure titillation, pandering to the mass market, they in their turn reveal more than one suspects about the inner lives of those who choose to read them.

Whilst Enid Blyton has for many years enjoyed a unique place in popular children's fiction she has been vilified by those who would much prefer children to read classics, both old and new. And yet children continue to read her, and to read Dahl. This book tries to explain why. It also explores other favourite authors, like Judy Blume, R. L. Stine and Stephen King. Whilst each has his or her own approach they also have a lot in common.

This is, then, a book about readers, explaining them through what they read. There is so much material that could have been used that there have been many choices to be made. What has been chosen is representative of a great deal more, but more could have meant mere deductive repetition. The examples given are analysed not for their own sakes but for what they reveal about children, and about children as representatives of the human experience.

There have been a number of librarians in the past who have tried to ban some of the books described here. It is a position I fully understand. I too would prefer children to enjoy my own favourite authors and come to appreciate my own favourite books. But banning certain books has no effect. They continue to be as popular as ever. Nor does the fact that they are read prevent the possibility of children developing into truly mature readers and exploring great literature in all its intellectual and emotional strength. The connection between the two 'levels' is the fact that both types of literature are sought out because of the same inner needs. The potential of developing sophistication, insight and compassion is always there.

Over the years I have had help and support from many librarians who care about what children read. Most recently I have appreciated those in Kirklees who keep reiterating their commitment to the reading public, to people rather than profit. I have also learned a great deal from those who not only care about children's reading but have made the study of children's literature a respectably intellectual attention, like Marion Brown, Jan Mark and Trevor Harvey. But most of all I have appreciated the insights provided by the dedicatees of the book, Emma and Isabel.

For Emma and Isabel

1
A Secret World? Children's Response to Literature

We all imagine ourselves as 'perfect' readers, almost as perfect as reviewers, responsive, intelligent and alert. Anyone who writes seriously would like their readers to be like this, with the addition of immediate sympathy and understanding. So much trouble has gone into creating the text that says exactly what it should that the thought of misinterpretation is undermining. The perfect reader implies the perfect text.

But is the act of reading actually like that? The more that the responses of readers are studied the more complicated they become. Readers bring all their individual idiosyncrasies to bear. They do not *become* the text, but connect the text in their own ways to their own interpretations. Even the most impressive of texts that deserve the closest and most intense of studies, like *King Lear*, evoke any number of individual interpretations and personal responses, according to both levels of understanding and experience. When we see the way in which critics interpret plays such as *Coriolanus*, we have to acknowledge that the individual response of the reader is embedded in the cultural ambience of the time. Some texts transcend the time in which they are written, but they are still subject to the temporality of the circumstances in which they are read: is Coriolanus, the proud hero, a tragic figure brought down by the mindless mob, or is he someone who, in his sheer pride, is responsible for his own failure? Not only the time in which the reader lives but the political outlook he holds will influence the interpretation.

If the critic or the reviewer pays professional attention to the text and arrives at such individual interpretations, what of reading at a quite different level? We are dealing here with imperfect readers and imperfect texts. The levels and styles of response are quite different. There are a number of texts which deal with the complex ways in which the readers operate, but they are usually with the supposed reader who interacts with the writer of the text, constantly alert, detailed and erudite. What about the more common act of reading? There are two major differences between the material we are dealing with here and that which has been previously the subject of attention. They are opposite sides of the equation. Here we are concerned with popular literature, which does not 'abide our question'! No one, the authors apart, would pretend that the literature studied here has anything to offer that would elevate the mind of the reader, or would deserve critical literary scrutiny. Popular literature is there to entertain, to seek out what the audience would like. It is a mass medium offering quick gratification by responding to the tastes of the audience of the time. It therefore reflects rather than changes the interests of the reader.

There is always a tension between those attempts by the individual artist to explain him or herself, to retain the integrity or the purity of what is to be communicated, and the endeavour to create a mass appeal. Those who remain too arcane, or too self enclosed, or even self-indulgent have no audience. Those who seek solely to please the audience have nothing original to say. The idea that the great work of art will always find an audience is the result of wishful thinking or a romantic dream which even a quick history of publishing would dispel.[1] The reception of any literature is a matter of chance. However intensely thought out or felt, the great work will not convey its message until, by fortunate circumstances, it finds an audience willing to listen.

Popular literature, however, is based on the assumption that the audience is understood. Whilst it takes certain kinds of people to produce it, and whilst many try and fail, the appeal rests on having designs on the response of the reader. Given the recognition of what the readers seek, the idea is to gratify them as simply and unselfconsciously as possible. This suggests that there is nothing sacrosanct about the text. If it succeeds in its own terms this is enough. Its own terms are only that it fulfils a certain formula of popularity and that by its very lack of uniqueness meets the criteria of expectation.

This suggests that popular novels reflect something about the nature of the audience, that they represent the author or the time. To a great extent they do. But we must not target the individual reader. In the case of learned and demanding texts the reader dwells on the true interpretation to discover the essential truths. But light novels never gain such attention. They would not stand up to it. Instead, the reader seeks out only what he or she wants; to be entertained rather than taught, to be eased into the obvious rather than cajoled into something new. The whole style of reading is different. Lapses of concentration do not matter. There can be no misinterpretations. All must be obvious enough for the sensation of reading to be at once rewarding and ephemeral, to pass the time of day and to be forgotten.

The readers of popular fiction are by their very nature the most 'imperfect' of readers, if the perfect reader is interpreted as someone who pays close attention and who seeks to be intellectually stimulated, who respects what the author is attempting to convey and who consciously reflects on its meaning. The levels of meaning or interpretation are quite different. Not only are the texts at a different level, but the act of reading them even more so. Children approach books with both advantages and disadvantages. They have a strong belief in story. At the same time they are conscious of the art of reading, of the skills employed. They become easily engaged in the idea of the completeness of the word of fiction and yet read easily and very fast. They know what they seek and what they look for in a text but also become easily bored.

There are a number of what appear to be contradictions in the art of reading. The recognition of the familiar is balanced by the seeking out of the startling or different. The sudden shocks or excitements are embedded in the everyday. Reading is a lonely pleasure based on observation of the social world. The very ease of gratification leads to boredom, but anything too demanding is rejected for fear of boredom. What young readers learn is the dichotomy between reading because they want to and reading because they ought to. Children are voracious readers but they read what is essentially the same text again and again and again. Does the text then reflect their taste or help to form it?

There are two areas of concern and each interacts with the other. The first is the audience, the children who are the readers and who display their tastes so clearly. The second is the texts they choose and which seek to meet their tastes. What we seek to explore is the way that children become active readers and what makes them react so positively to certain authors. The exploration of this, however, is embodied in the examples of the texts themselves; what makes them popular and what is the effect? Books are recognized as a formative influence but we cannot pretend that every book or every experience of reading, including magazines and newspapers, makes an indelible impression. What they do is to reflect and extend the collective tastes of children by their accumulating impact. There is an iterative process between the anticipation of the reader's taste and its gratification. But books do not merely reflect the taste and embody it; they reinforce it.

In the complex interaction between the reader and the text proper recognition needs to be given to both, rather than to one or the other. At different times, in the many books devoted to literature, there have been tendencies to concentrate on the sacrosanct nature of the text, or the recreation of the work of art inside the reader's head, as if the text no longer mattered. The concentration in our time of relative values is on the latter, but it was not long ago that the idea of a canon of literature, an accepted corpus, was the basis on which English was studied. The perfect reader would share in the recognition of the great tradition and acknowledge the emotional and intellectual mastery of the author. Robert Graves tells an anecdote of his experience at Oxford when his tutor says to him, 'It seems, Mr Graves, that you are eccentric. Indeed it seems you prefer some books to others'.[2]

It is easy to see why there should be such a respect for certain texts. One has only to mention Shakespeare to demonstrate it. But this mention itself draws attention to the importance of interpretation. Shakespeare's greatness lies in the multi-dimensional nature of his work. There will never be an ultimate or final reading of it, even if the moral and psychological messages he gives are clear. What is being said is both profound and complex. This does not mean that it is obscure, but that it is never obvious. But here we are dealing with readers' responses to quite different levels of text where even the designs on the reader are obvious, as well as the devices used to fulfil them. This means that they are far easier to understand and analyse and that far less respect needs to be paid to them. But does it also mean that one can also understand the exact nature of the reader's response?

Before we explore the ways in which children read their favourite authors we should remind ourselves of an already large and constantly growing literature on the complex nature of the interaction between the book and the reader, with all the manifestations of ideology and culture, psychological associations and chance. The previously dominant view of literature as a reality expressed by an unusually perceptive author, to be accepted by the attentive and alert reader as 'true', when the reader's duty was to try to gain access to the meaning, has been superseded by a sense of the text as a cultural or ideological artefact.[3] The irony of this is that instead of reading literature as something to be interpreted and learned from, books have been analysed for their structure or their style as if they actually embodied something significant in themselves – beyond even the intention of the author but in Bourdieu's sense expressing the dominant culture.[4] This has meant that literature has been studied for its latent messages, for its mythical properties and for its collective subliminal messages as well as for its imposition of ideologies.[5]

Let us take some examples. Lévi-Strauss suggests that myths live on in men, unknown to them, and find their expression in language, passing on collective meanings. When folk tales are analysed – *Little Red Riding Hood* is one of the favourites – it is suggested that they are being used, by reinterpretation, to mould readers into the contemporary social messages.[6] But these messages are supposed to work at a psychological level. For Zipes, the changes made over time to *Little Red Riding Hood*, by Perrault and the Grimm brothers, suggest the intention to transform an ancient and disturbing tale into one fit for civilizing children into more stringent codes of behaviour.[7] He suggests that:

> educated writers purposely appropriated the oral folk tale and converted it into a type of literary discourse about morals, values and manners so that children would become civilized according to the social code of the time.[8]

It could be argued that this tradition of teaching children about standards of behaviour underlay the work of writers like Strang and Westerman, but whilst that is a much stated moral intention, it is not in fact what drives the construction of the book. For even modern popular books are a kind of myth-making, giving expression unselfconsciously to a shared assumption about the world. We can see very clear ideologies in the books – but they are an expression of a collective will rather than the author's wish to do good.

There are, after all, some values which are shared by all. The sense of the happy ending; the closure that comes about with the victory of the hero – the good – over the many dark forces which he (or she) confronts leads to an underlying structure which holds all popular writing together. All fairy tales, and all books since, are battles between good and evil, sometimes simple and sometimes more complex, but all driven by the need for one to prevail ultimately over the other.[9] This implies of course that the hero is the reader, not necessarily good but definitely the winner. The acceptance of the hero as in some unspecified way morally superior is a necessary suspension of disbelief. The hero wins. It does not mean that the actions that he (or she) carries out are in their nature any more upright or fair than that of the enemy, especially when analysed in any detail. The collective assumption is that we accept through some obvious signal that there *is* a hero and the point of the book is that the reader knows that all will be well in the end.

It is important to draw a distinction between the recognition of a hero and identification. It was once common to suggest that children learned through simple imitation, modelling their behaviour on others. The role model and therefore the behaviour of the hero was crucial. Far more significant than the moral outlook of the hero is the acceptance of the role. The hero can be neutral but prevails. Children do not copy the main characters but control their own version of the hero in their imagination and give this a personal meaning.[10] The hero never has too much of a personality to become someone distinct, and therefore other. He or she will have typical characteristics, but it is the tone and the point of view which is attractive, the sense of the 'I' who looks out on other people. In those adventure books written before the Second World War, where the heroes stand for national values, they see the most horrific sights but are utterly unaffected. More recently the heroes of stories see little that is frightening but are always affected. There are different versions of the 'I' of a story, but they are essentially the means to the plot, the bringing in of the personal point of view of the reader, with ease and without disturbance.

The text therefore provides an opportunity for self-indulgence rather than self-exploration, for confirmation rather than discovery. Nevertheless, the attraction of the folk tale is still supposed to be at a less neutral level. If for some, like Zipes, tales like *Little Red Riding Hood* are explorations in changing ideologies, for others they are redolent of deep psychoanalytical meaning. The wolf becomes the male sexually rampant, a representative of a father's sexuality or symbolic of instructive nature. The woodcutter becomes the super ego of the father, and symbolizes different aspects of the same person, or is part of an Oedipal myth.[11] One would never have thought that a simple tale had so much in it.

But has it? Do texts really carry with them so much symbolic weight, of the collective subconscious or of the ideologically dominant? About fairy tale and myth there is perhaps no point in speculating, but whatever forms the text there are still readers undergoing them, lightly, personally and repeatedly. Fairy tales might carry such meanings, or, more pertinently, be used to display them, but in their structure and their pace and familiarity they are not essentially unlike the popular fiction that children read.[12] The one might be told and retold, the other read and re-read. But there is the same expectation. The story told is each time slightly different. The series of formula books like *Baby-Sitters Club* is each time slightly different. But the pleasures looked forward to, and the experiences anticipated, are liked because they are expected and familiar.

This puts the more emphasis on the reader. Whilst there are subconscious influences at play the level of gratification and the pleasure sought are more obvious. Although there are many books that demonstrate the difference between the reverence for the author's meaning and the book as an artefact of a particular ideology, the concentration of interest has turned towards the reader as an interpreter. This is not a new point of view. Vico in 1725 talks about the idea of what later was dubbed reflexivity – 'that which man recognizes as true is what he himself made'.[13] If the text was once taken as sacrosanct, full of meaning to be interpreted by the person who paid the closest and most reverential attention, it has now been replaced by the ideal of the sacrosanct reader bringing with him or her a bundle of personal requirements, at a psychological or social level.

There are two difficulties with this vision of the perfect reader, both at contradictory levels. One is that the reader is always alert, interpreting, connecting, aware and responsive in an individual way. The other is that the reader is driven by subconscious needs, devouring the text for the revelations of hidden needs. Both points of view are forged on an anvil of intensity, the seeking of meaning, the answering of needs. The problem is that most readers do not approach books in this way.

Theories of reading concentrate for the most part on the idea of a perfect adult reader, like the author himself. This means that the attention being paid to the act of reading is paramount. Since I. A. Richards' first explored the response of his students to literary texts there have been many accounts of the imperfections of response and the misinterpretations of text.[14] Influenced partly by Lévi-Strauss and Barthes, there is a growing awareness of the plurality of readings that a text will provide.[15] Every text has more than one meaning, although I would argue that multiple meanings belong, at one level at least, to more complex texts. It should be recognized that each reader brings his or her own prior experience and individuality to the reading, and will take unique associations from it, but Barthes actually argues that whilst there are individual responses these are dictated to some extent by the text. Barthes draws attention to five different 'codes' of interpretation, including suspense and action. He suggests that readers seek a kind of justification of their own sense of logic in human behaviour, and want the text to comply with their own experience. The match, or mismatch, between the text and the reader is crucial.

But all this still suggests that the reader, far from being a passive recipient of meaning, is an active interpreter of it, bringing a powerful array of expectations to bear. Is this how we can describe the gratification of pleasure? There is perhaps a third style of reading which does not take the text that seriously and certainly does not bring any powerful concentration to bear. The many descriptions of the reader talk of the 'creative relation between reader and work'[16] as if the readers only made sense of the text by transforming it according to their own character. This must be true up to a point, but discussion of creative tension implies a deep level of involvement, again suggesting psychological impacts. Interpretations of the act of reading, therefore, concentrate either on psychological or intellectual needs, but always on needs which go deep.

The suggestion that reading can be interpreted at a psychoanalytical level has often been taken up. Subconscious fantasy is supposed to be transformed into conscious meaning through the text, seeing the latter as a type of relief from the hidden activities of life.[17] Or the book appeals to the super-ego, the ego and the id, by dealing with the actuality of conflict.[18] Books, even popular ones, are seen in terms of deep levels of engagement, in the struggle to have inner conflicts resolved or mollified. This all depends on the idea of reading as a very special activity, on the assumption of a profound and individual experience. For some, every text is an 'event'.[19] In this event what the reader brings is much more significant that the textual meanings:

> The asymmetry between text and reader stimulates a constitute activity on the part of the reader; this is given a specific structure by the blanks and the negatives arising out of the text, and this structure controls the process of interaction.[20]

The suggestion is so far from the notion of the sanctity of the text that it is even the 'blanks' and the 'negatives' that are the most important. The asymmetry puts the reader with the commanding, controlling and defining position, restructuring what is read and almost reconstructing the text. The irony is that such a 'deconstruction' of the text only draws the more attention to the text itself.[21] There is so much analysis of the response to the text it is as if the text had no 'effect' in itself.[22] But the text remains, giving its own insight into the reader and the act of reading. It is not merely a blank page. Out of this fact derives the fascination with the reader.

There are many different styles of reading and this is crucial if we are to understand children's approach to books. Not only do they bring with them their idiosyncratic expectations but a whole array of moods. Books pass time. They fill up moments that remain forgettable. They gratify simple pleasures. They do not constitute constant revisions of the interpretation of life. Much of what children read is repetitive and familiar. And yet the assumption underlying the analysis of the reader is that each reading is a powerful and mighty event; thus there are clear reasons for the act of reading beyond the text itself.

The essential point about the importance of the reader – where after all would a book be without one? – is by now well understood. Books constitute an interpretation of the world that people need. They offer a structure and meaning. This would have no purpose did it not serve to help the individual come to terms with circumstances, either in the early years as a person trying to make sense of the complexity of experience, or later on in understanding it. The making sense in the formative years of childhood is the recognition of structures, of formulas and certainties, of categorizations and answers. These structures are a kind of ritual, which are not just about the real world which books represent but part of the rhythm of books themselves. Books are looked *into*, not seen through. Whilst the favourite books for young children are ostensibly versions of what they do every day, they give that rhythm of normal life a point, and an outline. Young children expect the same words in the same order when they are told a favourite story. They anticipate the significance of the story in itself, including not only the sense of an ending, but the certainty and inevitability of the order in which events happen. In the chaotic and traumatic series of experiences which constitute childhood, stories give a sense of structure and wholeness.

To suggest that the reader is all is to leave out the act and experience of reading itself. It is a reaction to the dominance of the text, but it is not altogether a replacement of it. The whole point of semiology is to suggest that even if the text is not as significant as the reader, it carries with it ideological and cultural meanings beyond itself, which the reader has to find his or her way through. Literature is seen as an ideology which in turn is part of the 'condition of experience of our world'.[23] For some the ideology of the text is an interpretation of the world which is embedded in contradiction and conflict. Literature is seen as echoing the entry into the contradictions of our present circumstances – not of life, but of culture.[24] Thus a divided society, full of conflict, is presented not just in terms of a resolution of the contradictions – or even the sense of moulding the reader into accepting them – but as the essential reconciliation of needs. For some semioticians all books (and all readers) reflect the structural actualities of society into which children come into conflict and which books seek to, or inadvertently, resolve. These are seen as temporary social conflicts arising from a capitalistic system, rather than the eternal realities of the human condition. Books, after all, in contrast to the age old myths and stories, are recent.[25]

The interest in the relationship between the reader and the text is often expressed in terms of the shared ideology, as if there had to be a coming together of beliefs. Clearly this is true in a number of ways. As Eco points out, any reader must accept the meaning of the words on the page before anything happens.[26] There is a sharing of conventions like the opening 'Once upon a time', implying not only the fact that a story will be told but that it is both present, immediate and now, and repeatable, eternal. The tone as well as the structure needs to be shared between the writer and the reader. The question is how deep this sharing goes. In the most profound of books the sharing is intense and individual. Each reader takes something different from it. In popular literature, however, there is a more common understanding. The ideologies which are shared are not those of profound belief as much as those of gratifications, the realization of what is wanted, the response by the writer to an impulse or desired interpretation of the reader. Readers draw on those common assumptions they share with the author, making inferences on the basis of them and reading on to find out if they are correct or not.[27] Of course there is a meeting of minds, but at what level?

Eco suggests that there are ideological factors. He suggests that readers can assume the ideology of the text and imbibe it as they wish, or they can introduce their own ideology into the text and create their own meanings and understandings, or they can question the text and actually reject it. Both the perfect and imperfect reader create a balance between the text and themselves. Those who 'reject' the text simply cease to read. But the distinction between the acceptance of, and belief in, the text, and the 'aberrant' reading of it, the introduction of personal meaning far removed from the author's intention is, in fact, a very fine one. Both belong together. All texts are, in Eco's sense, 'open'; that is, for interpretation. They are also 'closed', trying to fix a distinct meaning. What excites critics is the tension between the two.

Children are often voracious readers. They read so much and so fast that one text must run into another. One cannot image each experience of reading as a unique event, although it might be, given the associative power of the individual mind. In popular literature, repetitive and familiar by nature, it is the accumulation of experiences that are more important than the individual gratification. In the short term the startling, the specific and the unusual make a strong impression. But this impression is short-lived. In the long term it is the general themes, the familiar and the general that we recall.[28] What children seem to seek from story is the generic rather than the episodic, the familiarity of theme and tone, rather than the challenge to their perceptions. They like to have their expectations and their anticipations met.

Discussions of semiotics and structuralism point out at some length the complexities of a text and the variabilities of a reader's response. It is difficult, if not impossible, to give a summary of all the erudition. But for the main part the books are about the high ground of reading, the intellectual convolutions that the person gifted enough to write about the art of reading must undergo in order to explain himself. The problem is that there are many different types of styles of reading. The usual readers seek an expected and familiar work which reflects their own experience. Books are read fast, the pages turning over faster at some passages than others and the moment when the book is 'snapped shut', the ending, is positively looked for rather than dreaded.[29] The irony is that those texts which most easily enclose the reader in a familiar and all embracing world, the world of assumption, are just those which demand the least attention. The texts which really want to convey a complete picture of actuality distance themselves from interpretation by their very challenge. One can assert that there is nothing written that gives as much as the plays of Shakespeare – but how many people read him?

We are dealing here with exploring the minds of the 'common readers' at a time when they read more books than they ever will again. Reading is an essential part of childhood. Reading provides a coherent and recognizable depiction of the real world, reminding children of the shared human experience and of the fact that no one lives in isolation. The patterns of daily life are explored, even if the protagonists are animals or the turn of events fabulous. Stories, through the structure of the text, remind and comfort. They suggest that there is a familiar world of rhythm and meaning, of understood perception and shared understandings. At the same time that children are learning about the importance of story they are learning the skills of decoding the text. This is part of the problem. Young children easily associate reading with failure, and forget the pleasures of the book in the problems of the interpretation of phoneme and grapheme.

The time when stories are of most significance in the lives of children coincides with the time when they are struggling with the mechanics of reading. For some this is a problem easily overcome. For many it remains a blight on their reading habits. Reading is associated with difficulty, with doing what the teacher wants rather than with the pleasure of story. In all the discussions about fairy tales and the psychological impact they have there lies an essential truth. Young children need stories to outline, structure and clarify their own perceptions of the world. To receive this sense of story they need reading adults, people who will share with them, by telling or by reading the familiar outlines of meaning that enable children to cope with the challenges of the world. At the same time they are detecting how it is that the adults keep placing the words in the same order in the same way. For some children the connection between being read to and reading is apparent and the transition easy. For others, the act of reading is not associated with pleasure but with failure.

The differences in taste between those who yearn for literature which is demanding and emotionally exciting, and those who seek the least challenging of gratifications, begin very early. The differences are connected in many ways with the disjunction between the excitement that the art of reading can generate and the difficulty that the act of reading can cause. Reading is a barrier or a way through. For those few who take to the higher ground – this is often associated with 'cleverness' as if there were an innate gift involved – there are many who seek comfort in the familiar. Given the difficulties put in the way and the lack of encouragement, this is no surprise. There are very close connections between the familiarity with story and the belief in reading, between the earliest influences and experiences and the subsequent personal development.

There are many reasons why children and adults seek out the familiar pleasures of popular and undemanding texts rather than the most complex experiences of the books which ask for a far deeper intellectual and emotional response. Given early experiences combined with the difficulties of interpreting the letters into sound it is no surprise that the usual experience of reading should be a longing for the experience of ease. This type of reading is connected to, but quite different from, the reading that requires the exploration and interpretation of a text, and the accumulation of new fields of knowledge. Children are voracious readers, once they know how to do it easily, but also mostly superficial readers which, often, they will remain. Theories of reading only apply to them obliquely, but then some would argue that arcane theories of reading and deconstruction do not apply to anybody. Children need their habitual pleasures in the texts they read. They know what they are looking for. Their discrimination is between the books that give them exactly what they expect and those which are unreliable. Unreliability, in the sense of new and disconcerting challenges, is exactly what 'serious' literature seeks. But the habitual sense of everyday reading is another matter.

We have, therefore, children reading in their own way, and books provided to reflect both their styles and tastes in reading. It gives insight into both the needs of children and their views of the world in which they find themselves; the connection between what they want and what is provided for them. There is, in fact, possibly a closer analogy between the reader and the text than there would be with older people. The voracity and the certainty of taste is a clear insight both into the mind of the individual and the cultural habit of the time.

There is a clear distinction to be made between the careful and erudite reading of the page of text, interpreting, responding and connecting, and skim reading, the speedy scanning of the text for familiar signs and for immediate excitements. Most people pace their reading according to the text. For some this means the frustration of not being able to understand it, a frustration born not just of distrust of the text, but distrust of self. If I cannot easily understand it, is it my fault or the author's? The *art* of reading lies in knowing how to vary the pace. Some books demand and deserve careful scrutiny. Others clearly display their ephemeral pleasures as lightly given and lightly taken. The way children approach books varies between the two, since their experience is on the one hand that of being given books which cause difficulties in the deciphering of text and on the other that of the pleasures of passing the time. For most children reading is divided between the confrontation with the impossible and the ease of the familiar.

In discussing aspects of semiotics and response the emphasis is invariably on the complexities of the interchange, and how difficult it is to arrive at a true interpretation. Even ostensibly simple stories, like fairy tales, are seen to carry deep cultural and psychological messages. Such interpretations suggest that the act of reading is a deep intellectual and emotional experience. But when we observe the ways in which children read books, or comics or magazines, we have to accept that the pleasures of books are not at a profound level. There are certain comforts to be had from books, but they also pass the time, something to do when there is nothing better to do. There are, in the psychology of response, a number of different levels, not only to do with the text itself but with the approach of the reader.

At one level the text is a mystery to be unravelled, or a new territory to be entered. For young readers the shadow of the first difficulties with the decipherment of the letters can remain with them for a long time. There is always a potential as well as an actual barrier to the act of reading. There is the remaining antipathy to the struggles of reading, even if the fear is transferred from the mechanical aspects of reading to the intellectual demands the text makes. For many people the experience of reading includes bewilderment with the text, the struggle to make sense of it, depending on what the text holds. The greater the gain, the greater the demands. But some children who read hold on to the distinction between the different books; those that terrify them by their impenatrability and those which give an easy welcome. This is almost an analogy with those books they *ought* to read, and which are recommended by adults, and those they actually want to read, whether anyone approves or not.

Books can exclude as well as embrace the interests of the reader. When they do the latter they can seem a kind of solace, but this must be an easy kind, a rapid comfort rather than a complex unravelling of the personal meaning of life. For this reason popular books present a unique insight into the immediate needs and desires of their readers. They gratify not the individual and unique attempts to make sense of the world, but the more generalizable and common concerns of a kind of collective and cultural consciousness. They both present a mirror of reflected tastes and a kind of artifice of experience where the solace comes not from the answering of questions but the promise of a happy ending. Unlike the lives of the readers, popular books always have a happy ending.

Children listen to stories told to them with profound attention; and interpret them as reflecting their own lives. If they see the connection between the experience of listening and the mechanics of reading, they will to some extent look for similar gratifications and repeated pleasure. But even the most fluent reader will have experienced the barriers of misunderstanding, the lost clues, the impossibility of knowing where to begin. There is never an altogether easy transition from the idea of the story to the decoding of the personal experience in scripts. This means that once the breakthrough is achieved the pleasure in the ease of reading is the more acute. Children look for the familiar, for the signs of meaning as they construct their interpretation of the world, for it is by connections that they intellectually survive. They then look for support in the acts of familiarity and recognition of what they already know.[30] The very ease of reading becomes important for them.

There are psychological connections between the hidden themes of books and the interests of their readers, but these can only be understood in terms of the tenuous and collective pleasures of children. Popular stories have particular formulae and outlooks which come easily to some writers like Enid Blyton. There is also a connection with the dark side of childhood, the traumas of understanding and, despite understanding, trying to survive, by adapting. The books they read are a sign of their adapting. The books ease, and reflect, and fulfil expectations. But the way they do so, and the way that particular writers succeed so well, is the secret. Popular books have an instinctive recognition of misery, and we see signs of this, but also as readily suppress it. There might be excitements but there is a greater security, at least within the book.

The most important security of the popular books lies in the way they are read. Books become for children the overcoming of loneliness, the portable video, the entry into friendships which do not depend upon other people. When children were asked about their leisure habits very few said that they would choose to read a book as the most significant pleasure.[31] There were far more popular distractions that came about through actions,[32] like riding or making models. But reading was always there in the background, something to do when you were 'alone'. There is, as we will see, an association of reading with loneliness, with passing time when there is nothing else to do. Reading is not just an individual but a private pleasure. When children read their comics, for example, they do not wish to share them. Comics are not unlike the most popular books. Their pleasure is anticipated and familiar. They can be read again and again. Indeed, one is very much like another. It is not as if the recognition that the material has been read before makes any difference to its rereading. But reading comics in particular, and all popular books to some extent, is associated with boredom. It is done (as in Enid Blyton's own books) when there is nothing else to do.

Books are read fast. This is not the same as skip-reading or fast reading. They are read as material that does not challenge or cause reflection. Children cannot say much about what they read not because they are inarticulate but because they assume there is not very much that needs saying. Just as children reading comics rely on visual clues (they can return to the text in the bubbles later) so they rely on the familiar details in the texts: the details that are the fulfilment of expectation. This should not suggest that they do not read every word, but that the layout and presentation of the text and the tableau of the plot is of a known and familiar entity. Whilst some readers reduce and simplify an account of the story in their own minds, and others expand and elaborate upon it, the plot is something that each mind can use as a starting point, not too challenging and yet full of certain excitements, with at once a definite presence, but little real actual detail.

In the debate on 'effect' and 'response', the material that books provide and the experience that readers bring, the crucial questions are how conscious is what takes place, and the extent to which more secret forces are at work. It is only with hindsight that a person can say 'that was the moment I was influenced', or 'that was the moment I made up my mind'. Even such insights would be questioned as being wholly valid given all the chances of illogical experience. So it is impossible to know the exact effect of any reading, even if the books that are read in their millions leave nothing to chance, except the experience of their being written. What we have to recognize is the lack of intellectual seriousness with which the reader approaches the text. The great fear of the effects of horror comics depended on the assumption that the reader would take them very seriously indeed.[33] But the reader understands and accepts the convention, however weird. The reader is aware of the act of reading, of the palpable absurdity of what is being read.

Popular books are, after all, an obvious formula. Orwell discussed the formula as 'good poor man defeats rich bad man' as a version of pie in the sky.[34] But there is nothing obviously sociological in the books: riches and poverty do not come into them. Money and designer clothes definitely do. But as in the boys' stories of the 1920s and 1930s disseminated in *Boy's Own Paper* and *Chums*, the assumption is that *all* are rich, whether the readers are or not. Not all go to private schools, but the readers enter into that world. Not all can afford the most expensive of clothes, but all readers are happy to imagine the possibility. The important part of the formula is that the hero defeats the enemy, whether the hero is fighting a battle, overcoming a murderer or winning the undying loyalty of the person he or she loves. The greater the difficulties the greater the sense of justification and jubilation as well as relief at the outcome. It is a curious fact that there is a sense of familiarity even in the absurd. The more far-fetched the idea, the more certain the outcome. It is no wonder that even the most absurd of fantasies; the Marvel series of comics full of creatures like Superman, Batman, Daredevil, Captain America and the even more incredible Hulk, should have devotees who see in them the most secure of familiarities. As one reader expressed it,

> They really are a sort of inspiration . . . that the good guys really do win out in the end, that the decent and clean life bears its own reward. But, most of all, they have the ability of putting things in perspective.[35]

This disingenuous account of the triumph of decency and cleanness actually points to the perspective that the exaggerations of popular stories bring – the perspective of comfort in the face of reality, an alternative to thought.

The sense of the happy ending, of the good person defeating the bad, was dismissed as 'pie in the sky' by Orwell. It is not the usual experience that people have that the poor underdog overcomes the rich and powerful. And yet that remains the essential formula of films as well as stories. Against all the odds the hero emerges in the end unscathed physically or emotionally. The fact that characters do not change whatever amazing events they witness is a clue to the way in which these fantasies are viewed and read. In everyone's emotional imagination, when faced with some kind of rejection there is an element of self-pity, well caught by Mark Twain when he depicts Huckleberry Finn lying outside the window of the girl he loves, holding a rose to his chest and hoping to be dead in the morning. He imagines her opening the window and seeing him. 'Then she'll be sorry!' Life is full of powerful and impossible wishes: 'if only!'[36] Popular books with their tribulations and their ultimate success for the hero provide a type of emotional sustenance. But they do so on a superficial level, giving a framework of emotional reward or emotional distraction rather then engaging the emotions deeply.

There is a strong distinction to be made between the world as depicted in popular literature and the real world. This is not to say that popular literature is pure fantasy or pure escape, running away into the realms of science fiction rather than dealing with everyday concerns. Judy Blume and Paula Danziger try to capture as closely as possible the daily concerns and interests and tastes of teenagers, and they rely on, and acknowledge, the advice that their acquaintances give them. Even Enid Blyton's stories, however undescriptive, are located in something one can visually and individually put together. The unreality of popular literature lies not in the focus of attention but the ease with which problems are overcome, of emotional rejection put right. Suddenly the difficulties disappear and all is relief. Without this essential fantasy popular literature would not be what it is. It is an alternative to the emotional and intellectual struggles of the everyday.[37]

This suggests that the act of reading is one which does not deeply involve the reader as in, say, Henry James. There is still a close relationship between the reader and the text, but it includes a level of ease as well as the other responses we will be exploring. Children can be voracious and fast readers. They often read essentially the same text again and again, like the *Baby-Sitters Club* series which offer the most familiar of experiences. But this is true of all popular literature. Readers know what they are looking for. They want the book to suit them, rather than the other way round.[38] This makes books representative of a certain level of taste or need. It also means that whilst the reader knows what he or she is looking for, the writer can manipulate or stage manage the reader. Popular literature guesses what are the easiest types of gratification and what is not so much a transcending of ordinary experience but an alternative, preferred interpretation of it.[39] This suggests that the style in which it is written is close to everyday speech, making full use of dialogue. It does not challenge by making use of the extraordinary powers of language. The distinction between the literature that challenges and the literature that gratifies lies not only in the emotional comfort of the happy ending, or in the lack of the emotional and intellectual engagement with real concerns, but in the style in which it is written. It is as close to having no style of its own as possible. In some cases this very absence of characteristics strikes one, as in the case of Enid Blyton, as remarkable.

The lack of complexity or challenge in the style means that the essential narrative drive, where the end is implicit and inevitable, is the more important. But this was always so; in oral stories or in fairy stories.[40] The reader or the listener is engaged with the question of what will happen next. 'And then?' When young children tell stories they demonstrate their awareness of the importance of the narrative drive. They parody the crucial structure of stories by concentrating on the phrase 'and then'. Just as they respond to stories that use the device of having a series of similar incidents before arriving at the denouement, so they quickly grasp the way in which stories are based on a clear and important structure. This lies at the heart of popular literature. The same pattern explicit in stories told to young children is used as the most essential device. Sometimes, as in the *Point Horror* stories, the reader is mercilessly manipulated with each chapter ending with some sort of mysterious or frightening event. 'And then?' In these stories the question of what happens next ends in bathos, in false alarms. For it is not the events themselves that matter but the asking of the constant question: what happens next?

The structures of popular books are, like their style, simple, even primitive, compared to 'serious' literature. They rely on the ancient, folk tale device of a series of events leading to the unravelling of a problem, by some kind of intervention that puts all things right. This intervention always comes, in a sense, from outside. It does not have to be a fairy godmother or a kiss. It is the manipulation of the writer, the ability to make sure that the enemies do not prevail, or that the heroine finds true love. In those books which are ostensibly about real life, as lived in the present, where the adventures are of the everyday, there is just as much intervention as in adventure stories. It has been argued that children like stories set in worlds like their own and with characters like their own.[41] But the worlds of popular literature are like clothes to wear. It is the reader who is, in a sense, in control as well as controlled. The characters are like companions alongside whom the readers engage in the story. Much has been made of the notion of identification, as if the reader looked for characteristics in the heroes that related to their own. Like the notion of imitation, the automatic copying of what is seen or read, it is impossible to sustain.[42] Readers are far too diverse. No book would be popular if the reader needed any close identification with a complex character. Whilst a book like *Middlemarch* sustains both emotional engagement with, and intellectual understanding of, complex characters, the sense of identification as such, even if people might liken themselves consciously to Lydgate or to Dorothea, is objective. The world depicted is made actual because we are led to understand it, and can only do so through its relationship with our own experiences. Popular literature has few such sustained objectivities. A book like *Middlemarch* provides an objective correlative to ones own life. Popular fiction is a natural part of it.

Identification, in terms of children's reading, lies not so much in the characters as in the events. The reader is 'there', not in the sense of understanding the thoughts and emotions of the heroes but in accepting them as their own. The fewer the characteristics of the protagonists the easier it is to be engaged with them. All that happens does so to the reader rather than to the heroine. Occasionally there are no characters that children say they can or do identify with. But these are because of some physical attribute rather than personality. A child who has diabetes will suggest that the fact that Stacey in the *Baby-Sitters Club* has the same condition justifies her reading the whole series. There are those who particularly like Enid Blyton's character George, the 'tomboy'. But does this suggest actual personal identification? Any recognition of similarity is with a condition or a type.

When children devour books they do so by entering familiar territory in which the act of reading, the excitement of 'being there' without distraction is what they are looking for. They judge a text by the feeling it gives them and find it very difficult to conduct a review or assessment. This is not surprising given the nature of the texts and their styles of reading. It is the excitement that matters rather than the understanding.[43] The theme or the plot is far more important than the credibility. Thus the act of reading is not comprehensive or imaginative, but circumstantial and restricted.[44] Reading has to be easy and undemanding. If children read literature for emotional escape from particularly difficult circumstances then children who come from tense home atmospheres would read more.[45] But emotional difficulties affect the child's capacity to derive pleasure from the act of reading. Just as home circumstances affect the ability to learn to read, so it affects the pleasures of reading. The kind of emotional engagement that a book demands is not one of deep psychological need. The book might offer alternatives to the real world of traumas and difficulties, but they are alternatives to the world that all children share, rather than individual pathologies.

The level of engagement with the text of a popular book needs to be such that all readers derive a similar pleasure, whatever their own characteristics and circumstances. This means that the safe worlds books offer are not laden with too much reality. The sense of escape that pervades them are from the difficulties that all children experience: disappointments, misunderstandings, unfairness and a sense of not being as clever or as fortunate as others. But children do not merely experience their own narrow worlds. They are aware of the news, laden as it is with individual and collective depravity. Popular books take the reader away from this. Whatever the subject matter, from war and crime to horror, there is an essential distancing of effect. The books do not try to do more than use the excitements or threats of the circumstances to gloss them over, to keep the reader safe in the midst of all that goes on.[46]

The safety of popular literature does not rely on ignoring the actual events of the world. Like the news, they deal with the difficulties, with untoward events. Percy Westerman dwells on wars, Enid Blyton on criminals or spies, *Point Horror* with depravity. But unlike the news the actualities of the world are turned upside down. All is essentially safe, for the reader, because he or she will come through anything unscathed, and just as important, unaffected. Like the heroes who see the most horrifying of events in pirate stories and remain exactly the same as in their early innocence, so the reader is left untouched.

It is, however, important to recognize the context in which this literature rests. At one level the appeal of popular books lies in their depiction of a world arbitrary and cruel. The reader or heroine is unscathed but others are not. Part of the appeal of Roald Dahl lies in the very lack of compassion for discardable characters, the depiction of horrible behaviour and the relish with which the unjust or the unfair are cruelly punished. Nor is this a recent phenomenon. Many of the most popular authors from the chap-books of the eighteenth century have dealt, through slapstick and satire, with the misadventures of unfortunates.[47] There are different ways of reflecting children's sense of the arbitrary and the unfair. They can be distracted from them either by being led safely through the events themselves, or by seeing justice done to wrong-doers, or, usually, both. In contrast to the world of actual experience popular books depend on justice. The happy ending is a constant.

There have been those who have characterized children's literature as being essentially a search for a mysterious, elusive good place, a secret garden.[48] It is as if there were always a sense in which children (and the writers, like Kenneth Grahame or A. A. Milne) were supposed to need an alternative to the imperfect world. Carpenter depicts the tradition of writers for children from Carroll onwards as depending on a rejection of conventional Christianity with its sense of a divinely ordered world.[49] But if those writers were attempting to find a replacement, can we say the same for more contemporary ones? The most popular books as opposed to the 'classics' are set in a world not full of animals but people, not suggesting some arcadia but a place where dreadful things happen. The 'secret garden' lies in the mind. The hero/reader is safe, whatever events take place, just as the super-hero overcomes the most incredible odds. Terrible events take place, but they do not matter.

When one considers some of the great books for children like *Through the Looking Glass* or *Wind in the Willows* one realizes that they are engaging the reader at a number of levels. Adult readers are still fascinated by them since they give parodies of a recognizable and actual world. There we find characters we recognize, like Rabbit, always donnishly busy, or characteristics we are familiar with, like Humpty Dumpty's political logic. These books might seem to be set in a secret garden but they link directly to our understanding of experience. Popular books, in contrast, present an experience in themselves. They might seem to deal with the actual world, but they do so in a way which, ironically, displaces it. They give far more of a sense of a secret alternative by their restrictions of reality. Some of the classic texts for children have been characterized as giving readers 'consolation' and 'critique'.[50] They both offer an alternative and better world and compare it with the more familiar one. Experience is seen in a new light. But popular books seek to distract rather than console. They do not present a world which is any better than the real one. What they offer is the power to survive or get the better of it. Instead of a critique of reality they present an escape from it. Their heroes and heroines are always the same, and end happily through events which happen to them rather than by their own judgement.

The attractions of popular literature lie in the ease with which it is read, the very lack of conventional literary demands. This does not mean that the books do no more than pass the time, like some comics, or fill a gap that would better be used to have an adventure, as several Enid Blyton characters curiously declare. The very need for fantasy for the opposite way of dealing with the experience, for a world in which all dreams come true and where all wrongs are, from the point of view of the hero, put right suggests something about childhood experience. Very young children like stories that reflect and confirm their perceptions of their environment. The telling of events, like getting up and going to sleep, are what young children seek out. It does not matter that the protagonists happen to be elephants or mice. What does matter is that they go through familiar experiences. But as children get older they are given books which, instead of placing the element of the fanciful, like an elephant, in a real world, place the real world in the light of fancy.

Gradually as children interpret their alert perceptions of the world they are taught to discriminate between work and play, between being engaged in necessary interpretations and with forms of avoidance. Again, to very young children there is no such distinction. They play hard and constantly, as a form of engagement. But popular literature draws a sharp distinction between effortless pleasure and the chore of intellectual understanding. Whilst children are learning to read in terms of deciphering text they are at a stage when they would intellectually be ready for the most demanding concepts and insights. But they are offered banalities instead. By the time that they are able to read fluently they tend to turn back to the more easy and more banal habits of the popular. This is not a criticism. There is a need in children for an element of escape, of unreality, of the undemanding and slight experience of conventional curiosity.

Popular literature answers a general need. Children's lives, despite the conventions about the innocence and optimism of childhood, are not uniformly happy.[51] There are many, too many, cases of children deeply traumatized by their upbringing. But in one sense all children suffer from the traumas of childhood. There are moments of extreme pain; of being ostracized or being humiliated, just as there are extremes of other emotions like excitement or embarrassment. The dream world of literature is not so much an escape from one world to another, as an act of escape. The pleasure is partly in the act of reading, in not thinking about other things. This juxtaposition between the characteristic experience of childhood and the comfort of reading is well illustrated by Enid Blyton herself. Her childhood was a nightmare which she dealt with through denial and suppression. She replaced her nightmare quite completely with her dream world of perfection and happy endings. But she would not have done so with such conviction if she had not been driven by hidden trauma. Like all children she needed to have the terror opened up and understood, but she preferred to escape.

Whilst the act of reading connects so closely to the demands of the texts, and books are sought out which meet the needs of children, there are subconscious connections between the books and the actual conflict that children experience. These books recognize the excitement of conflict and difficulty as well as overcoming them. They might not explore them in depth but they acknowledge their existence. The very superficiality of the text means that each child can make his or her own connections. When young children first learn the mechanics of reading they undergo a complex interaction between their knowledge of shape – a doll is always a doll from whatever angle it is seen – and their knowledge of graphemes. There is only one way to see a letter: 'd' does not carry the same meaning when upside down. They also have to learn that phonemes – those sounds which carry meaning – can be extracted from a number of different letters – 'I' or 'eye' or 'aye' etc. This complexity means that when they learn to decode script they make many guesses and often make mistakes. What is interesting is that the mistakes they make are often as valid and sensible as the original; the mistakes are valid and personal interpretations of the text.[52] They might not be 'correct' from the text's point of view. Indeed they are wrong, for there is only one true way to read script. But their mistakes reveal their attempt to adjust what they see to their own understandings. These interpretations or guesses have their roots in the subconscious. They are not arbitrary.

This understanding of the mechanical aspect of reading is an analogy of the act of reading as interpretation. The text has one ostensibly true meaning. The simpler the text the more apparent this meaning should be, although the more complex it is the more trouble the author has gone to in trying to make a particular meaning clear. There is always the intention, the aim in a serious work, of revealing the 'perfect' reader. The 'perfect' reader is for most theorists the reader who studies and studies until every nuance of argument is followed. But in reality the 'perfect' reader is the one who agrees with the author, especially from the author's point of view. In this sense the perfect reader, even the author himself, cannot be said to exist. For everyone brings an individual interpretation to the act of reading. The psycholinguistic guessing game characterizes the average reader, looking for clues, making their own connections, recognizing some information, and ignoring other parts.

Reading is a personal act and a private pleasure. But there is little ostensible room for interpretation in texts which give just enough clues to help the reader construct his or her own mental picture. The irony lies in the fact that popular texts have clear designs on their readers, and assume certain styles of response. They manipulate and cajole. At the same time they do not give much away. There is little there to interpret. The act of reading is both an act of personal reconstruction and a thoughtless response to, and therefore absorption into, the expected and recognizable interior of the text. Popular literature provides a different kind of interaction. It also provides a clear insight into both reading habits and reading preferences and into the collective, shared and subconscious experiences of people.

Any question about desires: what would you like to have, or what would you like to be, can elicit responses which are realistic – 'I want to be a bank manager' – or fantastic – 'I want to be a film star'. When children are posed with such questions they understand the distinction but opt for the real. They know they can fantasize but ultimately such questions are pragmatic. And so their answers can be considered modest, seeing their own futures in real terms. What is interesting about popular literature is that this important distinction is largely overcome. Readers know they are dealing with a fantasy. But they accept that its basis is a kind of reality. But this is only a starting point. In adventure thrillers the heroes can do whatever they want; they are both detectives and fighters, they understand the intricacies of technology and the uses of physical action. In a sense the readers become like the film stars that are part of their fantasy world. For this is where reality and fantasy connect. Every magazine and every film reminds children not only of the fantasy worlds that are quite distinct, but of the fact that for certain people they are real. There are pictures and stories of pop stars and film stars. Then there are pictures and stories of what the magazines call 'hunky' men. The response is supposed to be 'Isn't he gorgeous!', and fantasy turns into dreaming, and into wishes.

Popular literature for teenagers has a lubricious connection with all these elements. It occupies a kind of middle ground. It relies on the essential fantasy of success but it includes all kinds of elements of a type of reality – what is trendy in speech and clothes and sex and the ideas that are supposed to occupy the minds of the young. But there is always a connection with a personal reality as well as with escape in all popular literature. One cannot suggest that any 'alien' world can be created in the minds of actual people, since we are all embedded within society. The comfortable landscapes of Enid Blyton and the lists of food that people eat, the historical backgrounds of Herbert Strang or the manic behaviour of Roald Dahl's characters all connect with the experience of their readers, as with something recognized. Only it is recognized in a certain way, not with the shock of the new, but with the acceptance of the familiar. It is fantasy made safe.

The yearning after a better life – winning money, or being famous – is a common characteristic. The more ordinary the circumstances the more understandable this is. Popular books sustain the fantasy of the 'right' or the satisfying outcome. The protagonists are rarely 'heroes' in the old-fashioned sense of carrying some special virtue or power. They are the entry points into the story. They are the ones who win. They are the reader, whoever it is. There is therefore both a sense of connection with their own lives and an acceptance of its convention that stories offer not a different world but an alternative experience to the world. Stories are 'other' to the extent that they have their own expressive language. Young children follow the conventions. When asked to tell a story they will dutifully begin 'Once upon a time' and end 'Lived happily ever after'. These very phrases point to the attractions of the stories and the mixture of fact and fantasy. 'Once' is definite. 'Time' is eternal. 'Lived' means they came to an end and died. 'Ever after' assumes they are still alive.

This balance between the real and the imaginative lies at the heart of reading popular literature. There are many texts – associated with work – using referential language, classifying and interpreting fact. But the texts of the imagination are equally important at whatever level. They are not an escape from the actual world but an interpretation of it, an interpretation dependent not just on the text but on the reader. Children as quickly interpret the world they live in through exploring the fantasies – why else should fairy tales remain as popular – as well as through living the everyday. For them it is hard to make a clear distinction, and in that they are right. Those who assume that there is one immortal reality create a fantasy of their own. Children do not move gracefully from the known to the unknown.[53] They are constantly speculating on the possible, for what we subsequently declare are actualities are in fact our collective interpretations, our agreed definitions. Egan suggests that

> children's strongest conceptual grasp on reality begins at its extremes.[54]

When they explore their environment they have to push the imaginary boundaries of what it contains. They are aware of the tension between the agreed and the personal points of view. Indeed, they very early on understand the distinctions between truth and falsehood. In a way, popular literature develops these distinctions. Readers are not deceived. But they would rather like to be.

Truth and falsehood, deception and self-deception are at the core of children's learning about their environment, about the social world. All relationships depend on trust and suspicion, on certainty and uncertainty. Fiction provides an obvious account of all these social relationships, doing so, in popular terms, by providing simplicities in the place of complexities. People change their minds. They can rewrite their own histories by reinterpretation. What for years was love can overnight be put down to pity. In such an uncertain world, a world that children undergo as a kind of trial before they embark on long-term relationships, fiction offers a kind of certainty, a safe haven. In books there are the certainties of personal victory and success. But these are not mechanistic certainties. They are embedded in an acceptance that there are actual uncertainties and insecurities. What would be exciting if there was nothing but an inevitable outcome? What would be interesting if a story were as certain as fact? It is the very acceptance of the fragility of relationships and the possibility of being undermined that feeds the security of fiction. There is excitement, but it is safe. There is fear, but it is controlled.

In one way at least the reader is entirely in control. He or she can choose to read or not, can believe what he or she reads or spurn it, make connections with the story or find it emotionally antipathetic. All texts are read with both deliberate credibility and constant detachment. At the heart of reading is the control of the reader, the personal response, the individual meanings. This does not prevent the text from being powerful and having a life or world of its own. Far from being 'deconstructed' it is a palpable entity of its own, the connection between the one creating it, and the nebulous world of a half-imagined, half actual audience. The audience in terms of taste and style, temperament and belief can be studied to some extent in the text. But the uses to which the texts are put are of a different order.

Popular fiction, like soap opera, is powerful in its repetition. Any effect, like any symbolic meaning, is cumulative. Readers know what they are looking for and in the sharing of instinctive taste the needs of one are embodied in the other. In many analyses of the readers there is an assumption that there are different 'types'; not just those who read seriously and those who read lightly, those who look for truth and those who wish for entertainment. In addition to those noted as 'paraphrasers' – limited and superficial – or 'problem-solvers' – entering into the spirit of the novel – are those who are seen as cracking the code of the text and those who take merely what they want to.[55] But I would argue that there are any number of different readers, bringing their own concerns and interests to bear, looking for the fulfilment of expectations on a number of levels. They know what to look for and know what to take. They are not passive receivers any more than they are perfect instruments of intellectual appreciation. What they have in common is a habit of reading that combines different levels of response.

The essential formula is of readers interacting with a text.[56] Each of these:

People (readers)	→	doing (reading)	→	Art (story)

has more than one level. In the story, for example, there are characters, environments and events. These interact in a complex way. The reader clearly follows the events (what happens next) and has sometimes personal and sometimes manipulated attitudes towards the characters, imbuing them with the necessary personal interest but no more. Readers also bring with them a whole array of responses. Some are dependent on the self-consciousness of the act of reading. Readers are critics. At any moment he or she is able to analyse, to say 'this is nonsense' or 'this is too far-fetched'. Readers remain self-conscious. They can lapse their concentration, be distracted by other more immediate events. They are able to draw back, to look at the text in a far more critical manner, analyse the style, explore the clichés or note the understated messages. At the same time the reader can enter into the text, to create a series of personal images that remain so powerful that anyone else's version of the same book visualized on film must be a disappointment. The valuing of the text, the acceptance of make believe, is centred on a kind of visual imagination, a play of the words on the page with actualized figures in which the reader is central.

Readers both imaginatively enter the text and critically stand back from it. There is a constant tension between imagining and criticizing, between the awareness of the act of reading and the valuing of the would be actualities of the world that is being presented. But in between these two forms of reading, or alongside it, lies that crucial and individual response of personal associations. We never know exactly what impact a particular scene might make because it triggers an associative response with a personal experience. Each reader will imagine the text in an individual way, but also connect it to scenes or experiences which they have undergone. The story not only provides a text to criticize, or a world in which to enter, but a series of sub-conscious associations with personal events and personal places. No book is so visually detailed that it is possible to frame an agreed or consistent series of pictures, not even film scripts. They provide the framework, the suggestions, even the desire to make the matters plain. But it will depend in the end on the individual association of the reader.

Popular texts, at one level, provide far fewer visual or emotional clues than more complex books. There is little description and little delineation of character. On the other hand they provide more. There are assumptions that the reader will share the same taste and the same outlook. The associative reader therefore has a greater chance to take exactly what he or she wants, no more and no less. The reader also has the chance to be less critical and to rely on imaging, entering into the heart of the story. The irony is that popular texts are premised on the assumption that they know what personal associations their readers might make. This is what makes them often so dated and so revealing of the mores of the time. Reading, at any level, is a way of reinterpreting the experience.[57] But this is done sub-consciously rather than deliberately. Those who deliberately study the text presume that their personal experience should be eschewed in favour of a detached criticism of the book. Those who like to 'lose' themselves in a story like to forget that they bring their personal associations with them. But both extremes of detachment or involvement actually cohere together. When young readers talk of books they talk of projections into a character or situation and of detached evaluation.[58] But at the heart of both are the associations they bring with them. Reading is a process that combines imaging, associating and criticism. The extent to which one predominates over the others depends on the reader.

But the style of reading also depends upon the book. The distinction between the concentration needed to appreciate, say, late Henry James or a Barbara Cartland could hardly be greater, let alone the difference between a work of logical philosophy and a tabloid paper. This brings us to the abiding concern about education and the reading public. What teachers wish children to read and what children actually like to read are not the same. The aim in teaching children to read is not merely the mechanistic one to enable them to read bills or take exams. There is always an underlying desire to enable children to become educated, cultured people, sensitive to issues and able to hold an intellectual dialogue with others through books. To those who inhabit the comforting zone of cultural relativism where it not only does not matter what people read but where all literature has the same worth, there is nothing to say.

Whilst we are concerned here with popular literature and the insights it gives into children's reading habits, this is not to imply that there is no desire to elevate children's tastes in reading so that they can be intellectually stimulated rather than undergoing a repetitive and familiar gratification. Anyone reading books of this kind will consider the question of how to create an educated reading public an important one and is unlikely to feel that what people read does not matter. That there are great differences between the wealth of great literature and the world of the best seller is clear. The question is whether two different styles of readership is inevitable. There are those who consider that demanding literature will always be confined to a small elite.[59] There are many more who yearn for the time when all people look to literature for personal development and social understanding, like the heroes of Hoggart's *The Uses of Literacy*, people who, whatever the disadvantages of their circumstances, develop a taste for erudition.

The nineteenth century was the first time when universal literacy was experienced. This might have been assumed to be universally welcomed, but it at once led to the great debate about what people should read. Coleridge explained as early as 1817 that nine-tenths of the reading public confined themselves to periodicals or short extracts from books.[60] From then on, and especially from 1850 to 1900 the question was how 'the spread of the printed word contributed to the spiritual enrichment and intellectual enlightenment of the nation at large'.[61] As Altick goes on to comment:

> More people were reading than ever before; but in the opinion of most commentators, they were reading the wrong things for the wrong reasons and in the wrong way.

Just as today, people were depressed to witness an apparent decline in reading for a serious purpose. They were also prone to idealize the past, thinking back on those who learned to read through studying the Bible or *The Pilgrim's Progress*, just as we wonder what happened to the successors of all those people whom Hoggart describes.

It seems that the taste for tabloids rather than newspapers, for the ephemeral rather than the challenging, has long been with us. It says something about the human condition and about 'culture'. When the mass reading public was first recognized, it was not always welcomed. At first it seemed like a threat, as if it were something that not all classes should undertake lest they should begin to understand more about their condition and no longer accept their 'place'. But the lack of pleasure in the rise of the reading public was not so much to do with threat as with entertainment. All the belief in the advantages to be gained from access to great literature, all the investment in mechanics' institutes and libraries and all the motivation to use learning in order to advance seemed to come to nothing in the face of a seemingly inexorable preference for the lightest of entertainment. Dickens made in *Hard Times* a plea for 'fancy' and 'pleasure', rather than the utilitarian learning of hard facts. But he had in mind novels like his own and Wilkie Collins. He did not mean the chap-books, the extracts, and the 'penny dreadfuls'.

If the concern for standards has a familiar ring, there is one great difference between the nineteenth century and the twentieth. In the earlier time there was a problem of the availability and accessibility of good books. They were expensive and difficult to come by. The lazy reader would not only have to learn to read more assiduously but had to find the material to do so. This is no longer so. There are any number of editions of 'classics' that are cheaper than glossy magazines. But the excuses for not reading remain familiar: other forms of entertainment, from dances and circuses to cinema and television.

We have, then and now, two conflicting themes which are constantly at war. One is despair that people will ever have an interest in serious reading. The other is the hope that, if only there were a real education system, they would be enabled to develop their pleasure to a high level. What is clear, then and now, is that the desire and ability to enrich one's life through reading are not contingent on occupation, weekly wage or family background.[62]

Any attempt to educate, to help children to be fluent and thoughtful readers must be based on an understanding of their needs, a respect for their abilities and a knowledge of their social milieu. If we are to help we need to know something about popular literature rather than just dismiss it. If we are to have an insight into the tastes of children we need to acknowledge that there are certain pleasures they seek out. If we wish to understand the social pressures of the peer group we need to recognize the latent or overt messages of their favourite reading. Many are agreed about what children ought to read. But we also need to understand what they do read, and why.

Notes

1 Even Coleridge outlined the way that an original writer needs to 'create' the audience that is prepared to read him; the earliest sign of modern marketing.

2 Graves, R. *Goodbye to All That.* London: Chatto and Windus, 1923.

3 Belsey, C. *Critical Practice.* London: Methuen, 1980.

4 Bourdieu, P. *Destruction. A Social Critique of the Judgement of Taste.* London: Routledge, 1984.

5 Hawkes, T. *Structuralism and Semiotics.* London: Methuen, 1977.

6 Summerfield, G. *Fantasy and Reason. Children's Literature in the 19th Century.* London: Methuen, 1984.

7 Zipes, J. *Fairy Tales and the Art of Subversion.* London: Heinemann, 1983.

8 Ibid., p.8.

9 Ames, L. Children's stories. *Genetic Psychological Monographs,* No.73, 1996, pp.337–96.

Applebee, A. *The Child's Concept of Story, Ages 2–17.* University of Chicago Press, 1978.

10 Egan, O. In defence of traditional language: Folk tales and reading texts. *The Reading Teacher.* Vol.37, No.3, 1983, pp.228–33.

11 Fromm, E., Bettelheim. B., Klein, M., Yung, G. and Freud, S. respectively.

12 E.g. Sarlend, C. *Young People Reading Culture and Response.* Milton Keynes: Open University Press, 1991, analysing *Carrie* and the idea of menstruation.

13 Vico, G. *The New Science.* London: Cornell University Press, 1968.

14 Richards, I. A. *Practical Criticism.* London: Routledge, 1924.

15 Barthes, R. *S/Z.* London: Cape, 1975.

Lévi-Strauss, C. *Structural Anthropology.* London: Allen Lane, 1968.

16 Holland, N. *The Dynamics of Literary Response.* New York: Academic Press, 1968, p.117.

17 Holland, N. Op. cit.

18 Lesser, S. *Fiction and the Unconscious.* New York: Vintage Books, 1962.

19 Iser, W. *The Act of Reading: A theory of aesthetic response.* London: Routledge and Kegan Paul, 1976, p.125.

20 Ibid., pp.169–70.

21 Derrida, J. *Of Grammatology.* Baltimore: Johns Hopkins Press, 1977.

22 Cf. the word 'Wirkung'; an active 'response' rather than 'effect'.

23 Belsey, C. Op. cit., p.5.
24 Sarland, C. Op. cit.
25 Ong, W. *Orality and Literacy. The technologising of the word.* London: Methuen, 1982.
26 Eco, U. *The Role of the Reader.* London: Hutchinson, 1981.
27 Ibid.
28 Slackman, E. and Nelson, K. Acquisition of an unfamiliar script in story form by young children. *Child Development,* Vol.55, No.2, 1984, pp.329–40.
29 Cf. the way that Blyton uses this phrase.
30 Cf. Chapter 6, Cullingford, C. *The Human Experience. The Early Years.* New York: Teachers College Press, 1998.
31 A.P.U. Survey. Gorman, T., White, J., Orchard, L. and Tate, A. *Language Performance in Schools.* London: HMSO, 1981.
32 Quite apart from TV, the most popular distraction.
33 Wertheim, F. *Seduction of the Innocent.* New York: Holt Rinehart, 1954.
34 Orwell, G. Quoted and endorsed by Dixon, 1977. See n.37.
35 This account written by a Peace Corps volunteer at the height of the debate about the harmful effects of comics. *Daredevil.* 1966.
36 Winkley, L. The implications of children's wishes. *Journal of Child Psychology and Psychiatry,* Vol.23, No.4, 1982, pp.477–83.
37 Cf. Dixon, B. *Catching Them Young: Vol.2. Political Ideas in Children's Fiction.* London: Pluto Press, 1977, p.31.
38 Chambers, A. *Introducing Books to Children.* London: Heinemann, 1983.
39 Iser, W. Op. cit.
40 Ong, W. Op. cit.
Starr, C. Why folk tales and fairy stories live forever. *Where.* No.53, 1971, pp.8–11.
41 Nodelman, P. How typical children read typical books. *Children's Literature in Education.* Vol.12, No.4, 1981, pp.177– 85.
42 Bandura, A. *Aggression: A Social Learning Analysis.* New Jersey: Prentice Hall, 1973.
43 Protherough, R. How children judge stories. *Children's Literature in Education,* Vol.14, No.1, 1983, pp.3–13.
44 Peel, E. *The Nature of Adolescent Judgement.* London: Staples, 1981.
45 Richman, N., Stevenson, J. and Graham, P. *Pre-School to School: A Behavioural Study.* London: Academic Press, 1982, p.194.

46 With some clear exceptions, like the work of Jan Mark.
47 Spufford, M. *Small Books and Pleasant Histories.* London: Methuen, 1981.
48 Carpenter, H. *Secret Gardens. A Study of the Golden Age of Children's Literature.* London: Allen and Unwin, 1985.
49 Ibid., p.73.
50 Cott, J. *Pipers at the Gates of Dawn: The Wisdom of Children's Literature.* New York: Viking.
51 Cullingford, C. Op. cit.
52 Bettelheim, B. and Zelan, V. *On Learning to Read. The Child's Fascination with Meaning.* London: Thames and Hudson, 1982.
Goodman, K. *Language and Literacy.* Boston: Routledge and Kegan Paul, 1982.
53 Egan, K. *Education and Psychology: Plato, Piaget and Scientific Psychology.* New York: Teachers College Press, 1983.
54 Ibid., p.369.
55 Dias, P. Making sense of poetry: patterns of response among Canadian and British secondary school pupils. *English in Education,* Vol.20, No.2, 1986, pp.44–52.
56 Winkley, D. Children's response to stories. DPhil thesis, Oxford, 1975.
57 Fry, D. *Children Talk about Books: Seeing Themselves as Readers.* Milton Keynes: Open University Press, 1985.
58 Protherough, R. Op. cit.
59 E.g. Q. D. Leavis, T. S. Eliot.
60 Altick, R. *The English Common Reader.* Chicago: University of Chicago Press, 1957, p.368.
61 Ibid.
62 Ibid., p.374.

2
Reflections of Real Life: The Ethos of Schools

Popular books will always provide an easy and undemanding read, with pace and excitement, with action rather than description and with dialogue rather than analysis. That much they all have in common and we should not forget the essential neutrality of the experience of reading. It can be a repetitive and an unremembered gratification, like watching a series of soap operas on television. Popular books do not have as their central aim the seeking out of truths, or the dissemination of a moral message. But they also have an ethos of their own which can have an effect through the accumulating experiences of the sensations and attitudes that they provide. They not only reflect the tastes of readers but leave their mark.

The effects such books have, of course, are subtle rather than obvious, more a matter of tone and attitude than the presentation of a new idea. Their content is worth analysing, but their ethos even more so. Many of the books written about children's literature, especially those about schools, concentrate on the messages that they are supposed to convey, especially in the supposed art of preparing for the adult world.[1] This raises a gender issue in that there is a commonly held assumption that the world depicted in boys' stories is quite different from those for girls. There is clearly a gender divide in terms of sales and marketing. There have for a long time been books written exclusively for girls. Those set in single sex boarding schools clearly have a demarcation line. Boys would not dream of reading 'girls' stuff' or vice versa.

The analyses of stories set in girls' schools tends to concentrate on the extent to which readers are being subtly taught how to become good, possibly subservient, wives and mothers, to play a feminine role as clearly and simply as boys are being taught to be masculine.[2] Certainly, if there are any messages at all in books like *The Hardy Boys* it is that heroes, as always, are brave and tough and win fights.[3] The adventures that take place in girls' stories are rarely so 'macho'. Does this reflect or effect the outlook of the readers?

Given the gender divide amongst the authors one can only with difficulty believe that they have definite designs on their readers.

The books which remember, analyse and sometimes celebrate school stories, from *Tom Brown's Schooldays* onwards, deal with what now seems like a dated genre. That gives school stories an association with comfortable nostalgia and with old fashioned chauvinism. But when one examines some of the messages that they convey it is clear that they are not all full of 'sweetness and light'. They reflect a world that is far more complicated. Whilst there are plenty of examples of moral messages, exhorting 'decency and honesty', there are also many incidents where the opposite is clearly relished.[4]

Given the importance of school in the lives of children, it is surprising to discover that in the huge volume of books written for them, there are nowadays comparatively few which concentrate on schools as a location. When schools are depicted they are used as social meeting places, as a background to the real action which is centred on relationships.[5] Whilst there are a number of stories written about life in school, like the *Turbulent Term of Tyke Tyler*,[6] and whilst there is a continuing fascination with the more rumbustious and informal sides of school life of the kind that characterize the television series *Grange Hill*, there is nothing in more contemporary literature to match the sheer volume and consistency of boys' books before 1940 in creating a world of childhood which is distinct and with a shared outlook on life. This is not to suggest that present authors do not have insights into the thinking processes of children. Jan Mark – as in *Enough is Too Much Already*[7] – Trevor Harvey in *Operation Pedal Paw*[8] and others, have explored the social relationships and idiosyncratic views of children as they share them with each other. But although school is the background and is both a shared experience and social meeting point, the focus of attention is the children, in groups. As in the world of Enid Blyton, *Malory Towers* and *St Clare's* apart,[9] the school is an incidental aspect, not the centre of attention. There are few contemporary books which rest their case for understanding children on the depiction of their lives in school.

Even books which would appear to be about school, like Pinto's *School Library Disaster*,[10] take an unusual event as a starting point, in this case a bring and buy sale, and use a school less as a locus of attention than as a useful background. Looking through the works of some of the most famous names in writing for children – Robert

Westall, Rosemary Sutcliff, John Rowe Townsend, Geoffrey Trease, Alan Garner – one encounters hardly a sign of school life. The stories are, instead, set in unusual places or within unusual events. When they do deal with the more everyday world of childhood, they concentrate on children's lives outside school, in holidays mostly, or at least after school. It is as if the particular tradition of Arthur Ransome's *Swallows and Amazons* or Richmal Crompton's *William* books were the ones being continued rather than what used to exist as a substantial body of literature based in schools. With honourable exceptions, school life seems to be relegated for depiction in *Grange Hill* or the 'Bash Street Kids'.

This is a pity. School is a significant part of childhood experience. It can be a traumatic one, as conveyed through bullying and its effects on victims. It can be a dispiriting one, as revealed in the different forms of truancy. And it is also a formative one, learning how to adapt to groups as well as individuals and to the rules and hierarchies of school, as well as personal relationships. One could argue that the setting of children's literature is not a significant aspect of quality. An insight into the world of growing up can use any material as a starting point. But what literature reveals is on more than one level. At best, children's books demonstrate both personal individual experience and the general background of whatever milieu they are set in. At worst, books reveal, sometimes inadvertently, the ethos of school, the shared attitudes, the assumptions made about their purpose and habits of authority and discipline. Books of all kinds reveal a good deal more about the actual experience of school and the prevailing attitudes about schooling than they necessarily set out to do.

Ever since the success of Thomas Hughes' *Tom Brown's Schooldays* in 1857[11] there has been a fascination with stories about school life. The publication of Farrar's *Eric, or Little By Little*[12] in the following year ('"Bother" said Eric, swearing his first oath') established the genre, and helped to create a large readership amongst boys. The pages of the *Boy's Own Paper* and *Chums* are filled with school stories, tales of the tribulations and pleasures of boarding school life.

The fact that the school stories were about 'Public Schools', boarding schools which were very exclusive, might suggest that the world that they depict would be far removed from the majority of readers of boys' magazines. One might imagine a rarefied atmosphere, of a sense of the effete that is far removed from the common hurly-burly of life. In fact the books reveal an atmosphere and a set of assumptions that explain their attraction to all boys. The books and magazines also give a very clear picture of the ethos of schools before the Second World War. The question is not only to understand how a particular ethos is created and shared, but to know what happened to it.

In looking at a representative sample of books about schools it is interesting to note how similar and consistent attitudes are from the late nineteenth century to the Second World War. We might find some of these attitudes very different from those held today. But we might also find some striking parallels. The books reveal the strong sub-cultures of schools, the tendency to subvert authority as well as the need for firm discipline. In some obvious ways they are different, as in the pervasive nature of corporal punishment. But in other ways we gain an insight into a culture of schooling that remains the same; friendship and enmities, the exploration of relationships within peer groups that sometimes seem of greater significance to children on a day-to-day basis than the formal mechanisms of control.

In terms of physical appearance, the curriculum and the uses of educational technology, there are many differences in the schools. In an article on *School Life in the Future*, written in 1929,[13] some of these changes are anticipated:

> The marvellous advance of wireless and electricity will mean new wireless and electrical appliances in the school itself.
>
> Perhaps television will be installed in the class room.
>
> A series of living views of foreign lands would make Geography an alluring subject.

The article goes on to suggest the advance of scientific subjects at the expense of the classics, brighter decorations, more lessons taught out of doors – 'perhaps aviation will be in the school programme' – and then points out that one feature of school life will never change.

> The teachers ... will remain the hard-hearted, short-tempered, vitriolic tongued, but sportsmanlike at heart men that they were yesterday and today.

It is a useful corrective to the assumptions of teachers in their professional role to realize that whilst children are very acute in their observation of their behaviour and their authority, they also have agendas of their own. They are busy in the forming and testing of relationships, in pleasing each other. The formal curriculum is important – like guessing what the teacher requires – but it is also a background to peer group relationships. For example, children do not wish to fall behind in their work because that would hold up their peers. Nor do they wish to be too far in advance, for then they feel they would be deemed to be 'show-offs'. At the level of motivations and relationships, and in their attempts to understand themselves, children are less concerned with the formal curriculum than with each other.

One of the underlying assumptions behind the idea of the boarding school (an assumption that was supposed to be of relevance to the state day-school system) was that it helped to form character. The school was seen not as a place where a set curriculum is 'delivered' and assessed, as in the National Curriculum, but where other moral virtues are learned and imbibed. This places teachers in a subtly powerful position. They are there not merely as experts, not only as controllers of discipline but as examples. What is interesting about boys' books generally is how distant the teachers actually remain, how they are on the outer periphery of a circle of friendships and enmities.

The teachers themselves might not hold a central place in the plots of the books, but schools are nevertheless seen as extremely autocratic places. Many would argue that they still are.[14] But in these books power is embodied in the prefects as well as in the teachers. They are also the ones who set an example, who create the right tone. The prefects are, however, symbols of an authority that is centred on the headmaster and through him on the housemasters. The prefects have day-to-day power but only because power is invested in them, as if they were Non-Commissioned Officers, answerable to their superiors as the other boys are answerable to them.

Schools are always somewhat hierarchical institutions and children have always been aware of the power of the teachers, the presence of the headteacher, and even the outside controls over the head as witnessed in the governors.[15] In the boarding schools described in the books of this time the point is often made that at each level the individual has great power over his immediate inferiors:

> As far as anything concerned the individual house Fifteens, Elevens, Eights, etc., the Captain of each house was an autocrat, who consulted the other seniors more as a matter of politeness than necessity.[16]

The result of this autocracy is a system which creates a clear set of differentials: between boys of the same age in the same house, and, even more significantly, between boys of different ages. *All* who pass through the ranks of the school will eventually have the chance to show power over others. The system of 'fags', in which the most junior children were virtually the unpaid servants of prefects, was seen as an initiation ceremony through which all would of necessity go, slowly and painfully. It was seen as a way of teaching the importance of recognizing authority and differentials; the power of some over others.

The fagging system so dear to the hearts of older boys in public schools was open to abuse and many books of this period include episodes which demonstrate this:

> 'Come, say it's fair!', commanded Thorpe, and by way of urging the fag to speak he seized his cane, which always lay handy, and dealt him a blow across his shoulders which made him stagger backwards.[17]

The moral tone of the books is clear; that only bullies would abuse a system in which some boys have power over others. Nevertheless, there are two significant factors in this. The first is that it is taken for granted that such a system exists and should exist. There is no questioning the right of some boys, like prefects, to have power over others. The second is that the books are commonly written from the point of view of the younger children and are stories in which they, at last, get the better of the bullies. There is therefore an immediate structure of story given to the books by virtue of the fact of fagging. How the fag gets the better of the older boys – virtually always in a fight – is a common plot. The prefect, however, demonstrates at some length his right to mete out punishment and wield the cane like a master, before receiving his 'come-uppance'.

> Thorpe rushed upon his wretched fag and beat him with his clenched fists 'till he was tired . . . not so satisfied with this ill-treatment, however, . . . the prefect pounced upon him and started at him with his cane.[18]

The theme of fagging and prefects is, however, only one form of the ritual of boys' stories. Far more significant than the power of prefects and the abuse of power over fags is the constant battle for authority evinced by rival peer groups. It is the early years in the boarding school that command the interest of the writers, and 'The Fourth Form at . . . ' or 'The Upper Remove at . . . ' are common titles. In the arcane world of public schools, of course, the Fourth Form is the first year; the boys are aged about 13. Then comes the Fifth Form, followed by the Lower Sixth, Sixth and the ultimate pinacle, the Upper Sixth. The 'Upper Remove' is a special category for those who do not make the usual progress.

The central core of many of these stories, then, is the battle for power between rival groups, a battle on which most prefects look with distant indifference, and the masters with ever more distant distaste. This explains why so much fighting takes place. It is very much a boy's world, boys being defined as naturally aggressive and quarrelsome. Girls simply do not intrude. There seems little curiosity about them.[19] The only way they impinge, even in books published by the Religious Trust Society, is as a threat or punishment:

> I was to go up and learn Latin and Arithmetic at – oh, how shall I say it? – a girls' school![20]

What marks out the boyishness of the boy's world is the assumption that *one* part of 'manliness' that must be learned is to be tough. All the fighting, the beating and the caning are seen to be a necessary part of school life.

> You see, boys aren't like girls, and they must rough it, or they wouldn't be worth anything.[21]

Girls are associated with the softness of home life from which little boys must be weaned. Whether from the point of view of the new boy who has to learn to fend for himself, or from the point of view of those who inflict punishment, beating toughness into little boys is a duty.

> It was the first time within my recollection that anyone had even struck me at all, and the sensation was so vastly unpleasant.[22]

(*Jefferson Junior* goes through the intimate details of how the eponymous hero learns to cope with being caned.)

> Together, like men with grim and resolute purpose, he and Griggs rose. Together they approached Eric. Followed a brief struggle, then the squawking Eric was across Griggs's knee and there came a healthy [sic] slapping sound as Jinks waded in with the window strap.
>
> 'If', said Griggs conversationally, across the squirming forms of mama's darling, 'there is one thing', – Thwack! – 'which I abhor', – Thwack! – 'it's cheeky new boys'.[23]

Battles for control and power can be at a number of levels. In these boys' books, however, the battles are literal. Fighting abounds. It might be thought that fighting could be used by the authors as a simple way of creating a climax or as an obvious way of rewarding the hero, like climactic gun battles in Westerns. But, as in many Westerns, fighting is seen not just as a means to an end but symbolic of some greater justice. Furthermore, the fighting that punctuates these books is deeply imbued with the ethos of the school. It is not a matter of fighting for fighting's sake but fighting as a natural way of sorting things out. It is as if the fight were a part of a boy's way of reasoning:

> After a lot of argument, and a fight between Bilks and Wulgar Minor, it was decided . . . [24]

> . . . but I flung him off on to the floor and started swiping into him with the bolster and that knocked a bit of sense into him and calmed him down a little.[25]

Ever since the famous fight in *Tom Brown's Schooldays* confrontation between two individuals or two groups can seem like an epic of almost mythic proportions.[26] Fights are seen as almost ritualistic:

> It was the most famous fight the School had ever seen, for, by some mysterious manner, the Fifth and Sixth got to know that the strange battle was going on.[27]

Many authors describe fights with relish. They talk of the 'fistic art' and the 'scientific pugilist'. They also stress how fiercely the boys fight. There is no sense of holding back. Fights might be rituals in themselves but they are not carried out in a ritualistic way.

> The clash was fierce . . . hard knocks were exchanged . . . and black eyes and cut lips were brought away.[28]

In some books, like the tale of *Jefferson Junior* who started innocently ignorant about how to fight but who is defended by others until he learns how to cope, there are many successive pages devoted to describing fights until someone has 'received a very fair portion of the sound thrashing which he had been yearning to see inflicted upon my tender person'.[29] Jefferson is not the only person, however, who

> gained strength from the very act of fighting

and

> was enabled to stand firm

or

> becoming more accustomed to cuts and blows and sneers.[30]

The idea of needing to fight in order to be 'made a man of' is a ritualized form of an attitude which still prevails in schools today. The ability to 'take care of myself' is cited with pride by boys who find themselves caught up in bullying. Assertiveness and self-protection are held in respect, and the ability to command the attention of others, even in physical terms, held in awe as well as fear.

Since fighting is so prevalent and so useful, it follows that all boys must be able to join in. The admiration for a really good fight is in part the relish of seeing justice done in the most obvious manner –

> Russell minor had even gone so far as to say that he couldn't remember a prettier blow than the one which had floored Stevens for the second time.[31]

– and in part a sense of conniving in the symptoms of 'boys will be boys':

> It was a good fight while it lasted. In fact, quite one of the briskest fights which had ever been witnessed in Dormitory Three.[32]

The almost formal nature of fights which define both individual and group relationships give a rhythm to the flow of these boys' stories. They punctuate every significant action and climax. But the books are also punctuated by even more formal and institutionalized forms of violence. We have already noticed that in addition to the weaponry of fists, rulers and window-straps, prefects possess canes. It is taken for granted that caning is so much a part of school life that boys are actually proud to have been caned. 'Six of the best every day; made me what I am!' It is certainly apparent that caning is much preferred to other forms of punishment like being given extra work to do, or lines.

> The three principal culprits took the licking that the Head gave 'em like men – and he gave them a pretty strong dose, I can tell you . . . but, not satisfied with them, old 'Flatfeet' has been bullyragging us at every possible opportunity, setting us lines by the cartload.[33]

'Taking it like men' is part of the rite of passage that boys undergo. They must be seen to take the pain without flinching. It is not only that boys want to do anything to avoid lines, but that they are proud of taking a 'licking'.

> I've decided that the next time a master bags me for an imposition, I shall simply cheek him, so that he'll be bound to send me to the Head for a licking instead. I'd far rather have that because its over sooner, and you don't have to miss grub.[34]

Sending the boys to the head for a caning is one of the few aspects of the repertoire of teachers that impinge on the stories. A boy is sent, and the head then 'lays on lustily' and the boys 'bear it' even with 'smart and cries and tears'.[35] The reason for such easy acceptance of the cane is the strong belief that caning is good for boys, that it makes men of them. They can be literally 'licked into shape'.

> Give him a good caning for his disobedience; he's worth it, for 'though he is a disagreeable oaf we must give him his chance. If he can't be licked into shape, why then we must consider the matter later and see what can be done.[36]

> And that the mischief about your schooling is that you've not been smacked as often as you ought.[37]

Physical punishment, like fighting, is a central tenet in the ethos of these schools. It is used to teach a lesson, to punish, and to toughen the boys up so that they can accept pain. There is little if any moral judgement about what the boys have done to deserve such a punishment. Every boy, hero and villain, is caned. There is no talk of prevention, since caning is more relished than avoided. The young Jefferson Junior has to undergo his first experience having said, like other boys, 'I'd rather you swished me, any day in the week' as opposed to other punishments. This is too great a temptation for the prefect to resist. He makes great play of getting ready as slowly and with as much relish as any torturer. In the end:

> Reluctantly I extended my other palm and received two more cuts, that made me execute a sort of impromptu war-dance. But I remember with pride that I did not squeal.[38]

It seems that caning the hands is deemed a more satisfactory, perhaps easier part of the anatomy than the behind. The boys reappear bravely with their 'hands redder than ever. The old firm when they came out shared but one thought, namely, to blow on their fingers as hard as they could'.[39] But the 'old firm' (or gang) seem to feel this kind of escapade is a normality.

> [The head] employed two media to drive home his point. One medium was word of mouth. The other stung more.
>
> 'But he might have jolly well slat us six!' Page cried jubilantly.[40]

Caning is seen as an essential means of enforcing the authority of the head and others over their juniors. The use of the cane still fascinates people today, as evinced by old Etonians writing to the newspapers about their memories of the headmaster Chenevix-Trench. But the fascination seems to be with the idea of the cane as a weapon, as a mode of punishment. There is little mention of the cane as a symbol of authority, of the real rituals of power. Power, or its abuse, might not nowadays be reinforced in such physical ways, but it still exists, as do bullies and the ability of teachers to 'pick on' particular individuals. The cane is essentially the symbol of hierarchical authority. Prefects also play an important role in this hierarchy. For the school is seen to symbolize order – an order that young pupils wish to disobey but which they must, in the end, respect. The excitement of the school stories lies in the fact that the young are seen trying to beat the system, and they 'get into scrapes' but within the security of school discipline. For even caning comes across as a symbol of security. It is part of the order of things.

Far more worrying than harsh discipline in a school is any sign of 'slackness', since the boys look up to and imitate those in authority over them. In *Tom, Dick and Harry* the head boy has trouble with some masters, but would not dream of subverting their authority by appealing to the head. This causes problems to him, and through him, to the school as a whole.

> No news flies so fast in a school as that of a responsible head boy being slack or 'out of collar'. And . . . so it was, slackness reigned supreme.[41]

The concentration on a rigid hierarchy in which everyone plays their part rests not only on obedience, but on the fact that everyone knows their place and accepts it, together with the responsibility they have for others. Whether through the toughness of accepting punishment, or the willingness to fight, the books preach 'manliness'.

'Manliness' is an important concept that appears and reappears on the pages of boys' magazines. It is a quality that is often invoked but rarely defined, partly because it is seen to be an innate part of good character. One of the few attempts to write about 'Manliness' appears in the *Boy's Own Paper* of 1901. The anonymous author writes about his son.

> My parting advice to him, when we said goodbye at Southampton, was 'Live clean, be straight, do your duty, and act the man'.[42]

The important point about the concept of 'manliness' is that it combines a concern for others and rectitude with a certain degree of toughness, or 'stiff upper lip'. All those canings at school will have been useful. 'Unselfishness is a "manly" duty'[43] but so is the ability to stand up for yourself. The ability to fight is not seen in an aggressive light, but as a way of not allowing others, however rough, to get the better of you. For this reason boxing was a sport much admired and developed in schools before and after the First World War. It was seen as a form not only of self-defence, but self-restraint.

> Self-discipline – and a person can have no more valuable quality in life than that. A man who is master of himself is rich indeed.[44]

Here again we see the combination of physical ability and self-control that is so central to the ethos of the public schools.

The ability to box meant that when necessary the schoolboy could stand up for himself.

> One big rough was particularly offensive and insulting in his remarks. When young Mursell had divested himself of his pads and gloves, he walked up to the individual and said 'Look here, my man, you've had a lot to say at my expense. I don't mind chaff, but I'll be hanged if I'll stand insult. Put up your hands, if you think you can fight'. For a moment the rough looked taken aback.[45]

Needless to say the 'rough' had 'a rude awakening' in store for him. Here the 'gentleman', the schoolboy, completes the picture of the ethos of these school stories. The readership was spread far and wide, with many more readers who did not go to boarding schools than those who did. But there is a definite sense that the schools are striving to make 'manly' people, who carry real virtues. The heroes are invoked for emulation, they are generous and kindly as well as strong, fair as well as tough. The school stories have villains as well as heroes. This distinction is put down to 'types'.

There are different kinds of character within the school and outside. The point is made again and again that people vary – they are not, as in many a modern novel all equally bad or indifferent. The sense of right and wrong is powerful. But in this world, which combined morality with a sense of hierarchical order, it is sometimes easy to make distinctions:

> Never had Arthur looked a more perfect little gentleman than he did as he stood thus at bay, surrounded by these worthy youths, most of whom were of a very different type ... their faces and bearing contrasting unfavourably with his intelligence and refinement and childish grace.[46]

Right and wrong are easy to see, a combination of breeding, status and upbringing. There are some who possess 'innate cruelty', who are 'cowardly souls', whose 'brutal instincts' show clear signs that their 'previous associations had not been elevating'.[47] It is this last phrase that is particularly important. In the ethos of schools people are made, not just born. There might be many a mention of the 'Bill Sykes house-breaking type'[48] or the 'Brutes' who gamble, but these are seen not only to be rough in class but rough in behaviour.

The same Major Charles Gilson who talks of the Bill Sykes type (and was governor of a military prison) talks about the majority who are 'the best chaps in the world'. The distinction between 'manliness' and 'meanness' is not only a class distinction. Those who are privileged enough to go to public school must also learn to do their duty, to 'play the man'. The message is one that is directed at everyone, not only those who have to undergo such strenuous rites of passage. The school stories try to give a flavour of how these peculiar circumstances can help form character:

> Allow me to introduce ... Vyvyan ... Treherne. If you follow his fortunes in these pages you will in due time find out that he is a better sort of fellow than at first appears, and you will recognise how true it is that 'changed circumstances produce changed characters'.[49]

The circumstances of the boarding school might seem peculiar. All the books about them suggest a toughness that informs the public discipline of the school and the private associations between boys. It might be that in contrast to schools today these schools are fairly brutal, with corporal punishment and many fights. It could also be true to say that the schools depicted here share a particular vision and sense of purpose. It is certainly easier to define what it is.

The books that are centred on school life give insights into a particular morality and a distinct ethos. No other form of writing, however erudite, can capture quite that mixture of personal experience and social relationships. The surface matters – what is being formally learned – are subsumed in the everyday experiences, which teachers also need to recognize. For it is easy to forget that for pupils there is a great deal of personal anguish, self-doubt and struggle embedded in the school. Some of the real experiences of learning and understanding are hidden from view like the 'invisible children'[50] who slip out of the memory as if they had never been in the class. These books, like contemporary ones, present both a reminder and an insight.

The books of the pre-war years, however, differ from contemporary accounts of school life in one important respect. They suggest that there is a strong and explicit morality which is shared by the formal structures of school and by the informal attitudes of the pupils. However violently expressed, one set of values is embedded in the other. There is a common sense of purpose and a belief that all are trying to make 'real men', however brutal the process might be. To that extent, there seems to be a contrast in the present day. The formal work of school, expressed in SATS and the National Curriculum, in financial management and appraisal, seems to be one world; the world of the children, another. And it is not a world in which we detect a prevailing ethos, or a common sense of purpose in the system of education as a whole.

It is, perhaps, the absence of shared attitudes that make schools a less popular subject today, or perhaps the declining interest in boarding schools. All readers aspired to the idea of the boarding school even when only a tiny minority actually attended one. The attitudes which are conveyed in these boys' books contain clear moral messages, even if they also carry more than a hint of the absurd. In this, their tone, like those of Strang and Westerman, contrasts with the outlook of more modern fictions. However complex a mixture of 'manliness' and chauvinism, violence and kindness, the books do suggest a world of story from which the readers are supposed to learn about certain ways of behaving. However far in the background, the adult world exists. There are examples to be followed, and virtuous adults to be admired. Such books are no longer being written. They seem dated not because they are embedded in such a different world but because more contemporary fiction presents a quite different attitude to adults, and to behaviour. Instead of rules and hierarchies the interest is on the difficulties of inter-personal relations, or the pleasures of the group. As we will see in later chapters the adult world is more likely to be ignored or attacked.

Notes

1 Quigley, M. *The Heirs of Tom Brown's School Days.* London: Chatto and Windus, 1982.
Musgrave, A. *From Brown to Bunter: The Life and Death of the School Story.* London: Routledge, 1985.
Auchmuty, R. *A World of Girls: The Appeal of the Girls School Story.* London: Women's Press, 1992.

2 Auchmuty, R. Op. cit.

3 See these themes in several chapters.

4 Darton, H. *Children's Books in English. Five Centuries of Social Life.* Cambridge University Press, 1982. Darton does, however, draw attention to the high ideals of the *Boy's Own Paper.*

5 E.g. *The Baby-Sitters Club* series.

6 Kemp, G. *The Turbulent Term of Tyke Tiler.* London: Collins, 1981.

7 Mark, J. *Enough is Too Much Already* and other stories. London: The Bodley Head, 1988.

8 Harvey, T. *Operation Pedal Paw.* London: Harper Collins, 1991.

9 Blyton, E. *Malory Towers* etc. London: Dent. Always in print.

10 Pinto, Y. *The School Library Disaster.* London: Puffin, 1988.

11 Hughes, T. *Tom Brown's Schooldays.* London: 1857.

12 Farrar, F. W. *Eric, or Little by Little.* London: 1858.

13 Anon. School life in the future. *Chums,* 1929, p.60.

14 E.g. Bowles, S. and Gintis, H. *Schooling in Capitalist America.* London: Routledge and Kegan Paul, 1976.

15 Cullingford, C. *Children and Society.* London: Cassell, 1992, pp.40–1.

16 Elrington, H. *The Red House of Boville.* London: Nelson and Sons, 1925, p.136.

17 Mansford, C. *The Fourth Form at Westbourne.* London: Jarrolds, 1927, p.102.

18 Ibid., p.245.

19 But see Chapter 6.
20 Reed, T. B. *Tom, Dick and Harry*. London: Religious Trust Society, 1894, p.44.
21 Silke, L.C. *School Life at Bastrain's*. London: Religious Trust Society, 1897, p.86.
22 Fletcher, M. *Jefferson Junior*. London: Blackie and Son, 1905, p.88.
23 Rochester, G. *Adventures at Greystones*. London: The Popular Library, 1936, p.14.
24 Anon. 'A Communication from The Society for the Suppression of Piffle in Public Schools'.
25 Ibid., p.734.
26 Hughes, T. Op. cit.
27 Mansford, C. Op. cit., p.107.
28 Mowbray, J. *The Feud at Fennell's*. London: Cassell, 1930, p.11.
29 Fletcher, M. Op. cit., e.g. pp.95–110, p.96.
30 Silke, L. Op. cit., p.74.
31 Rochester, G. Op. cit., p.74.
32 Ibid., p.115.
33 Anon. 'Punishment in Schools' Part III. *Boy's Own Paper*, 1901, p.778.
34 Ibid., p.779.
35 Colbeck, A. 'The Mystery at Stockwell Lea: A Christmas Story'. *Boy's Own Paper*, 1925, p.302.
36 Elrington, H. Op. cit., p.215.
37 Reed, T. B. Op. cit., p.44.
38 Fletcher, M. Op. cit., p.258.
39 Mowbray, J. Op. cit., p.214.
40 Ibid., p.137.
41 Reed, T. B. Op. cit., pp.176–7.
42 Anon. 'Manliness'. *Boy's Own Paper*, 1920, p.412.
43 Ibid.
44 Anon. 'Boxing for Boys. The Art of Self-defence. How to excel at it'. *Boy's Own Paper*, 1914, p.57.
45 Anon. 'Amateur Boxers'. *Boy's Own Paper*, 1924, p.314.
46 Silke, L. Op. cit., p.38.
47 Ibid., p.41.
48 Gilson, C. 'About my Own Stories'. *Boy's Own Paper*. 1921, p.21.
49 Butcher, J. W. *The Making of Treherne*. London: Charles H. Kelly, 1911.

50 Pye, J. *Invisible Children: Who are the Real Losers at School?* London: Oxford University Press, 1988.

Note: A version of this chapter appeared in *The Use of English,* Vol.46, No.2, 1995.

3 Deliberate Appeals: For Children or to Children? The Case of Herbert Strang

The human tendency to seek the undemanding and the familiar might seem to be growing, but it is not a new invention. There are certain tastes in reading which do not change; the love of a secure formula, incidents of danger and excitement in the knowledge that all will come right in the end. The safety lies in the ending, in the almost inevitable passage towards that moment when truth, justice and rewards prevail. This is the deep structure of popular literature.

The provision of emotional security through reading and the placing of the self in imaginative fantasy is, however, comparatively new. The rise of the reading public meant a thirst not so much for the best possible literature offered in libraries, but for the entertainment provided by chap-books and 'penny dreadfuls'.[1] Those providing the reading material soon discovered what people liked. They did not seek to mould so much as to reflect taste and preference. Even those tracts produced to bring about religious conversions were often read for the 'wrong' reasons, for instance for the description of a crime, rather than the moral message of repentance.

There has always been an ostensible tension between the desire of the author to do good and the desire to attract and please the reader. This tension is a constant between the awareness that the personal feelings and ideas of an author are important to him or her and have no interest to others unless they can be expressed in such a way as to communicate, and the realization that the way to appeal to a 'mass' audience is to expunge anything individual. This tension underlies all art – between originality and immediacy of communication, for instance – but is less serious in popular writing. In the authors and examples cited in this book we will see how easily blended, in successful authors, are their personal tastes and their appeals to other people.

Children have clear tastes but these are rarely if ever consulted. We find out about them obliquely, through discovering which books they like to read and keep re-reading, despite any admonitions. For however formulaic popular books might seem, they are not based on conscious or deliberate research. The publishers and the children's writers produce what *they* think will appeal, and these books are based on understandably conservative, proven ideas. There seems at first to be a real tension, true of serious fiction, between the desire to communicate something original and writing for money, but in the case of children's literature, let alone elsewhere, this is almost a false distinction. From Dr Johnson onwards authors might have scorned writing for any other motive than to make money, but in the case of writers for the children's market, the two – expression of ideas and appeal to others – go so closely together that the only way to discover whether that expression is worthwhile is by popularity – by sales. The adult critics of children's literature are after all speaking on behalf of others; their only credibility or authenticity is in being proved right in terms of popularity, and sales.

The fact that the appeal to a large audience of children is so important makes the author's voice and ideas no less significant. The deep structure of fiction might seem constant, but the surfaces, the beliefs and the assumptions which pervade so many books create their own impact. They have clearly changed over the years in ways which are significant in understanding contemporary experiences but they carry beliefs which are the more powerful for coming almost as a matter of course, relatively unexamined and, by being so clearly assumed, the more readily shared with the reader.

There has always been a hidden imperative to do more than merely entertain the child reader, although the balance between moral designs and entertainment for its own sake has swung violently from the former to the latter. Nevertheless the sense of potential responsibility, of the position of teacher in relation to the reader, has been widely shared by children's writers. They might not have thought of themselves as literary but they certainly wished to be moral. They wrote deliberately for children, and they had a strong sense of their audience.

Whilst these writers had a clear idea of what they wished to convey they were probably more aware of their audience, and the taste of their audience, as a distinct entity. They were not so much driven to convey their unique vision as to attract the reader. Children knew and know what they like. Their criticism is demonstrated not in reviews but in their choices. The satisfactions they derive are personal and cannot be forced on them. The distinctions between the 'design' of the author and the taste of the reader cannot be clearly drawn. All successful authors for children do not set out *merely* to exploit the market. What they write with such appeal must come to them as naturally as leaves to a tree. The child audience might be a distinct one, but it does not exclude the adult, the shared experience of being human. The adult author brings his or her own concerns to bear, often as idiosyncratically and revealingly as in any other form of fiction. How else can we explain Lewis Carroll or A. A. Milne?

Despite the difficulties of drawing demarcation lines – writing for oneself or for children – the sense of children as a distinct market is a significant one. It grew as rapidly as the rise of literacy which led to a greatly increased demand for children's books.[2] The nineteenth century demonstrates not only a fast growing market but also a constant change in taste, towards the more and more immediately attractive; those books which had, above all, 'appeal', as well as reinforcing shared assumptions. By the beginning of the twentieth century we already see children's literature as an important market, ready to be exploited by those who could appeal directly to children's tastes, rather than to the school and Sunday school teachers who chose prizes.

When G. A. Henty died in 1902 many people felt that he had symbolized all that was good in children's literature. He had displayed patriotic fervour and moral uprightness, and combined it with exciting stories and historical accuracy. The young men and women of Great Britain and the Empire were felt to have had a great talent for entertainment and inspiration taken away from them. There was certainly no one else who wrote so many novels so steadily, or so fast, and with such a large guaranteed audience. His death left what publishers saw as a distinct gap in the market.

Two business colleagues working in a large publishing house not only saw this gap in the market but decided to do something about it. These were G. Herbert Ely and C. J. L'Estrange who decided to collaborate in writing books to appeal to the large market, especially for boys. Their first book, *Tom Burnaby* (1904), appeared a little more than a year after Henty's death. Their agreed strategy was that L'Estrange wrote the plots and gathered the ideas and materials, and Ely did the actual writing; but in fact both made suggestions to the other and both criticized and corrected the writing. The result shows no hint of dual authorship. Indeed the sense of an homogeneous whole is true even in those books in which there is 'dual' authorship acknowledged by the introduction of an additional specialist historian.

It is significant to know what 'Herbert Strang' thought would, and did, appeal to children, and especially to those who bought books for them. It is the more so because the amount of press attention and praise they received was unusually excessive. It is instructive to learn what particular virtues they were deemed to represent. Many of their books, from the beginning, carry endorsements from most of the leading papers of the day; the *Church Times, The Spectator*, the *Manchester Guardian, The Daily Telegraph, The Saturday Review*, the *Gentlewoman* and so on. The reasons for these endorsements are unequivocally clear, and each seems to support the other. There is no doubt that Herbert Strang (from henceforth 'he') 'replaces' and is superior to G. A. Henty:

> It has become a commonplace of criticism to describe Mr Strang as the wearer of the mantle of the late G. A. Henty . . . we will go further and say the disciple is greater than the master. (*Standard*)

> We have said before – every critic, indeed has said – that in many respects Mr Strang is greater than Henty. His craftsmanship is always praiseworthy: 'though he writes with ease he writes well . . . and of the fullness of his knowledge he gives unsparingly. (*Academy*)

> If the place of the late G. A. Henty can be filled it will be Mr Herbert Strang, whose finely written and historically accurate books are winning him fame. (*Church Times*)

> This is the literature we want for young England. (*Gentlewoman*)[3]

It is almost as if there is an agreement in the press that Strang should be supported and endorsed, that Strang was the appointed successor, that Strang fulfilled the almost formulaic needs perceived at the time. These needs were seen to be a combination of three factors. The first was the moral uplift invoked by being British and all the superiority and responsibility that this privilege implied. The second was the historical foundation and proof for such superiority. The third was the conveying of this message in as entertaining a manner as possible.

The entertainment lay in understanding the nature of the hero; not just the fact that he or she would prevail, that he is bound to do so, but that he would undergo exciting trials before the end. There was a time when much was made of 'sugaring the pill', as if the whole point of entertainment was to make the moral attractive. In the case of fiction of this type the central messages are so heavily covered that they are the more easily swallowed without being aware they are there at all.

The essential need in this enterprise is the old one of combining instruction with sweetness; of conveying a moral and patriotic message in such a way that young readers would enjoy it. Herbert Strang was not only seeking to meet this criteria but was strongly praised for doing so by the critics – and they were justified in their praise by the sales. He was seen to represent all that was good and most typical in children's literature, as well as the spirit of the British Empire.

The authors themselves occasionally introduce their own aims when writing historical fiction:

> First, to tell a good story; that of course.
>
> Secondly, to give some account of the operations that resulted in one of the most brilliant victories gained by our British arms.
>
> Thirdly, to throw some light . . . on life and manners two hundred years ago.[4]

'Instruction and Education'; these are the twin aims that are felt to be uniquely fulfilled in Herbert Strang's books. Again and again the 'blurbs' surrounding the books draw attention to this.

> Few writers have known as well as Herbert Strang the exact proportions to allow of amusement and information.[5]
>
> It is not easy to say whether schoolboys or schoolmasters owe the greater debt to Mr Herbert Strang. Certainly the schoolmaster owes a great deal to an author who can combine the art of interesting boys with writing of excellent literary qualities.[6]

What nowadays would be called 'hype' for a 'No.1 best seller' is concentrated on historical fidelity and an uplifting tone that combines with excitement.

Before we analyse how this is achieved it is important to note that Herbert Strang does not deal only in historical fiction. In this lies the essential difference between him and his predecessors: Henty is always historical and the lists of his books emphasize the wide range of history employed but also reveal the absence of contemporary flavouring. The other influence on Strang was the success of the contemporary novels of Jules Verne. He is like the cusp between the ancient world and the new. The novels of the past, of historical events, are interspersed with novels that are up-to-date, dealing with futuristic visions of advances in mechanical expertise, or predicting future political possibilities – on the one hand mechanisms like gyro-cars and fast aircraft, and on the other a Chinese invasion of Australia or an ethnic conflict in the Balkans. As one contemporary commentator put it:

> Mr Herbert Strang . . . proves that the modern world is as full of wonder and romance as the ancient.[7]

When it comes to the past the authors often put in a little disclaimer about the tension between excitement and accuracy.

> The object of this series is to encourage a taste for history among boys and girls up to thirteen or fourteen years of age. If in these little stories historical fact treads somewhere closely upon the heels of fiction, the authors would plead the excellence of their intentions and the limitations of their space.[8]

They nevertheless see themselves as instructors as well as collaborators. Their authority derives from combining authentic historians with their own name. Thus *With the Black Prince, A Story on the Reign of Edward III* is by Herbert Strang and Richard Stead, Fellow of the Royal Historical Society; *For the White Rose, A Story on the Reign of Edward the Fourth,* is by Herbert Strang and George Lawrence.

Why then, did 'Herbert Strang' achieve such fame and such success? How did he acquire such support? When the plots and the sentiments are analysed it is possible to see something very formulaic; the means to achieve an appeal based on very basic principles. An early eulogizer praises the plots:

> Mr Strang stands alone; he is nothing like so mechanical as his predecessor; this tale stirs the blood even of a grown-up reviewer as Henty's heroes never did. (*Morning Leader*)[9]

What is being referred to here is not unlike the praise given to countless films. They are predictable but exciting. They invoke the slightest frisson of fear, but are safe. They balance a hint of horror with security. The psychology follows a predictable pattern.

Whilst Herbert Strang is praised for not giving us 'mechanical' plots, the fact is that they all follow a particular pattern. The most famous of the novels is perhaps *Humphrey Bold.* Whilst this is set in the eighteenth century, and uses an historical background – in this case Admiral Benbow – the essential plot is in many ways typical. The small details and little incidents surround an essential framework. First the particular plot: the eponymous hero is adopted on the death of his parents, has two enemies who bully him, Cludde, son of a Baronet (and therefore redeemable) and Vetch. Bold is cheated out of his inheritance, whilst learning to be a good swordsman – and growing into a handsome young man. When they see Bold becoming capable his enemies arrange his kidnap in a privateer from which he is captured and imprisoned in France. Bold escapes (having learnt fluent French in a matter of weeks) and steals/captures a ship. He joins the Royal Navy and is made a Lieutenant (at 18) and one of Benbow's men. It is worth noting that Admiral Benbow is a particular hero for combining being a gentleman without being a snob; he gives the example of coming from an 'ordinary' background and yet being both powerful, respected and 'clubbable'. When the daughter of his mentor flees to Jamaica to escape the clutches of Bold's enemies, Bold follows them, undergoes a series of fights, captures and escapes. Bold wins. Vetch dies. Cludde behaves properly again.

Whilst there will be glimpses of the spirit, style and attitudes implicit in such a story, it is worth mentioning that there are some important minor characters. There is Joe Punchard, a strong and faithful servant. There is Captain Galsworthy, a fencing master. There are people who 'adopt' Bold as their charge and return him to his inheritance. There are various faithful and fearful natives, now full of spirit and now full of cowardice. And, unusually, there is a heroine.

There are elements here of the typical plot but also some unusual ones, which is, perhaps, why *Humphrey Bold* stands out as a monument to Herbert Strang's particular genius. The key elements emerge again and again in various books. One is the formation of a gang around a leader (our hero), spontaneously recognizing him as superior. The rough and hardy seamen, for instance, see his moral and intellectual class.

> 'Be 'journed if it [following the hero] be aint a right merry notion', cried the mariner.[10]

Another is the support and admiration given to the hero who has style and dignity by the ordinary person, the 'mechanical', the person who in Shakespeare's plays speaks prose rather than verse;

someone who either is a good and faithful servant or who has a genius of the everyday kind that complements the hero's 'dash'. The Honourable Raymond Oliphant, who has 'dash', for instance, joins up with Tom Darvell who has practical ability and who makes a plane in *The King of the Air.*[11] It is as if the world were divided between the 'grammar' school and the 'secondary modern' – but a world in which each type accepts his or her place.

In the historical romances there are invariably faithful, and older, servants who help support the hero. *Martin of Old London,* however, is supported by an Indian boy (*c.* 1666).[12] But usually the ultimate success of the hero depends on clear factors. One is the overcoming of a tragedy – the losing of an inheritance, often by the dastardly cheating of their enemies.

> But he realized now that he was another wanderer, in danger of arrest by the law and with no name to turn to. The wealth of the Thynnes was fallen: their honour alone was left.[13]

Two elements then intervene. The first is a chance to shine at some outstanding act of courage, like stopping a rampant horse and thereby saving a small girl who turns out to be the Queen/Princess/Duchess/very rich.[14] The second is the appearance of the supporter:

> 'Master', said he, 'while thou't have me, I'll no leave thee'.[15]

As a result of all this the hero re-inherits his land, lives happily ever after, and basks in his own honour.

> Blushing with delight at the honour done them, the two young knights left the tent with the baron, and returned to their own quarters to celebrate the happy event. [They have just been knighted by Richard I.][16]

Reviewers praised Herbert Strang for not having mechanical plots. It is certainly true that despite the formulaic approach to the outline – someone disinherited but since he is a gentleman he shows his mettle by an act of high courage and is sufficiently recognized eventually to return to his proper position – there is a 'wealth of incidents', a host of different locations and a cornucopia of extras, mechanical and human. What Herbert Strang provides, however, is a unifying style and tone. The latter is not unlike the contemporary comedy thriller – scenes of danger in the security of knowing that all will be alright, with the additional realization that it does not really matter. But in terms of style Herbert Strang makes sure that it *does* matter. He has a message. The heroes, after all, take themselves very seriously.

> Luckily I was not born without a certain sense of humour. It had not deserted me under stress of what I had gone through during the last two days.[17]

This kind of portentousness also affects the text, with juxtapositions of vernacular and commentary on the excitement. One chapter ends:

> There's queer things happening in the parish lately, and that's a fact!

The next begins:

> Excited at this surprising turn of events, the boys . . . [18]

There are, as in subsequent literature, a series of markers, of direct reminders to the reader that what is happening is exciting, stimulating and worth reading. Whilst not going as far as Enid Blyton, or nearly as far as the mechanics of *Point Horror*, the reader is constantly cajoled. Part of the sense of earnestness that informs the plots comes about because of the need to put the adventures into an historical context. The readers after all must learn. That is why 'Fellows of the Royal Historical Society' are called in to give their authority to the text. The result is 'authenticity' of fact.

> In December the King set sail. Immediately after his departure William of LongChamp entered on the high-handed course of action which was destined to bring such trouble upon the country.[19]

> The state of England had gone from bad to worse.[20]

Part of the flavour of this striving for authenticity is to put in deliberate archaisms:

> Prithee, let me be thy Squire. I can carve full featly.[21]

The narrative style is very steady. There is a regular pattern of incidents and happenings, with few sudden surprises. There are no juxtapositions of events, no jumps from one place to another. The reader follows the progress of the hero with a secure sense that all will be well. As in the case of the most popular of later children's writers like Enid Blyton there is a sense of slight danger soon balanced by security. Dick Trevanion and his rustic companion are in a cave with the sea water rising inexorably and the light fading when

'I've found the opening!' he said . . . Dim as the light was, he recognized almost at once that he was at the end of the mine.[22]

This steadiness of progression is a result of the simple narrative drive of following the hero: there are no contrasts of point of view, nor are there any other perspectives. What seems like a linear description, with its sense of the objective narrative is, in fact, a subjective point of view externalized into a series of circumstances. The 'He' who said something is actually the 'I' of self-identification, the loose clothing of story into which the imagination can enter. At the same time this loose covering also has a metaphorical strait jacket of would-be historical realism. The adventure is balanced by historical verisimilitude. Books which deal with the past tend to begin like this:

It was a grey bleak evening in May 1455 . . . [23]

Somewhere about noon, on a hot August day in the year 1757 . . . [24]

It was a fine autumn morning at Southampton in the year 1338 . . . [25]

The text is interspersed with the occasional explanation:

It is now time to see how it had come about that Englishmen were at war with one another.[26]

It should be noted that Herbert Strang relished the use of old terms. It was not only a matter of needing to give a flavour of a period. The term 'doughtily' – used in historical romances in the sense of killing many people – 'They laid around them doughtily' – also appears in descriptions of the 'art' of boxing and in more 'modern' texts.

The new-comers laid about them doughtily . . . Many were cut down as they fled.[27]

The sense of purpose that drives the historical romances is the same in all the books: to give an idea of what it means to be British. Rather as the British government has been doing recently in trying to make the history element in the National Curriculum reflect past glories (and eschew the rest of the world) so Strang concentrates on elevating the British spirit above all others. The view of history is the standard one provided in *1066 and All That* – a steady progress towards as near perfection as any people can get, despite lapses and despite setbacks. There is a constant sense of right against wrong, 'us' against 'them' even if it is *within* the country – Richard the Lion-

Heart versus King John; Saxons versus Normans. This implies that there are 'foreigners' and that they are automatically to be suspected. This is as true of the contemporary stories as the historical ones. It is a thread of 'Englishness' that remains undiminished. The 'native race' will always do sensible things; one can tell a stranger easily.

> Who but a foreigner would live there alone with a wild-looking blackamoor?[28]

The ability to detect foreigners remains a useful commodity. What might begin as sheer observation –

> I've had a jolly spin, said George; Nearly ran into a foreign fellow in the village: there appears to be a little colony of foreigners there –

soon leads to suspicion:

> Did you notice the greedy look on that fellow's face?[29]

and so to confirmation that they are up to no good. Fortunately the heroes of these books can always tell when there is a foreigner around:

> Out of sight of the harbour were a score or more of men whom he recognized by slight indications in their dress to be foreigners . . . there lolled against the bulwarks near him a stranger whose hat and coat were manifestly Cornish, but his lower garments were as unmistakenly of foreign cut.[30]

In many of the stories the villains are foreigners. This is both a version of history and a sense that other people cannot be trusted. There is a suggestion that there is something distinctly odd as well as different about 'them'. It is not only Enid Blyton who uses the stereotypical idea of the foreigner. That sense of personal identification with the familiar is very strong. It is the preaching of group security.

> He was inexpressibly glad of the company of a fellow-countryman; the presence of a group of men of strange races was somewhat embarrassing.[31]

Does suspicion of foreigners imply an automatic racism? The answer to this question is more complex than it would first appear. That racism will have existed as an attitude then, as it so manifestly does now, goes without saying. There was certainly an automatic assumption that some 'races' were better than others. But there was also an assumption that British superiority was moral, and it had outcomes in terms of standards of behaviour. Whilst we see clear traces of an unexamined sense of stereotypical superiority we need to bear in mind the terms in which it is expressed. The superiority of the white man over the black man is at once assumed –

> They were stupid enough to be sure: from what I saw then and since I cannot but think they are no better than children in intelligence.

[This is thought by the hero] – and also questioned –

> 'Why, he is only a black fellow', said Cludde. 'And black fellows are flesh and blood, like you and me. But they haven't our feelings; come now, you can't say that?'[32]

But it is only questioned up to a point. Whilst the British in particular are deemed to be more advanced and more civilized, this gives them a certain responsibility over others. The assumption of virtues which cannot be obtained by others, except by emulation, is based far more on national characteristics than on racist lines. Remarks are thrown away with abandon and with ease about a whole typology of different peoples – cruel Spaniards, untrustworthy Italians, dastardly Germans – partly because whilst these sentiments are so easily said, and possibly deeply held, but partly because each nation *can* have mitigating factors. The most revealing attitude to genetic characteristics appears in *Barclay of the Guides* in which the hero is taken for, and has grown up as, a Pathan in Northern India, but is actually English:

> One observing him would have marked certain differences between his features and those of the Pathans among whom he dwelt. The observed conclusion would probably have been that Ahmed was a Pathan of a particularly refined type ... [33]

The quality of difference isn't as simple as good or bad. The Pathans are, after all, respected:

> He was a magnificent specimen of a Pathan, tall, handsome of feature, well made.[34]

The attitude towards 'primitive' peoples is part of the Victorian inheritance. What were part of the reported experiences of individuals who had been all over the world and whose attitudes of surprise and superiority were so clearly recorded were also supported by the science of the time. The sense of essential difference, and the distancing of strange customs from the moral integrity of the white man, was strengthened by the pseudo-scientific ethnography: as if there were a Darwinian hierarchy of race through evolution.[35] Many books of the late nineteenth century – *Tarzan, Allan Quartermain, Prester John* – see some 'types' as superior to others, as if 'primitive' religions were akin not only to 'primitive' politics but 'primitive' morality. But, given the moral and class differences within English society, there is no simple sense of 'us' and 'them'. The 'natives' are not mere specimens. Strang shows an awareness of the need to treat them properly.

> Attempts to graft Western ideas and customs on an Oriental people had embittered the population generally.

> Their officers had shown such tact and wisdom in respecting their religious scruples that the men had no fears of enforced conversion to the Christian faith.[36]

To each his own. There is an underlying acceptance, even respect, for the beliefs or the fighting qualities of other people. In fact there are many more unguarded mentions of other Europeans and their foibles. After all, these are the stereotypes nearer home:

> The Italians will do anything for a tip.[37]

> Of all men the Spaniards were the most superstitious.[38]

Whether in the past or in the present, the enemies present very clear moral reasons for antipathy. 'Spaniards are cruel'.

> It was not a pleasant introduction to the race dominating the Americas.[39]

It has been suggested that suspicion of foreigners depends on their power.[40] Thus Spaniards were the most hated when at the height of their dominance of Europe as well as the Americas. Conversely weakened nations are those about whom jokes are supposed to be made, as if the Irish and the Poles were always to be the butt of silly jokes. In fact, the books of Herbert Strang and others show a sense of universal superiority beyond the realms of power, and a typology of stereotyping which makes no distinctions according to perceived effectiveness in an enemy. This is, after all, before the days of Westerman and the use of chauvinism as propaganda.

The problem for Strang is that there are, on the one hand, clear distinctions between the 'white man', the European, and others, but even more subtle distinctions between the British, and that includes all within the Empire, and those outside it.

The equivocation of attitude derives from the fact that whilst the Europeans generally have a moral superiority over others, there are certain 'types' who are also seen to have their virtues. The North American Indians, like the Pathans, have heroic characteristics, even if these are undermined.

> His brother . . . was in the hands of a man entirely unscrupulous, wholly without compunction . . . a miscreant in whom the savagery of an Indian was mingled with the base qualities of the white man.[41]

These Indians are recognized to have qualities; they are respected. They are brave. They are honest. And yet they are seen to lack that final edge:

> The race was won. But with how small a margin! It had been won by the moral superiority of the white man over the red. Rob and his friends had known the danger and risked it . . . the Indians . . . the possibility of failure, of arriving too late had paralysed their will.[42]

These illustrations all imply the juxtaposition between the 'white' man – the European or the Australian or the Canadian – over other people. But the real stereotypical battle is, as in the case of Italians and Spaniards – foreigners – within Europe. They do not after all belong to this substantial moral world which is essentially 'British', which include all the Anglo-Saxons of the historian J. R. Green's vision.[43] In *The King of the Air,* a story about a speculative flight to Morocco in 1907, the battle lies between an Oriental, a German, and a Jew. The German is seen as stupid – he loves food like sauerkraut, is untrustworthy and a coward. The Moor has all the usual qualities – 'with true oriental discrimination . . . oriental duplicity' – he is lazy. But both are clear about the real fear:

> They were a strangely assorted trio. Schwab only half trusted the Moor; the Moor despised Schwab; both disliked the Jew.[44]

But why? It is an instinctive reaction.

> 'A Jew! A dog of a Jew! I don't like his *looks,* Tom.'
>
> He's not prepossessing, certainly; a little too glib, don't you think?
>
> 'A *rascal,* Tom, mark my words.'[45]

The typology of people into a set of distinct characteristics includes a sense of hierarchy, a sense which seems to have been lost in favour of just 'me' against all others. The 'top dog' in every way, morally as well as physically, is the Englishman. This sense of difference is also revealed in a strict class system. The heroes are nearly always well-born – even if disinherited. They immediately gain the recognition and submission of their 'inferiors'. The distinction between the refined hero and the more mechanical subordinate is often drawn out. Young men therefore find themselves with older servants who wish to serve them. In *Humphrey Bold*, for instance, it is Joe Punchard – strong, reliable, honest – who attaches himself to him. There is something about class which stands out.

> T'was the spirit that prompts a gentleman, however puny, to despise the churl, however big.[46]

'Gentlemen' have superior virtues and they also think faster.

> The door stood open; only the lackey was in the direct line between the prisoner and freedom. Before the man's slow rustic mind had accommodated itself to the situation he was sent reeling against the wall by a straight blow between the eyes.[47]

The ability to keep cool in a crisis and to act fast are just two of the typical virtues. But there is also an 'aura' around those with class. One can detect it in the physical appearance.

> He would scarcely have been distinguishable from the fisher lads of the village but for a certain springiness of gait and a look of refinement and thoughtfulness.

And there is also the respect for family.

> But the name of Trevanion, in spite of the fallen fortunes of the house, was still a moral power in the country-side.[48]

These being adventure stories, set in the past or the present, the heroes need to have physical courage and speed of thought so that their enemies are overcome. This is explained by the fact that English gentlemen are not only more refined, but that their enemies, however many in number, are slower-witted and not as brave. They haven't the same class.

> During this little encounter the bearers had done what might have been expected of men of their class. They had set the pathi down and stared in open-mouthed confusion, irresolutely watching the course of events.[49]

Speed of thinking and calmness in the face of danger imply a certain control over feelings, unlike volatile 'foreigners'. This does not, of course, imply that the heroes do not feel. On the contrary, their feelings are deep and steady, but they are kept in check, or put in a laconic way. As with other writers for boys, much is made of the understated British way of putting things.

> 'Hello, kid!' he said, in the young Briton's casual manner of greeting.[50]

This is to imply really charged feelings, firmly controlled but not suppressed. It is *control* over feelings – a clear head – that is important:

> I endeavoured to compose my countenance so as to betray no sign of the excitement through which I had passed.[51]

The assumption is that feelings are as strong as they are under control.

> And 'though he said but little, and never once raised his voice, I knew by the set of his lips and the gleam of his eye that it would go hard with anyone who baited me again.[52]

Indeed the point in the stories is that the passions evoked might be bridled – but they are the stronger for that. The heroes evoke not just sympathy, but as in a modern film, a strong sense of outrage when they suffer. The feelings encouraged in the reader are supposed to be strong – 'it makes my blood boil' – not indifferent. The fact that the hero suffers only elicits the stronger sympathy. In a curious way there is an encouragement not only to the 'stiff upper lip' but to what it is covering. An outlet of these passions is the 'doughty' way in which people fight.

> And then ensued as pretty a bit of close fighting as ever I was engaged in. We laid about us right lustily with our clubbed muskets, and I will say for black men that they were not a whit less doughty than the white. Our firm success had, I suppose, given them confidence.[53]

But restraint, or control of the emotions, also leads to a certain etiquette. You might feel strongly but you reign in your passions so that even if the best man must win he does not inflict too many injuries on the other.

> I ever regarded duelling as a barbarous and foolish way of settling a quarrel. If men must fight, let them use their fists, and so be quit of it for a bloody nose and a few bruises.[54]

This is rather like the message of *Tom Brown's Schooldays* in that the British fight with their manly fists, and that only nasty foreigners use knives.

Fighting, however, in one form or another, abounds. One of the most emotionally rousing forms it takes, in terms of the sympathy of the reader, is bullying. There are times when subtle forms of bullying are part of what the hero needs to go through, a rite of passage:

> They took a delight in threatening me, conjuring up all manner of imaginary horrors, and so working on me that my sleep was disturbed by hideous nightmares. I told nobody of what I suffered.[55]

The heroes in these stories, in fact, are far more exposed to real physical suffering than their more modern counterparts. But there are also occasions on which the reader is worked up not through sympathy as much as indignation.

> The lash hissed in the air and descended on the poor thrall's back. A livid weal rose across the flesh and he screamed with agony. Again and again the cruel thong beat upon his body, till it was a mass of blood.
>
> And all the while Prince Richard and the Lady Constance sat laughing harshly at the man.[56]

This callous ability to find cruelty amusing is, however, only the extreme pathological end of a general acceptance of fighting. When schoolboys get together it is assumed that they will fight, and that this is somehow jolly. It is the British way of doing things – not with knives like foreigners, but with their fists.

> Romsey, whose nose was spurting blood . . . knocked his tall antagonist off his feet. For five minutes the fight went on merrily [sic].[57]

Fighting is not confined to war. It is part of a general background in all the stories. A school is mentioned where

> there was more fighting than learning, and where such boys as had strength made a place for themselves and held it, while the weaker ones went to the wall.[58]

After all, as in the outline of the plots, 'let the best man win'. The 'best man' is, of course, British. There are certain virtues that gives him an advantage:

> I have always had reason to thank Heaven that my brain is quickest and my resolution most cool at the moments of greatest stress.[59]

> But behind the breakwater waited British Officers, cool, unemotional, with their men, British and native, seasoned warriors, disciplined, the best soldiers in the world.[60]

Strang uses the word 'unemotional' but it is meant to stand for control of emotions. Again, it is the understated that is rated so highly as a peculiarly British characteristic. Whilst many writers of the time talk about this trait, they also draw attention to the way in which the British can unleash emotion. The same 'cool' officers and men 'sprang to their feet with a cheer', and there is something special about the cheer.

> Surely there was an English ring in those cheers; it was no mere Spanish yell. It was coming nearer, swelling into a roar.[61]

The 'coolness' and 'discipline' that does not allow feelings to get out of hand is also held to be the virtue that makes the British behave in a more civilized way than others. Revenge and cruelty are frowned upon.

> If we fight, let us fight like Englishmen and not like savages, and treat our enemies according to the manner of civilized nations.[62]

Few of Strang's books do not demonstrate this particular virtue. 'Fair-play', the upholding of civilized values, is one of the underlying themes. In the structure of the books there needs to be an enemy to overcome. The books written about early English history also have the same element of 'us' against 'them'. The enemy might be a corrupt king, or a Roman invader, or a Norman. In each case, however, 'we' stand for decency.

> The Norman states: Well, I would rather be counted the worse man, so long as I have victory.
> The Saxon asserts: And I would rather be counted the better, even if I be defeated.[63]

There is therefore an attempt to give a moral basis to British superiority. The books have clear messages that add to their appeal to those that recommend them. They are not just jingoistic, although jingoism plays its part.

The time at which Herbert Strang received the most praise was before the First World War, and one of the reasons for this praise was the clear patriotism he expressed. Strang's modern stories, wherever they are set, have a political dimension. They express the growing concern with the might of Germany and the ambitions of the Kaiser. They also see the threat of the 'yellow peril'. They preach the need for the Empire to stand up for itself.

The Cruise of the Gyro-Car (1911) deals with a Balkan crisis, analysed in this way: Austria, backed by Germany, absorbs Bosnia and wants Montenegro. Behind Serbia, on the other hand, stands Russia. It is considered an explosive situation. In *The King of the Air or To Morocco on an Aeroplane* (1907) the book ends with a German (the despised Schwab) saying that the Kaiser will soon make war. Strang gives this as a warning, and also expresses clearly his opinion of what should be done about it:

> Didn't I *tell* you the country was going to the dogs ... it wants a fleet, an expedition, a few quick-firers and Long Toms. We're sinking into a state of jelly-fish; anyone can poke us and smack us and we simply *go in.*[64]

The clearest expression of this belligerent attitude towards national sovereignty is in *The Air-Scout: A Story of National Defence* (1912). The book begins, unusually, with a preface. It warns of German power and it suggests that the Dominions realize the need for Imperial defence:

> The race will still be to the swift and the battle to the strong ... but the speed and strength that will win the great struggles of the future must be the fruit of long and patient training. Our national genius for making good lost ground by spasmodic effort is likely to avail us less and less as time goes on. Organization must be our watchword.
>
> The ensuing story will have served its purpose if it succeeds in directing the thoughts of the boys of the present day.[65]

The story is about the way that the Australians with the help of two British heroes – one a gentleman and the other a mechanical genius – fight off a Chinese invasion around Darwin. 'Not a man hesitated to respond to the call.'[66]

The reason that the Australians win is in part due to the heroic actions of the air-scouts, their use of barbed wire, trenches and bombs, and, more significantly, their moral fibre:

> Basically it is this. The Anglo-Saxon has a native energy far exceeding that of the Oriental. The Australian in particular, accustomed to an active life in the open air, enjoys a physique, with its accompanying moral stamina ... [67]

The book ends with a homily about loyalty and patriotism and

> As England has helped us, so we will help England if the call comes.[68]

Not all that Strang predicts happens but his books give a strong sense of the concerns and attitudes of the time. They are especially interesting for several reasons. They were certainly most popular and widely read. They give very clear indications of the general moral outlook of the time towards European and international politics. They delineate what characteristics of behaviour are to be expected in the youth of the time. They shape a clear attitude towards history. And they do so in a way that has, apart from popularity, two other significant features. Herbert Ely and L'Estrange deliberately set out to fill what they saw as a gap in the market – vacated not only by Henty but by Jules Verne. And they clearly succeeded in their aim. They were taken up as the leading authors, the most representative of those feelings, attitudes and opinions that British youth would best learn from. As the *Gentlewoman* said:

> This is the literature we want for young England.

At the same time Strang, in 'his' popularity, shows an awareness of the needs of the market. He pleases the gatekeepers – the adult reviewers and buyers of the books. He has clear messages. But he also meets the reading tastes of his audience. Beyond the subtle messages are the everyday excitements; the predictability, the familiarity and the security of the hero within an uncertain world.

Notes

1 Altick, R. *The English Common Reader. A Social History of the Mass Reading Public 1800–1900.* Chicago: University of Chicago Press, 1957.

2 Bratton, J. *The Impact of Victorian Children's Fiction.* London: Croom Helm, 1981.

3 Quoted in flysheets of *Humphrey Bold. His Chances and Mischances by Land and Sea.* London: Henry Frowde and Hodder and Stoughton, 1908; also published by Bobbs Merrill, USA 1908.

4 This refers to the battle of Blenheim. Preface, *The Adventures of Harry Rochester.* London: Oxford University Press, 1944 (reprinted).

5 From *The Cruise of the Gyro-Car.* London: Henry Frowde and Hodder and Stoughton, 1911.

6 *Preparatory Schools Review,* quoted in *For the White Rose.* Herbert Strang and George Lawrence. London: Henry Frowde and Hodder and Stoughton, 1912.

7 *Romances of Modern Invention,* ibid.

8 Introduction to *With the Black Prince; A Story on the Reign of Edward III.* Herbert Strang and Richard Stead. London: Humphrey Milford, Oxford University Press, 1920 (reprinted).

9 Quoted in *Humphrey Bold.*

10 *With Drake on the Spanish Main.* London: Henry Frowde and Hodder and Stoughton, 1908, p.226.

11 *The King of the Air or To Morocco on an Aeroplane.* London: Henry Frowde and Hodder and Stoughton, 1907.

12 *Martin of Old London.* London: Oxford University Press and Humphrey Milford, 1930 (reprinted).

13 *Claud the Archer: A Story of the Reign of Henry the Fifth.* Herbert Strang and John Aston. London: Humphrey Milford and Oxford University Press, 1929 (reprinted), p.67.

14 E.g. *For the White Rose.*

15 *Claud the Archer,* p.111.

16 *Lion Heart: A Story of Richard the First.* Herbert Strang and Richard Stead. London: Humphrey Milford and Oxford University Press, 1917 (reprinted), p.147.

17 *Humphrey Bold,* p.100.

18 *Young Trek: A Story of Road and Moor.* London: Humphrey Milford and Oxford University Press, 1925, pp.96–7.

19 *Lion Heart,* p.43.

20 Ibid., p.103.

21 *Claud the Archer,* p.106.

22 *The Adventures of Dick Trevanion, A Story of Eighteen Hundred and Four.* London: Humphrey Milford and Oxford University Press, 1927 (reprinted). Orig. Henry Frowde and Hodder and Stoughton, 1911, pp.64–5.

23 *For the White Rose,* p.7.

24 *Rob the Ranger: A Story of the Fight for Canada.* London: Hodder and Stoughton, 1908 and Humphrey Milford and Oxford University Press, 1923 (reprinted), p.11.

25 *With the Black Prince,* p.9.

26 *For the White Rose,* p.23.

27 *Barclay of the Guides. A Story of the Indian Mutiny.* Oxford University Press, 1908 (reprinted 1943), p.49.

28 *Young Trek,* p.16.

29 *The Cruise of the Gyro-Car,* p.20 and p.26.
30 *Dick Trevanion,* p.321.
31 *With Drake on the Spanish Main,* p.126.
32 *Humphrey Bold,* p.356 and pp.315–16.
33 *Barclay of the Guides,* p.12.
34 Ibid., p.52.
35 Street, B. *The Savage in Literature: Representations of 'Primitive' Society in English Fiction 1858–1920.* London: Routledge and Kegan Paul, 1975.
36 *Barclay of the Guides,* pp.139, 140
37 *The Cruise of the Gyro-Car,* p.59.
38 *With Drake on the Spanish Main,* p.85.
39 Ibid., p.71.
40 Leersen, J. 'The Anglo-German relationship in context', in Cullingford, C. and Husemann, H. (eds), *Anglo-German Attitudes.* Aldershot: Avebury, 1995, pp. 209–21.
41 *Rob the Ranger,* p.138.
42 Ibid., p.299.
43 Green, J.R. *A Short History of the English People.* London: Macmillan, 1874 (revised and enlarged 1916).
44 *The King of the Air,* pp.108, 113, 219.
45 Ibid., p.85.
46 *Humphrey Bold,* p.94.
47 *The Adventures of Harry Rochester: A Tale of the Days of Marlborough and Eugene.* London: Oxford University Press, 1922 (reprinted 1944), p.110.
48 *The Adventures of Dick Trevanion,* pp.18, 95.
49 *Barclay of the Guides,* p.148.
50 *The Cruise of the Gyro-Car,* p.11.
51 *Humphrey Bold,* p.22.
52 Ibid., p.26.
53 Ibid., p.358.
54 Ibid., p.259.
55 Ibid., p.11.
56 *In the New Forest: A Story of the Reign of William the Conqueror.* Herbert Strang and John Aston. London: Humphrey Milford and Oxford University Press, 1924 (reprinted), p.101.
57 *With the Black Prince,* p.42.
58 *For the White Rose,* p.28.
59 *Humphrey Bold,* p.127.
60 *Barclay of the Guides,* p.303.

61 *With Drake on the Spanish Main*, p.196.
62 Ibid., p.207.
63 *In the New Forest*, p.15.
64 *The King of the Air*, pp. 51–2.
65 *The Air Scout: A Story of National Defence*. London: Henry Frowde and Hodder and Stoughton, 1912, Preface.
66 Ibid., p.163.
67 Ibid., p.413.
68 Ibid., p.428.

4
Formative Years: The Novels of Percy F. Westerman

The level at which literature forms, as well as reflects, children's tastes is as difficult to detect as that balance between the designs of the author and the response of the reader. Much of what is read passes the reader by. They are not looking for ideas and are only rarely surprised into re-thinking their ideas or learning something new or memorable. Novels are predictable entertainment. They pass the time; time passes in a familiar fashion. Nevertheless there are subtle formative influences, in tone and outlook, in habits of association and unexplored assumptions that, because of the unselfconscious vulnerability of the reader, can have effects.

The significant point, however, is that of 'level'. It has often been noted that children read books happily enough without bothering about their narrow stereotypes of 'race' or gender. Adults worry themselves unmercifully about political correctness. To children they are beside the point. Nor can any subconscious influence be detected. The absurd foreigner or the behaviour of golliwogs are part of the convention of the literature, rather than the conventions of life. These simple self-images are seen by young readers for what they are, simplistic and mechanical.

There are, however, more subtle influences. These have much more to do with the author's tone rather than the plot or characters, with unquestioned habits of thought rather than the deliberate communicating of ideas.[1] Of course, there are times when these go together. Children are attracted to certain types of books and part of this attraction, as we will see, lies not just in the speed of the plot or the style but in the very approach the author takes; the tone of voice, the unexamined detritus of prejudice. Children respond to certain deep outlooks of life which certain authors include in their books, unaware.

Occasionally the author's tone of voice, distinctions between personal security and external threat, the proportions of safety and danger, will find expression in more apparent attitudes. When these are read with that same thirst and instant curiosity which children bring to their favourite books, then some of the influences can be deep and long lasting. Again it is hard to make a distinction between the author reflecting shared prejudice and forming it. But one can see the clear connection between the two.

In 1990 we were offered rare insights into the thinking – if that is the right word – of elements of the Cabinet towards their European partners. In particular, in an interview in *The Spectator*,[2] Nicholas Ridley, then Trade and Industry Secretary, revealed his fear and loathing of the Germans. This was not the only time that chauvinism and nationalism were revealed as so rife: indeed 'Germans' were the subject of Cabinet seminars. But never had stereotypical prejudices against the Germans been so clearly expressed by senior politicians – not, that is, since it was the prevailing practice to do so. After all, part of the war effort was the deliberate fostering of hatred against enemies. The only surprise was that such attitudes survived for so many years; that they went so deep that they could undermine the everyday political relationships of the European Union.

Yet such is the power of early influences that such prejudices and fear retaining their hold over many years should be no surprise. The kinds of attitudes expressed by Nicholas Ridley can be found in many pages of the novels written for children in the earlier years of the century.[3] Prejudice is not confined to the exaggerated headlines of the daily tabloid newspapers of our time, but insisted upon as a highly moral as well as 'politically correct' attitude. For not only was the integrity of the hero defined against other people's standards, but there was a sense of a collective superiority that marked 'us' against 'them'. This sense of an almost simplistic rightness of the hero set against necessary enemies is, of course, the stuff of the majority of tales of adventure and of popular movies. But in the case of novelists like Herbert Strang there is also a sense of definition that comes about from particular virtues, from a collective as well as a homely superiority. The heroes of children's fiction in the past, unlike, say, those of more recent years, actually exhibit moral codes. They don't just win. They are *not* heroes simply because they are the ones we identify with and who survive to the end. The prejudice that so affected Mr Ridley was so strong because it suggested that there were underlying reasons for believing it to be based on evidence.

The experiences of two world wars, let alone the holocaust, can only have underlined an already deeply held belief in collective superiority and collective guilt. But it emerges not from the wild propaganda of the world wars[4] as much as from the more subtle and assumed expressions of popular children's fiction. No writer is a better example of these attitudes than Percy F. Westerman. Whilst Herbert Strang combined the historical tradition taken up from G. A. Henty with more modern and political stories, Westerman concentrated on the latter. Certainly he echoes many of the sentiments of Strang and others but he does bring a particular focus and a range of subtle nuances to his stereotypes.

Percy F. Westerman was one of the most popular writers for British boys – and their colonial cousins – between the two world wars. His first book, *A Lad of Grit*, was published in 1909, after he had been working for some years as a clerk in Portsmouth dockyards. He went on writing for over forty years until his last book was published in 1958.

Westerman was one amongst many prolific authors for boys whose heyday was the period before and after the First World War. He was one amongst a number of famous writers who were intent on exciting their readers by extreme (indeed, often implausible) adventures and by appealing to them by an assumption of their British heroes' superiority over others. Writers like S. Walkey, Major Charles Gilson, and W. Gordon Stables all had large and devoted followings. There is a consistency of tone that they all share, and that Westerman exemplifies.

Most of the significant writers of the period, from Stables to Westerman, were to be read in the two leading boys' magazines, the *Boy's Own Paper*, founded in 1879, and *Chums*, founded in 1892. Both were full of adventure stories which exemplified the British imperial spirit, at home and abroad. Stories of public-school life were lined up against stories of heroism and bravery set in all the corners of the world. These stories, interspersed with articles on practical suggestions and interviews with leading sportsmen, were illustrated by engravings, often to a very high standard (for example, by Paul Hardy). Writers like Fenimore Cooper, Max Pemberton, and Robert Louis Stevenson were glad to write for *Chums* and the *Boy's Own Paper*. Their influence over the thinking of generations of schoolboys must have been very strong.

Westerman's books are distinguished for the consistency of their tone and style. They symbolize many of the attitudes of his generation and expose some of the chauvinism that supported imperial ambitions. But it was the atmosphere that led to, and was developed in, the First World War that gave him his real theme and impetus. His books were often based on a simple outline: two 'chums', usually in the armed forces, managing to overcome dastardly foreigners. Many of his earlier books were reprinted during the Second World War, where again the German 'race' provided the clear enemy.

As popular as Enid Blyton, Westerman also provides simplistic stereotypes of character and race. Like Enid Blyton's stories, his books depend on a straightforward tension between security and adventure. The heroes go through amazing exploits, but we know that they will be safe in the end. In fact, they seem to have a relish for excitement:

> 'A chance of seeing something exciting at last!' exclaimed Ross. 'Of course we've not had altogether a dull time, but this ought to be absolutely it.'[5]

'Not altogether a dull time' has by then included being captured by German spies, incarcerated in a submarine, almost drowned, mined, torpedoed, rammed, shot at, left adrift, and all the usual excitement of war. The pace of the books is uniformly fast, and the simplicities of the attitudes expressed are also uniform.

It is the attitudes of Percy Westerman, towards race in particular, that remain significant. Generations of boys have imbibed the spirit and assumptions that the books reveal. These attitudes are also a summary of many of those which, not long ago, were taken for granted. It is important to remind ourselves how widespread such attitudes were, not only to wonder at, but to ask ourselves in what ways things have really changed. For although Percy Westerman reveals many of the stereotypes of jingoism and superiority to foreigners, the national distinctions stand for vices or virtues. Being 'British' is not a matter of mere flag-waving or football chauvinism but a demonstration of 'decency'.

On one level at least, Westerman's purposes include propaganda. He has designs on his audience. He wants them not only to despise those who are not blest with their own virtues but to bolster a belief in those virtues which he associates with being British. Westerman has, therefore, an underlying message. The question is what influence it had.

It is always difficult to isolate the effects of particular books. As with all propaganda, the message goes down well with those who already believe or want to believe. Thus, with political parties, an audience will believe that their own candidate always wins the argument.[6] To that extent, the readers are having their prejudices reinforced. The fact that Westerman was so popular reflects what his readers wanted to be influenced by.

Westerman gives a consistent account of attitudes that bolstered the Empire, as well as revealing an innate conservatism that was suspicious of all change except mechanical advances, and especially suspicious of the 'clap-trap theory of social democratic equality'.[7] Conservative attitudes are balanced by an excitement in new technical advances in warfare. Many of his books include new kinds of propulsion; huge airships, some of which can become submarines; and all kinds of devices that help those who wish to become 'Fritz-Strafers'.[8]

Whatever mechanical inventiveness is shown by the heroes of the books, their virtue lies above all in their courage, their blithe indifference to danger and their willingness to take action:

> He may be a most clever inventor but he has not physical courage. His nerve failed him at the moment when it was most required.[9]

Physical courage is allied to a certain *sang-froid*, a French term used to denote a British trait – a coolness in the face of danger that is denied those of other races, even when they are showing bravery: 'though they lacked the calm deliberation of the British seamen, the men were not deficient in courage'.[10]

In particular the 'science of present-day warfare'[11] was a useful commodity for the cool heroes, since it meant that:

> It'll take more than a dozen gilded popinjays of a tenth-rate South American Republic to stop us.[12]

This attitude towards the particular courage peculiarly demonstrated by the British is also shared by foreigners:

> [He] believed it would be a comparatively easy matter, but he had learned to his cost that he had a brave and resolute Englishman to deal with.[13]

Given all the actions that his heroes undergo, it is no wonder that they have become finely tuned in dealing with strenuous circumstances. But there is also more than a hint that practice makes perfect and that there is nothing like war for keeping people 'up to pitch':

> Not that a mutual peace would be beneficial. They'll drift into a lazy crowd. War keeps them up to pitch, so to speak.[14]

It is the British in particular who manifest the greatest courage, that steady unswerving facing of danger, as opposed to sudden outbursts of frantic activity, often heightened by drink, that is the characteristic of all other races. In fact, virtually all virtues and characteristics are defined on racial grounds. The British are best and are the flower of the Anglo-Saxons:

> 'Peary's flag, by Jove!' ejaculated Whittingham. 'All honour gentlemen, to that intrepid American. Even if an Englishman were not the first to plant his country's flag at the North Pole there is no little consolation to be derived from the fact that an Anglo-Saxon established the priority.'[15]

The phrase often used about this racial characteristic is 'the courage and tenacity that marks the Anglo-Saxon race'. Against that standard, other peoples are clearly deficient:

> 'What else would you expect from Belgians? . . . No, Rollo, take my word for it, the Belgians are not a fighting race. Let me see – didn't they skedaddle at Waterloo and almost let our fellows down?'[16]

The notion that there is something about the Anglo-Saxon race so shared by the writers of this period is a reflection of many Victorian historians. Like J. R. Green, they trace back those peculiar characteristics of a blessed people almost apologetically to the curious mixture of tribes that made up the 'Island race'.[17] This sense of chauvinism was the more powerful for being described and defined as well as shared by philosophers, historians and distinguished writers.

The crucial assumption is that 'blood will tell'. When there is a villain who is not foreign, and this is very rare, there is almost bound to be some racial reason for this: 'Pengelly has dark curly hair and sallow features – legacies of an Iberian ancestor'.[18] The individual villains are normally taken as samples of their collective background. Westerman allows himself to ruminate on his opinions of various countries:

> He never had a high opinion of the modern Greek however much he admired the Greece of old, when it was a mighty empire that produced *men.*[19]

In fact, the author demonstrates his theory of Anglo-Saxon superiority – the race of 'men' – in an exchange which reveals some erstwhile common, and dangerous, theories about race.

'H'm! Let's hope the British strain is well-nigh eliminated', remarked the pirate captain. 'I never had much use for mongrels'. 'If it come to that', countered Kayburn, 'is there a more mongrel nation than the British? Saxon, Celt, Dane, Norman and half a dozen other strains, and the result holds its own with any other nation on the face of the earth'.

'Granted', acquiesced Cain, 'but all the races you name originate from districts north of the 45th parallel, and as a rule the farther north the better the strain. No, what I kick against is the mongrel with negro or Indian blood in his veins – a Paraguilian, for example'.[20]

Such a dislike of the 'mongrel' reveals an instructive belief in the importance of 'pure' racial characteristics, whether they are good or bad, for such stereotyping makes a world-view so much more simple. You know who is good and who is bad. You can be patronizing to those who are unfortunate enough not to share your own virtues.

The idea of the 'island' race as being strengthened by an historical mixture is counterbalanced by the notion of impurities elsewhere. There would be something faintly comic about these attitudes were we not reminded of the driving passion behind the writing of *Mein Kampf.* There is also already apparent the North/South divide, the richer, developed world against the poor developing one. What is important is to know your place; to own up to and admit inferiority – in fact to accept it. What is disliked is the muddle of a mixture, or a disguise:

I've no call to be down on a chap 'cause he's a Jew. In a manner o' speaking, a true Jew ain't a bad sort. It's the miserable blighters like yourself who won't own up to it that gets me goat.[21]

Westerman assumes that the typecast 'Jew' will be understood as a set of characteristics, as if it were something that had to be 'owned up to'.

Long experience had taught him how to handle white men; it had also taught him the futility of using his fist against the armour-plated skull of a nigger. He knew that the best way to deal promptly and effectively with a 'Son of Ham' was to tackle him in a weak spot – his shins.[22]

The typecasting of national and racial characteristics defines not only a potential enemy, and a distinction from the 'privilege' of being 'British', but also a series of actions towards them. This is made clear in Westerman's attitudes towards the 'Natives'. With a strong belief in the Empire 'on which the sun never sets', comes also a cavalier attitude to what he calls the 'uncivilized' world. He implies that there are few rules when it comes to dealing with 'skulking natives': 'Won't do, Mr Macquare. We aren't lying on an uncivilized coast where we can act off our own bat'.[23]

Rules of war are defined in European terms, and the distinction clearly made between the somewhat different British and German interpretations of the way in which people are expected to behave towards the 'natives'. In the 'uncivilized' coasts where the people aren't 'sportsmen', the rule of the firearm is more effective than anything:

> It was a desperate plan, but like most operations boldly undertaken against savages, its success depended upon initiative and the possession of fire-arms.[24]

The underlying assumption seems to be that the natives need brutal controlling, being always prone to outbreaks of savagery:

> A negro revolt had broken out in British Noyada. The blacks, easily influenced by a negro agitation, had risen and were attacking the white planters and traders up-country . . . maddened by unlimited quantities of rum.[25]

The answer to this distracting news is to send battleships and, for the sake of speed, Captain Cain in his airship to smother the rebellion with bombs.

Westerman expresses doubts whether the 'natives' can ever be wholly 'civilized'. They may be disciplined, but that is another matter. Given his stereotypes of other European peoples, and the gradations of character, it is perhaps not surprising to find 'natives' the lowest of the low. Attempts to civilize, defined in one instance as the introduction of the game of cricket (something has to replace war, after all), can end in failure: 'He made mistakes – chiefly on account of his endeavours to introduce civilized customs to his subjects'. Civilization is: 'The Natives, admirably disciplined by this ancient representative of the British Mercantile Marine'.[26] This defines the rank and status of each and the relationship between the two. We are offered advice about this:

> And remember; the less you do yourselves and the more you let these men do the better. The Natives will think all the more of you.[27]

The natives are typecast as subservient; both because they need controlling and because it is assumed they wish to admire the white man, being both 'fiendish' and 'simple-natured'.[28] Not that the general term of 'native' means that they are all bad, like Germans. The crew of the *Fusi-Yama* are very glad to acquire a cook whose ambition is to 'be coloured gen'lman at Barbadoes . . . Buy top-hole swagger hotel 'an get dollars from Yankee visitors'.[29] He is not only a very good cook, but faithful and cheerful. We learn that his name is Pete:

> 'You're making quite a fine show, Sambo', replied Villiers.
>
> The black's smile vanished and he pouted his lip. 'I would hab you know, Massa Villers', he exclaimed with studied dignity, 'dat my name is Pete, not Sambo Yankee niggah; me British born'.
>
> 'Right-o, Pete, I'll remember', replied Villiers and the black resumed his customary smile.[30]

So all is well. Pete is proud to be British, but he knows his place. He refers to himself as 'dis niggah'.

The contempt for foreigners is not just a matter of colour. Whatever their origins, South Americans are seen to be of a type. They might be upper or lower class, but Westerman's generalizations are as sweeping about his third favourite sphere of activity – small, querulous South American republics – as about any other. South America gives his heroes a chance to run an otherwise ungovernable country, at least until they return home, by dint of their military prowess and their integrity. We all understand the 'British' virtues. By contrast, South Americans have some distinctly unappealing characteristics. One is their volatility:

> making allowances for the mercurial Calderian temperament . . . But an important item in Calderian characteristics had been overlooked – revenge . . . A bloodless victory did not appeal to their hot-blooded instincts: they wanted revenge.[31]

Another, in contrast, is the laziness, a view often expressed by the British about those who live South of the '45th parallel':

> fortunately the South American habit of procrastination was as deeply rooted in these Valderian irregulars as it could possibly be. An hour or two made very little difference to them: 'tomorrow' was their creed.[32]

The advantage to Westerman's heroes is, of course, that they have a comparatively easy time of it, even if they are up against hordes of the enemy. The sense of superiority flows through all of them. They see South American generals and admirals as 'comic stunt merchants' who head a 'decrepit collection of coffin ships'.[33] They are no match for either the Royal Navy nor the individual with initiative. At the same time they are not to be trusted: 'I wouldn't trust a Paraguilian with half a dollar of mine, let alone fifty thousand'.[34]

Whilst Westerman expresses contempt, or worse, for South Americans and 'natives', he saves his real dislike for Germans. As his books indicate, he justifies this hatred by citing their misbehaviour during the First World War, but this attitude was developed earlier, during the rivalry that led up to it. The characteristics of what is habitually referred to as the 'Hun' are such as to make their 'wicked' and untrustworthy behaviour during the war inevitable. It all centres on the notion of total war, of 'frightfulness':

> These English are such fools that in their anxiety to observe the rules of warfare ... they play into our hands ... This is not a petty squabble between two nations. It is a struggle for existence; consequently it is where our frightfulness scores.[35]

The invasion of Belgium in 1914 and the well-publicized atrocities against the civilian population were the beginning of a propaganda war that Westerman never gave up. The 'bestiality' of Germans in the novels reflects a studied hate fostered by war. Whereas the honourable British fight by the rules, the Germans do not:

> 'It is against the rules of war to coerce a prisoner', [asserts the captured Rollo, who is a dispatch rider for the Belgians in 1914].
>
> A chorus of loud jeering laughter greeted this statement.
>
> 'My young friend', quoth the Major when the mirth had subsided, 'you do not understand. When Germany makes war she makes war: there are no half measures. Why should we, the greatest nation on earth, be bound by rules and regulations laid down by a self-constituted peace party – the Geneva Convention?'[36]

Of course, there has to be an explanation for Germans fighting successfully against a foe which man for man has the superiority of being British. Westerman's attitude expresses the tone of propaganda; a mixture of fear and loathing and a sense of inevitable victory.

Even if their behaviour is restrained, and decent enough, the Germans can only behave 'decently' under the threat of retribution, or discipline. In this way they are not unlike 'natives':

> But it was not chivalry that prompted Schwalbe to act with consideration. Had he been untrammelled he would have sent his prey to the bottom without compunction, for he had all the brutal instincts of the Kultured Hun. It was a superstitious fear that held his frightfulness in check – a presentiment based upon the Mosaic Law, an eye for an eye and a tooth for a tooth.[37]

Just as Westerman reflects part of the ethos of this time, so he echoes powerful voices that suggest that Germans are by *nature* evil. This was still being argued after the Second World War, let alone the First (for example, by Vansittart and Lord Russell of Liverpool). The proof for such an assumption was always drawn out of the actions of the 'Huns', first in Belgium and then elsewhere. At one level, Germans are held in great suspicion because of their attitudes to war – a suspicion that is sustained:

> Generosity to the vanquished has always been a Briton's strong point, but, unfortunately for Germany, her utterly vile conduct during the war, until she knew the game was up, is sufficient to put her outside the pale for the next generation.[38]

Every German is subsequently held under suspicion, and the German flag is a symbol of all that is to be loathed:

> As a Hun, von Giespert knew that 'his name was mud' in almost every important sea-port on the Atlantic and Pacific shores. A nation cannot 'run amok' and institute a policy of 'sink everything without trace' and then expect to be treated on a pre-war footing by the States whose flags she has wantonly flouted and insulted.[39]

Germans are therefore typecast and fulfil the poor expectations of all Westerman's characters. All ranks join in the loathing of the German flag.

> 'Blowed if I'll fight under that rag', declared the first speaker hotly. 'I'm an Englishman, I am. Don't mind the French tricolour, mark you, but the Hun ensign, – no thank you'.[40]

But at another level, the antipathy for Germans is stronger and deeper. It is the German character, the innate characteristics of bullying, untrustworthiness, cruelty, vindictiveness and vulgarity, that are seen to be shared by all Germans.

> Von Giespert was on the point of shaking hands with himself and abusing some of his crew – an indication that he was regaining his normal state of mind.[41]

> It was a typically German and consequently, one-sided view to take.[42]

In fact the propaganda image of the German, as portrayed in cartoons, prevails:

> a general, swarthy and heavy jowled, who scowled under his heavy eyebrows at the crowd as he rode by. He was the personification of German brute force, a stiffly-rigid figure in grey.[43]

Although it is impossible to single out the effect of Westerman's books in the minds of his readers, there are echoes of his attitudes in many people. Whether the books exemplify these attitudes or form them, there is no doubt that they symbolize unselfconsciously held opinions. They support attitudes of distaste against Germans, attitudes that might seem dated but nevertheless still exist. The connection of recent cases with Westerman lies not only in the attitudes but in the words in which they expressed.

Given Westerman's depiction of foreigners, the British sense of superiority towards them is not surprising. But Westerman does not merely show up the failings of foreigners. Like Strang he points out exactly what it is that he feels makes the British superior. He believes they embody peculiar virtues, virtues that all foreigners ought to possess but have not attained, and perhaps never can. The British are characterized as being honest as well as brave, quiet in their determination, restrained in their enthusiasm, and altogether feeling much more strongly than their self-control would suggest. They have a sense of duty and are 'decent'. This shows in their treatment of foreigners, contrasting with German habits: 'He was averse to taking life unless absolutely necessary'.[44]

Even the notorious Captain Cain 'was strongly opposed to taking life wantonly, whether it be man or beast'.[45] The reason for this disinterested concern for others is the sense of honour, of doing the 'right thing': 'It's not a question of ties of relationship . . . It's a question of duty'. Only one failing seems to be conceded – the tendency to despise foreigners.[46]

The British demonstrate a measure of self-control, which contrasts with the mercurial volatility of other nations. Even close friendships between chums are understated:

> Had they been of any nationality but British, the lads would have fallen on each other's necks and perhaps kissed each other. Instead, they stood a yard apart and laughed – but their mutual joy was none the less genuine.[47]

The stress is on the strength of feeling as well as the restraint of its expression:

> 'Hulloa, there, Gerald, old boy! How goes it?' This was the Captain of the 'Meteors' greeting to his brother, who for months past had been in danger of being put to death by an unscrupulous Dictator.
>
> 'See you later' was Gerald's equally unconcerned reply, although at heart the brothers were longing to shake each other by the hand.[48]

It is important to stress that beneath the restraint that Westerman praises there lies a strength of feeling, as if the two go together. Westerman believes in personal friendships and loyalties – to one's chums, ship, and country. This explains the special attention which is devoted to cheering:

> The next instant the first of three hearty cheers burst forth from the throats of the crew, with whom Ross was a great favourite.[49]

The bonding of enthusiasm, and the expression given to an outburst of spontaneous feeling is seen to be peculiarly British, despite the outward restraint:

> The visit was understood to be a purely unofficial one, but the British bluejackets, always eager to recognize a brave act, were not to be denied. As the barge approached the flagship the shrill trills of the bos'n's whistle rang out. In a moment the upper decks and superstructure of the warship were black with humanity and the waters of Zandoras Bay echoed and re-echoed to three deep hearty cheers that only Britons can do full justice to.[50]

Strength of feeling allied to restraint gives the edge of self-control that marks out what Westerman admires in the British character. Again, he echoes the messages of Herbert Strang:

> With a cheer the undaunted seamen followed their gallant captain, ready to face death with the grim determination that is ever the enviable possession of every true Briton when up against desperate odds.[51]

The British, then, are symbols of bravery and kindliness to others, slow to be provoked, but when aroused, not to be gainsaid. People realize that 'being in the power of the British, their lives were safe'.[52] They respect the 'word of an Englishman'. In the end, all ranks of the British – including pirates – are at heart jolly good 'sportsmen':

> Still a bit dazed, Broadmayne went back to his corner and leant heavily against his chum. The men were cheering like mad. It dawned upon him that they were cheering *him.* Tough, desperate ruffians they might be, but they were sportsmen, members of a race that produces the best winners and the best losers in the world.[53]

Captain Cain, hero of two books, shows himself to be essentially British. He is willing to kill anyone, if necessary, but he would prefer not to kill his fellow countrymen.

> Cain was a pirate, a freebooter, an absconding swindler; but there was this in his favour – he had never molested a British ship.[54]

His partner, Pengelly, has the equivalent of a 'touch of the tar-brush', which explains his comparative villainy and lack of redemption. If virtues are marked out as peculiarly British, one is led to the reciprocal assumption that to be British is to be peculiarly virtuous. All British, therefore, contrast with other races:

> 'They will shoot us!' exclaimed the terrified man.
>
> 'Nonsense!' replied Kenneth. 'British seaman are not like . . . ' He was on the point of saying 'Germans', but pulled himself up and added, 'Pirates'.[55]

Again and again Westerman draws attention to the contrasts in behaviour between different nations. We know the particular vices of foreigners and the peculiar virtues of the British, but the contrasts, about which presumably one can do nothing, are constantly brought to our attention:

> 'No guts!' soliloquized Broadmayne scornfully. 'Can you imagine a British ship with that sized crew chucking in the sponge? They'd rush the blighters even if they only had broomsticks'.[56]

Again, gentleness to the weak or fallen is tempered by bravery in the face of any odds. It is the constant contrast to the actions of 'Dagos' and 'Huns'. There is a point, in *The Submarine Hunters,* when a British dreadnought rams and sinks a helpless German submarine, killing all its crew (the two British lads having jumped off in time). Even this is somehow justified as the actions of a 'vengeful' battle-ship. On the other hand,

> When it came to torpedoing helpless merchantmen, and jeering at the death-struggles of the unfortunate crews, Jack Tar began to regard the *unterseebooten* in the light of pirates and murderers.[57]

Some actions are clearly more justified than others, but it is not only the actions that people undertake that matter. Other people can show 'dash' and 'élan'. It is in the way in which the actions are carried out, the *tone* of them, that the contrast lies:

> Above the noise of grinding steel and the hiss of escaping steam came a clamorous panic-stricken yell from hundreds of throats.
>
> 'Not British this time', commented Jack.[58]

Racial characteristics are clearly delineated in actions, but Westerman adds clear physical attributes in support. A 'touch of the tarbrush' is a sign of villainy in itself. People are what they are seen to be: the Germans both stiff and skulking, and the British upright and handsome. The villain will have developed physical features (almost inevitably foreign) that exhibit his character:

> His features were sharp and pointed, his eyes close-set, while his eyebrows, slanting upwards from the bridge of his nose gave him a saturnine expression in keeping with his character.[59]

Such typecasting extends even to the kinds of movements that people display, so that every physical detail is symbolic of character:

> He lacked the natural elastic stride of the British Naval Officer. His movements resembled those of a thoroughly drilled soldier, yet ever and anon he would glance furtively . . . as if in a constant dread.[60]

One can guess where he comes from.

So innate are the essential characteristics of races that even dogs, with a true sense of British robustness, discern those who aren't quite 'right'. A German's 'shuffling feet' upset the dog: 'The dog never could tolerate a slovenly gait'.[61] A spy is discovered by a dog's natural instinct to take a bite out of his behind. But such instinctive reactions are also demonstrated by people. Sir Hugh, who has to choose a crew for his expedition to retrieve the treasure of the *Fusi-Yama* judges men (correctly) on their appearance. The true British naval officer, after all, is a specimen of a 'powerful-looking face that betokened courage and sagacity'.[62] A group of Germans, on the other hand, are 'stolid-looking men whose faces looked like masks concealing a vulgar triumph'.[63] In describing a Dutchman, Westerman imagines him as a picture of stolidity, with a leisurely manner, corpulent , and smoking a pipe: 'The sentry was one of a type'.[64] Only occasionally, given the German mastery of disguise, can the truth be hidden. But true identities cannot remain hidden for ever: 'Unmasked, he was no longer an amiable Swede but an unspeakable Hun'.[65]

The Englishman's superiority over other nationals is paralleled by the superiority of one class over another. Westerman's heroes are all, essentially, 'gentlemen'. They have money and wealthy 'paters'. They have servants and friends in high places. The 'other ranks' are there to serve, or cheer, or be dogged. They know their place, when they make their occasional individual appearances.

> 'Anyone called, Brown?' asked his master, when the man-servant opened the door of Eckersley-Rennie's town abode.
>
> 'No, Sir'.[66]
>
> 'Governor in, Sparkes?' he asked as the footman opened the door and stared with amazement at the 'young master'.[67]

The lower classes make only the briefest of anonymous entrances. It is assumed that the hero is moneyed and taught to be a gentleman:

> In response to the summons, the garçon produced the bill and gratefully accepted the modest tip that Everest bestowed upon him with becoming public schoolboy dignity.[68]

Money is often involved as a mark of a gentleman; there are certain standards that need to be kept up. An 'awfully decent chap' is one who 'insists' on lending a hundred francs. And there are certain things that have to be maintained.

> He travelled first class, for in spite of his dwindling purse he resolved to maintain the dignity of his family. It was one of the few concessions he made to appearances.[69]

The appearance of servants in Westerman's books is rare, and they remain essentially anonymous. But they are acknowledged to exist. The appearance of women is virtually nonexistent. It is as if the world were made up only of men. True, there has to be the occasional landlady. But women do not intrude. There is one sister in *Captain Blundell's Treasure* who, by dint of stowing away, joins the chums' cruise, but she remains in the background. Yet very occasionally women do get at least a mention. In this masculine world it happens to be on two occasions when men are learning French, a subject presumed to be associated with women. One chapter opens with a French lesson:

> 'No, no, boy. Not "la silence" but "le silence".'
>
> 'But Sir', protested the boy, 'it's according to rule; it ends in a silent "e".'
>
> 'An exception, Beverley', explained Mr Jaques. 'An exception. One of the peculiarities of the French language. But this might help you to remember. Silence is one of the things that a woman cannot keep; therefore the French place that word in the masculine gender'.[70]

And now the young man knows and remembers.

In the other lesson, the hero of the book is an officer pretending to be a French teacher, which gives Westerman the opportunity for another schoolboy joke:

> Taking up a piece of chalk the instructor wrote in a firm hand – 'Mon frère a raison, mais ma soeur a tort'. 'How do you translate zat?'
>
> 'My brother has reason that my sister is a tart, Sir'. A roar of laughter, audible even in the Captain's cabin, greeted this information. The rest of the midshipmen nearly succumbed to apoplexy.[71]

Such is the humour. And such, it appears, are the limits of their thoughts about women. But Westerman's world is almost completely masculine, with the notion of 'chums' and other relationships being very much based on military loyalty and relationships.

The language of Westerman is consistent with the type of hero he describes, with public-school phrasing ('awfully', 'I say', 'rather') and the occasional bombast ('telephonically . . . ocular demonstration'). But in all the examples of old-fashioned 'isms' it must be remembered that whilst the British are held up as the one nation to possess all the virtues, it is clear that there are genuine virtues in which Westerman believes. We might deplore the chauvinism of the attitudes expressed and the consistent antipathy to other races, but Westerman's heroes also stand for 'decency', for 'playing the game'. This consists of giving people a chance, of not shooting anyone in the back, of sparing life whenever possible, and of living by a real code of honour:

> 'Besides, Rex, you've forgotten one incident that makes this intended *coup de main* impossible'.
>
> 'What was that?'
>
> 'We shook hands with him'.

'Oh!' There was a sincere tone of contrition in Hornsby's exclamation. He now realized, through his companion's arguments, that any course that necessitated force or coercion would be unworthy of the conduct of an English gentleman. Hitherto in his impulsiveness he had overlooked this fact.

'Hang it all, man; you're right'.[72]

The code of the gentleman is very important. To some, it comes naturally, as a matter of breeding, but this sense of decency pervades the British of all classes. They admire their officers, but all soldiers, sailors, and adventurers are supposed to be 'keen and reliable', united by a common cause, whatever their 'social grade'. The 'sporting' spirit is shared by all: 'He's a rough sort', thought Ken, 'but he's a sportsman for all that'.[73]

Class distinctions are taken for granted. The attitudes of officers and men to each other, with their different types of respect, are held consistently throughout the books. The 'gentleman' is, after all, a man who doesn't just exhibit a code of manners, but who has power:

'And I'll hand Mrs Pedlar a ten pound note to give to you if the boat's lost . . . '

'Very good, Sir', assented the man with an air of relief. 'I knew'd as you were a gentleman'.[74]

Provided this power is handled well, it is assumed that all people will be happy to accept it. Westerman assumes it is the lot of the majority to follow and respect their leaders. His social philosophy is very clear, appealing to people's better instincts rather than to legislation:

'They [the Government] threaten their employees with dire pains and penalties, instead of paying them decent wages and appealing to their sense of honour. I know that for a fact. My experience teaches me that so long as you pick your men carefully in the first instance, pay them adequately and treat them considerately, they'll stick to you through thick and thin with unswerving loyalty'.[75]

Fundamentally Westerman believes in the potential virtues of all British, and to some extent, some other 'races'. At least he knows what he thinks virtues are, and exactly what it is that 'Huns' fail to achieve. There are, after all, some British, untainted by foreign blood, who fail to make the grade:

> 'You'll probably think it's confounded cheek on my part giving you advice, but if you come across a rank outsider by the name of Twill, steer clear of him'.[76]

For all the 'isms' that Westerman parades, there is also a confidence in a set of beliefs, in 'decency', and in being a sportsman.

Westerman therefore exemplifies the attitudes held by generations of boys – at their worst and at their best. Their attitudes contrast in many ways with those held by the younger generations. But there is no doubt that Westerman helped to form the outlook of those who believed in 'duty' and the peculiarly British virtues of the gentleman. The research that has been carried out on effects – whether of literature or of television – has shown how difficult it is to isolate a particular cause in the mass of information the individual receives. But it has also shown the importance of 'recognition' as opposed to 'recall', that is, the way in which beliefs are supported and bolstered by experience.[77] The readers of Westerman will have recognized and imbibed the beliefs he expressed, including the unexamined feelings of superiority and the belief in particular virtues.

Westerman's books continued to appeal to boys (and girls) for fifty years not only because, like Enid Blyton's stories, they contain safe and predictable adventure, but because they are secure in their tone and in their beliefs. They do not confine themselves purely to action. Indeed there are glimpses of intellectual effort:

> Whittingham sprang to his feet, the muscles of his face working with excitement.
>
> 'That's serious – decidedly serious'.
>
> Whittingham paused to wipe his face. The perspiration was slowly trickling down his forehead. He was labouring under intense mental strain.[78]

But for the most part, the characters reveal themselves in their actions, in their behaviour in the face of danger and their demeanour towards enemies. The stories delineate Westerman's idea of the British gentleman. They appear to us today as ethnocentric and chauvinistic. But the contrast between a soccer crowd rooting for 'England' and attacking others for no particular reason, except that they come from another country, and the way in which Westerman believes in decency, couldn't be greater.

At one level we see in Westerman's stories all the virtues of conventional appeal; excitement and adventure within a safe and undemanding framework. On the face of it a book like *The Isle of Mystery* is not unlike an adventure of Enid Blyton's.[79] But he also adds a pervasive tone which has not continued in modern literature for children. It might seem old-fashioned and quaint. It might be dated. But it is instantly recognized:

> 'It's jolly cold and mightily uncomfortable, but we'll keep a stiff upper lip and show him what we're made of'.[80]
>
> 'The Oxford's midshipmen were made of the right stuff'.[81]
>
> 'He was a white man, if ever there was'.[82]
>
> 'I think I am right in assuming that I am speaking to an Englishman and a gentleman?'[83]
>
> 'The fellow hadn't played the game from the beginning'.[84]

The question with these phrases, of course, is how long their influence lasts, and what immediate effects they might have made. It could be, as in the case of political incorrectness in Enid Blyton, that readers simply ignored them. It could be that they were part of the attraction of the adventure stories, but a small one to the reader, even if an important one to the writer. It could be that the world of shared assumptions has fallen apart. It is, after all, impossible to think now in terms of the connection between class and money.

> Altogether he looked as unlike a man who habitually travels first class as anyone could possibly imagine.[85]

There are, however, many aspects of Westerman that, in terms of reader satisfaction, do not date, and his books were translated into many languages.

Notes

1 Cullingford, C. *Children and Television.* Aldershot: Gower, 1984.
2 See Moyle, L. The Ridley–Chequers Affair and the German Character, in Cullingford, C. and Husemann, H. (eds), *Anglo-German Attitudes*, Avebury, 1995, pp.165–80.
3 See *Anglo-German Attitudes*, Chapters 2 and 3.
4 E.g. Vansittart describing Germans as 'Butcher Birds'.

5 *The Submarine Hunters: A Story of Naval Patrol Work in the Great War.* London: Blackie and Sons, 1918, p.231.
6 For accounts of viewers' political prejudice see Cullingford, C. *Children and Television.* Op. cit.
7 Westerman, Percy F. *A Sub and a Submarine: The Story of HM Submarine R19 in the Great War.* London: Blackie and Sons, 1918, p.155.
8 Westerman, Percy F. *The Fritz-Strafers: A Story of the Great War.* London: Partridge, 1918.
9 Westerman, Percy F. *The Flying Submarine.* London: Nisbet, 1912, p.138.
10 Ibid., p.138.
11 Ibid., p.190.
12 Westerman, Percy F. *Captain Cain.* London: Nisbet, 1924, p.65.
13 *The Flying Submarine*, p.296.
14 Westerman, Percy F. *King of Kilba.* London: Ward Lock, 1926, p.163.
15 Westerman, Percy F. *The Dreadnought of the Air.* London: Partridge, 1914, p.138.
16 Westerman, Percy F. *The Despatch Riders: The Adventures of Two British Motor-Cyclists in the Great War.* London: Blackie and Sons, 1915, p.15.
17 Green, J. R. *History of the English Peoples.* London: Macmillan, 1874. 'No spot in Britain can be so sacred to Englishmen as that which first felt the tread of English feet', p.7.
18 *Dreadnought of the Air*, p.221.
19 *Captain Cain*, p.55.
20 Ibid., p.147.
21 Ibid., p.250.
22 Ibid., p.87.
23 *A Sub and a Submarine*, p.196.
24 *King of Kilba*, p.187.
25 *Captain Cain*, p.248.
26 *King of Kilba*, p.178.
27 Ibid., p.121.
28 Ibid., pp.80, 106.
29 Westerman, Percy F. *The Salving of the 'Fusi-Yama': A Post War Story of the Sea.* London: Blackie and Sons, 1920, p.247.
30 Ibid., pp.105–6.
31 *The Flying Submarine*, pp.252, 282.

32 *Dreadnought of the Air*, p.214.
33 *Captain Cain*, p.79.
34 *The Salving of the 'Fusi-Yama'*, p.79.
35 *The Submarine Hunters*, p.97.
36 *The Despatch Riders, p.143*.
37 *The Submarine Hunters*, p.55.
38 *The Salving of the 'Fusi-Yama'*, p.201.
39 Ibid., p.39.
40 *The Pirate Submarine*. London: Nisbet, 1923, p.118.
41 *The Salving of the 'Fusi-Yama'*, p.241.
42 Ibid., p.201.
43 *The Despatch Riders*, p.194.
44 *The Dreadnought of the Air*, p.333.
45 *The Pirate Submarine*, p.76.
46 *A Sub and a Submarine*, p.225.
47 *The Submarine Hunters*, p.268.
48 *The Dreadnought of the Air*, p.276.
49 *The Submarine Hunters*, p.269.
50 *The Dreadnought of the Air*, p.376.
51 *A Sub and a Submarine*, p.149.
52 *The Dreadnought of the Air*, p.376.
53 *The Pirate Submarine*, p.117.
54 Ibid., p.170.
55 *The Despatch Riders*, p.286.
56 *The Pirate Submarine*, p.83.
57 *The Submarine Hunters*, p.157.
58 *The Salving of the 'Fusi-Yama'*, p.122.
59 *The Dreadnought of the Air*, p.264.
60 *The Submarine Hunters*, p.32.
61 *A Sub and a Submarine*, p.11.
62 *The Flying Submarine*, p.4.
63 *The Salving of the 'Fusi-Yama'*, p.143.
64 *The Submarine Hunters*, p.253.
65 *The Salving of the 'Fusi-Yama'*, p.90.
66 *Captain Blundell's Treasure*. London: Blackie and Sons, 1927, p.12.
67 *The Dreadnought of the Air*, p.379.
68 *The Despatch Riders*, p.13.
69 *The Dreadnought of the Air*, p.44.
70 *The Salving of the 'Fusi-Yama'*, p.113.
71 *The Dreadnought of the Air*, p.19.

72 *The Flying Submarine*, pp.101–2.
73 *King of Kilba*, p.45.
74 *The Flying Submarine*, p.46.
75 *The Dreadnought of the Air*, pp.98–9.
76 *Captain Blundell's Treasure*, p.180.
77 Cullingford, C. *Children and Television*. Op. cit.
78 *The Dreadnought of the Air*, p.81.
79 Westman, Percy F. *The Isle of Mystery*. London: Blackie and Sons, 1950.
80 *The Submarine Hunters*, p.93.
81 Ibid., p.218.
82 *Captain Cain*, p.282.
83 *The Dreadnought of the Air*, p.66.
84 *The Salving of the 'Fusi-Yama'*, p.263.
85 *The Dreadnought of the Air*, p.48.

5
The Perfect World of Enid Blyton

Percy Westerman's *The Isle of Mystery* is in many ways typical of the genre of adventure stories.[1] Three boys take a holiday on a small island when, without looking for trouble, they become caught up in a mystery which involves kidnapping and a foreign submarine. At one stage:

> Following the almost horizontal tramway for about fifty yards, the chums found themselves faced by what appeared to be a dead end to the cavern.
>
> Pulling a lever, Dellifer opened a pair of double doors . . . [2]

This balance between adventure, including danger, and safety, for there is always a way out and a happy ending, is typical. However deep the cave, one of the heroes, like Enid Blyton's Famous Five, will always be carrying a torch, and will find steps and, indeed, find a vantage point to overhear the villains' dastardly plans.

There are, however, subtle differences which make Enid Blyton more attractive than her competitors. The level of adventure is the kind that would be enjoyed like a game. Her heroes positively *look* for excitement, and keep reminding the readers of what a good time they are having. The level of essential safety is far deeper. There is never any sense of real threat. In Westerman's books there are actual world events involved: atom bombs, foreign powers, governments, and newspapers. No such reality creeps in to Enid Blyton's books. Hers is a fantasy world complete in itself.

Enid Blyton's appeal is still very great. Part of it rests on the psychological balance in which adventure has all threat removed, in which security has the edge over excitement. To most writers their own sense of real emotion and actual adventure, imagining what people might be going through, inevitably intrudes. Enid Blyton remains immune. Whilst some might suggest that her success lies in her assiduous publicity – after all fame feeds on itself – there are more substantial reasons for her immense and continuing appeal to children.

The success of Enid Blyton remains a phenomenon in itself. In

1995, for instance, six million copies of her books were sold, translated into 40 languages. In 1996 a company bought the remaining years of copyright for £13 million.[3] To some extent this opportunity to make money is through the marketing of certain characters, like Noddy and Big Ears, reminding one that more is made by 'spin-offs' than through the original product. Enid Blyton herself endorsed a whole range of toys and souvenirs based on her *Noddy* books.

As in the case of many other famous authors, success and derision go hand in hand. For many years there have been attempts to ban her books from libraries, and their style and content have been the subject of much criticism.[4] One of the favourite lines of attack is on her stereotypes – of class, ethnicity and nationality, as if this were a new invention. This is an easy charge to lay for there are many absurd examples of mindless prejudice far beyond the limits of 'political correctness'. A character called 'Sniffer', a traveller – whose father

> What a nasty piece of work he is! Why doesn't he get a hair cut?

– is described as being 'more like an odour than something living', is in fact treated with affectionate contempt.[5] The three golliwogs – Golly, Woggie and Niggar – 'you can't tell one from another' – are infamous. As for foreigners,

> We've got two at our school. One never cleans his teeth and the other howls if he gets a kick at football.[6]

One could fill a book with such examples but such attitudes neither make her popular nor prevent her popularity. In a way, they are so absurdly innocent that they are beside the point. Unlike Strang or Westerman she does not have a point to make through her chauvinism. 'Innocent' might seem the wrong word but there is, within the stories, a naive unawareness that is undeliberate and symbolic of the way she approached her writing. Children so easily ignore the stereotypes that it is as if they did not exist, for once a book is read on that level of criticism it ceases to operate in the way it is meant to.

Enid Blyton herself tried to explain her appeal.[7] She likened herself to 'thinking like a child', letting her mind go 'blank' and letting the story take over as if she were not in control. To be able to write like that, with an almost uncanny sense of the mental wave-length of her readers, is something that cannot be artificially induced. Those who have tried to write those things they despise – like sentimental verses inside greeting cards – know how difficult it is for those to whom they do not come as 'naturally as leaves to a tree'. Blyton senses what her readers want, and what will appeal to them most strongly. This includes that balance of security and fantasy that translates the familiar into a strange but perfect place.

> My public, bless them, feel in my books a sense of security ... [8] All adventure stories are 'escapist' ... mine among them. I cannot think why some people use this adjective in a derogative sense – such stories fulfil a very real need.[9]

> It is as if I were watching a story being unfolded on a bright screen ... I simply put down what I see and hear ... I do not have to stop and think for a moment.[10]

> Another odd thing is that my 'under-mind' seems to be able to receive such directions as the 'story must be 40,000 words long'.[11]

Such automatic writing, without the need for corrections or second thoughts, is explained as if she were merely the medium through which the stories come. Enid Blyton finds herself in the

> happy position of being able to write a story and read it for the first time at one and the same moment.[12]

She even laughs at her characters' jokes. All this suggests what some people call a childish innocence. But it still does not explain the appeal, however naturally it comes to her. Enid Blyton exemplifies one style of reading, one form of gratification which children seek.

Whatever the naivety of her books, the term 'innocence' would hardly be apt in describing Enid Blyton herself. This is not because of her assiduous publicity, from advertising *Famous Five* books in the *Secret Seven* series, to starting clubs and magazines.[13] It is more to do with the contrast between the ways in which she describes herself and the actual circumstances of her life and behaviour. The 'official' biography, by Barbara Stoney, is remarkable in gaining the approval of one of Blyton's daughters whilst being a devastating critique.[14] That daughter, Gillian Baverstock, who had defended her mother's reputation in the foreword, describing the biographer as not suffering from being 'young and unmarried, or male', calls the book 'honest and detached'.[15] What it reveals are certain characteristics which help explain what made Enid Blyton uniquely able to write the books she did.

Much has been made of Blyton's cruelties to others, her ability to quarrel and abandon people. Much more significant, however, is the way she determinedly used her books as an alternative to the real world. She was driven not by untroubled innocence but by the desire to ignore, indeed to escape from, terrible events. The way she coped with tragedy was to pretend that it didn't exist. She heard her parents quarrelling before her father abandoned the family, and made up stories of fantasy.[16] She hid, even from her closest friend, the circumstances of her home. Enid Blyton had, in fact, a traumatic childhood. Relationships with both her parents broke down. She was a very angry person, but her rage was suppressed. She remained secretive and uncommunicative.[17] This was true throughout her life.

> As far as she was concerned the matter was closed and an unpleasant episode was best forgotten.[18]

She often told people never to mention the matter again.

Instead, Enid Blyton kept all kinds of matters hidden and threw herself into her books. These became a genuinely alternative world since she was successful, like Roald Dahl, right from the start. By 1923 she was able to buy a substantial suburban house. She never had difficulties with her writing, about which, for all her approach to it, she was very professional. This meant that she was driven.

> Her marriage made no difference to her prolific writing output.[19]

Others, including daughters, and friends, were not allowed to disturb her. The world she created for her fans was complete in itself, and separate. She wrote about the antics of her dog long after it had died. She created the image of perfect domestic bliss far removed from the sordid details of reality.

It seems unlikely that Enid Blyton would have appealed so strongly to children if she had not instinctively understood their reasons for reading. The particular type of 'escape' she offers, beyond that of other writers, is driven by the suppressed recognition of the actual traumas of childhood. There is an emotional need underneath those factors that have such an appeal to the readers. She did not set out to discover, intellectually, what that appeal is. But she demonstrates it comprehensively. Whilst her success can be seen in all her books, whatever the age range (her one failure was an adult novel), it can be seen as clearly as anywhere in her adventure stories including the Famous Five and the Secret Seven (or the SS as she calls them).

Enid Blyton always quickly establishes the tone and style that suggests a good read. Even the chapter headings – 'Exciting Plans' – are reassuring on this point. A typical example is *The Secret Seven.*[20] There is a lot of dialogue and a lot of action, and little, if any, description. Let us take the opening of the book as an example and comment on it.

> 'We'd better have a meeting of the Secret Seven' said Peter to Janet. 'We haven't had one for ages'.

This remark quickly establishes the important fact that in Blyton's adventures children are in control. They can make things happen. They can set up their own excitements.

> 'Oh, yes', said Janet, shutting her book with a bang.

This is the way that books are always shut in Blyton, with a sense of relief, so completely does the sense of the story take over from the awareness of a reader of the act of reading.

> It isn't that we've forgotten about the society, Peter . . . '

Note how often the names are reinforced. They need to be, since that is the major characteristic that defines the children as different from each other.

> . . . it's just that we've had such a lot of exciting things to do in the Christmas holidays we simply haven't had time to call a meeting.'

In Blyton's books there are always exciting things to do, and children are having exciting times, in contrast to real life with its boredoms, its longeurs, and the sense of being lonely or at a loss. Blyton's children soon find distractions. It is ironic that all the actions contrast with the act of reading. When a book is read it is like a sign that there are not enough things to do, so the book is shut with relief.

> 'But we must', said Peter: 'It's no good having a Secret Society unless we use it. We'd better send out messages to the others'.

Such societies are always possible to set up; all you need are some people and a few plans, like messages.

> 'Five notes to write', groaned Janet. 'You're quicker at writing than I am, Peter – you write three and I'll write two'.

Blyton readily acknowledges children's laziness and their preference to avoid chores. She doesn't seek to set a good example like stressing the importance of thank you letters, or doing homework. Instead her characters quickly and refreshingly desist from doing things that their parents think they ought to do. And they quickly confess they can't do certain things fluently.

> 'Woof!' said Scamper, the golden spaniel.

Another character is introduced although it has to be recognized from the arithmetic when the two wrote five letters that he is not a full member of the Secret Seven. He does, however, have his occasional, if limited, uses, and his part to play.

> 'Yes, I know you'd love to write one, too, if you could', said Janet, patting the silky golden head.

It is after all a *golden* spaniel, and its motivation, if not capacity, is not in question. He is, in fact, as much of a character as any of the others.

> 'You can carry one in your mouth to deliver. That can be *your* job, Scamper.'

Everyone has a function, a particular task, whether it is inventing a password, making notes, producing food or wearing buttons marked SS. For a secret society such badges might seem illogical, but then the whole point is that they are essentially playing a game. They are here to invent their next adventure. At one and the same time Blyton stresses the availability of domestic excitement – meeting in the secret shed (also marked with an SS sign) – whilst at the same time making sure that the reader knows that something is going to happen, even if he or she does not know what it is.

Whatever the reader's taste the book sets out to gratify it. Gratification of appetite is a very important theme in these books. We constantly witness the children's eating, and more precise description goes into food than anything else. In the course of one book we come typically across the following items: boiled sweets, chocolate, jam tarts, oatmeal biscuits, lemonade, ginger buns, potted crab paste, ginger biscuits, currant buns, home-made strawberry jam, peppermints, orangeade, honey . . . and a bone for Scamper.[21] Food and feasts punctuate the action. Food is a highlight as well as a reward. The satisfaction of dealing with hunger is almost as great as that derived from adventures.

> Soon the children were sitting drinking ginger beer and lime juice mixed and eating delicious ices.

> The five of them had a lovely time that evening. They had tea about half past five and then bought what they wanted for supper and breakfast. New rolls, anchovy paste, a big round jam tart in a cardboard box, oranges, lime juice, a fat lettuce and some jam sandwiches – it seemed a very nice assortment indeed.[22]

It has been suggested that these descriptions of food are a reaction to the austerities of the post-war years and a nostalgia for an Edwardian past.[23] But food is a constant theme in much popular romantic fiction and the most obvious and immediate reminder of physical pleasures. Enid Blyton knows that her readers will be interested, that (despite changing tastes since the 1940s) their mouths will water. But most of all, the eating of food, of having their appetites gratified, is the most significant form of reward. And each adventure is punctuated with the prosaic realities of domestic life. Children need to eat. They enjoy their food, their midnight feasts, their indulgences. In the middle of a kidnap –

> 'I'm hungry. That's all', said Richard.

> The others suddenly realized that they too were hungry. In fact, *terribly* hungry! It was a long, long time since tea.[24]

Food at such times is a reminder of being grounded in domestic reality. There are two distinct kinds of food that Blyton depicts. One is the food of necessity, provided by adults – in fact that is one of the parents' prime functions, together with approval or disapproval. Occasionally a meal has to be got out of the way so that they can get on with the adventure.

> All the mothers were astonished to see how quickly the children gobbled their teas that afternoon.[25]

The other kind of food is the alternative, the almost elicit pleasures of midnight feasts. It is this food, chosen and collected by children, that is so amply delineated in the books.

> 'What a spread we've got tonight! Apples, Ginger Buns, Doughnuts, Peppermint Rock and what's in this bag? Oh yes, hazelnuts from your garden, Pam.[26]

The food that is liked is the more attractive, less healthy type of self-indulgence.

Food is, however, also the most palpable form of thanks and reward. Approval by adults might be gratifying but it isn't quite the same as being given something to eat. As long as they escape the disapproval of parents and policemen children do not mind if they are praised or not. But they do appreciate rewards. Money can buy them food.

> 'Peter, here's some money. Take all the Secret Seven out and give them a thumping good tea, ice-creams and all.'[27]

> 'Now we want to make you all a handsome present for any inconvenience you have suffered – er – ten pounds for you to spend on ice-creams and so on.'[28]

> Ham and tongue and pies, crisp lettuce, tomatoes, a dozen hard-boiled eggs, a fruit tart and jam tart and two great jugs of creamy milk.[29]

These are the ways in which adults can demonstrate their appreciation, whether it is in the kind of food of which they approve or, more particularly, if it is in the form of the indulgences that children like.

Eating food is one of the central focal points that bring children together. Food is described because they are all sharing it; the idea of the 'feast' is the forming of the group. All these adventure stories depend on the idea of a close-knit (if also occasionally quarrelsome) group who 'belong'. The members of the group are not so much distinguished for their individual characters as for their membership; they are 'in' and have their functions. This makes them easy to identify with.[30] The reader does not look at one 'person' and say 'I'd like to be like that'. The reader is the extra, anonymous, individual presence in a collective of other children. Entry into the group is eased since the reader is not self-conscious or self-aware. It is as if he or she were simply 'there', acting and observing the actions of others.

The groups like the five and the seven are the more powerful because they operate outside the world of adults. Whilst the security of the domestic world surrounds them, they have time and space to be intrepid and resourceful. They are independent, but they are also bolstered by each other.[31] Membership of the group is all important and outsiders are not welcome.

> 'That's nothing to do with *you*!' said Jack. 'You don't belong to it, and what's more, you never will!'[32]

Even the dog is aware of the distinction between members and strangers:

> He hadn't at all approved of Susie being in his shed. He knew she wasn't a member![33]

The security that the books offer, in contrast with the too often traumatic social world of friendship and enmity, is their acknowledgement of being safe with others, unchallenged and accepted.[34] The groups are generally unthreatening. Whilst there are arguments the overall cohesion and consistency of the group is never challenged. Readers are therefore presented not only with malleable characters with personal characteristics and looks as generalized as those depicted in the illustrations, but also with the security of a permanent group to which a set number belong. Once again this sense of cohesion and security contrasts with the actual experiences of friendships and enmities that are usual at school. Any study of children's friendships reveal the miseries as well as the joys of relationships. There are always times when children feel like outsiders, when they are ostracized by others. If one child is busy with a friend she will show little compassion for the hurt feelings of others. The experience of being rejected is one that is shared at one time or another by all children. Enid Blyton's groups offer no such threat or possibility. The children that the readers imaginatively join are always with each other, a coherent and unthreatened whole. There is no question of ever breaking the security of belonging.

But then Enid Blyton's world of adventures in which the five or seven are placed is, as is the case in more recent literature for children, a long way from school. They are placed in idyllic surroundings, like the ever-changing world of fantasy that surrounds *Rupert*; a mixture of the homely, with meadows and deciduous woods and hills, a parody of the perfect English countryside. The fact that into this landscape appear a variety of strange characters, coming out of flying machines or castles or tunnels only reinforces the deliberate normality of the landscape. Whilst Enid Blyton makes copious use of islands and lighthouses, ruins and caves, these are all set in places that are fundamentally secure and, in a world of fantasy, familiar. Country lanes without traffic, fields to picnic in, high hedges and pretty cottages are all a safe playground in which the children can undergo their safe adventures.

The symbolism of place is very important for children. They associate particular places with definite atmospheres and find some places – dark, gloomy and windswept – off-putting.[35] They also have images of their favourite places which are associated with comfort and security. This includes a picture of the countryside as a state of bliss, a place where they can all roam.[36] The idea of open space and freedom of manoeuvre, away from the threat of the town, goes very deep and is shared by all children wherever they live. Enid Blyton naturally makes use of this. Her children might have adventures but they are never far away from the idyllic world of imaginary landscapes. Whilst it contains plenty of hiding places and obscure corners it is nevertheless like a theme part of the mind; a place to roam where trees stand in artificial copses rather than in a 'gloomy' forest, where hills are easy to climb and no meadow is compromised by the presence of animals or the soiling of the plough. This space in which they have such freedom is an important background to their fun. There is a shadowy world of darkness and caves and earth, and digging things up; but it is contrasted with the bright and beautiful world of sun and flowers. After all, as in the way that people are judged by their looks so children see places associated with either the upright or the shifty. At one point they suspect a man of stealing, since they find his spectacle case in a car which had been stolen, and then follow him. He lives in:

> . . . a little lane, set with pretty little cottages . . . a nice little place with a colourful garden.
>
> 'Well, it doesn't *look* like the home of a crook'.
>
> Somehow this pretty garden and trim little cottage didn't seem the kind of place those men would live in![37]

Rest assured, the man turns out to be all right. He proves that by giving them ten shillings. It is established in Enid Blyton that not only can you tell a person's character from their complexion, clothes, or gait, but you know a person by where he lives. All the words denote, without any particular detail, that 'pretty as a picture' cottage: 'little, pretty little, nice little, trim little, colourful, pretty . . .'. The diminutive undermines threat.

The actual crooks live, of course, in a very different style.

> A rather dirty looking eating house. 'Sid's Café' was painted over the top of the very messy windows. ... stuffy looking men, unshaved and dirty.[38]

Dirtiness is always put next to ungodliness but Blyton's blank visual sense relies on the word 'looking' inviting the reader to supply his or her own images. She does not distance the reader by objective description but appeals to that symbolic sense of place that contrasts darkness and light, the hard and the soft. What is most remarkable, however, is the assiduity with which she holds on to security. There are caves, but also torches. Caves can be made into havens:

> nice and big, and with a lovely sandy floor! Nobody would ever find it![39]

Comfort, security and excitement are all bound up together. It is like an invented dream in which, in contrast to the nightmare of reality, the child is never discovered. Instead he looks out from the safe place without being seen.

This psychological state of looking out from a position of security is also central to the plots. Much depends on overhearing.[40] The five or the seven almost invariably discover what is going on through listening to conversations, or possibly discovering notes. The villains are trying to be obscure and hide in dark corners; but our heroes, from the safety of their vantage points, learn all. The children always find out what the villains are up to because they overhear what they say. They might be disguised as a guy, or as a snowman – they are, after all, inventive – but they are inevitably successful. One might think there would be some moments of stress or danger but each prospect of the dark or a secret passage thrills rather than disturbs:

> A secret way ... the idea excited them all! Where was the passage? Nobody could imagine it!
>
> 'Careful now, Julian, there may be somebody lying in wait! ...'
>
> 'See that small hole? Well, I bet if we crawl through that we'll find it's the way up to the secret passage'.[41]

Despite the threat of an enemy and despite the darkness there is no sense of danger. This is for several reasons. One is that the children are seeking out the passage; they are in control. They are excited rather than frightened. Another is that there is always a back-up.

Even if one of them is caught or discovered, there is another one keeping a watchful eye. And even if they are in a cave, or even if they are captured and locked in a cupboard, they *always* have a torch. A torch is the symbol of safety, of their control of their environment. But it is also a symbol of the psychological safety net; Enid Blyton assures you she is in control.

The sense of sure control over what is happening is reinforced by the author's constant commentary. The readers are always reminded how exciting it all is, but before this they are assured that excitement will be provided. Again it is carefully controlled, sought out:

> 'But you can't have adventures in a lighthouse – it's out on the rocks, all by itself, as lonely as can be! There aren't any adventures to be found *there!*'
>
> Ah, you wait and see, Tinker! You don't know the Five! If there's any adventure about, they're bound to be right in the middle of it![42]

You are as reassured about adventure as you are about security. Adventure is something you look for as an antidote to the ordinariness of life. No wonder that what Enid Blyton extols as 'escapism' is so clearly and so persistently flagged. This is the promise of the books. Whilst the books within the stories are being shut with a bang, thereby turning away from boredom, in the books themselves the looking for a safe adventure, and the promise of it, is put before the reader.

> 'Can't we solve a mystery, or something like that?' suggested George. 'If we can't find something wrong to put right, we might be able to find a mystery to clear up'.[43]

The framework of security which surrounds the promise of anticipated adventure appeals strongly and continuously to children. It is, indeed, a form of play, or the boundaries of an activity in which their minds can roam.[44] The normal is depicted as dull.

> Absolutely nothing had turned up ... after having so many exciting adventures it was a bit dull just to go on playing games and talking.[45]

Or, in so many words, being a normal child with normal activities, includes the lacunae of boredom. If an adventure cannot alleviate the time – that might be too much – a simulation can. The tone of voice in the writing might be arch, but it shows an unaffected sharing of anticipated excitement.

> Be patient, Secret Seven. One may be just round the corner. You just never know!

But, of course, you do.

The distinction between actual excitement and controlled excitement is a fine one but very important. It depends on excluding any hint of the real world as seen through the media, or the arguments of the everyday. It means instinctively knowing just how far to go, and at what point to introduce the reminders of safety, the torch or the back-up. Occasionally Enid Blyton senses this distinction, as if she has gone too far. The Famous Five are safe but sometimes reality intrudes on outsiders.

> Richard had been having a much too exciting time.[46]

But then he did not *choose* what happened.

Based on the security and familiarity of the 'adventures' the reader is constantly reminded about what an exciting time is being had by all. 'They had an exciting time'. 'The meeting that afternoon was very interesting and full of excitement'. This might seen otiose in the circumstances, but it is an essential device for Enid Blyton. It gives both an enclosing and distancing effect. It is both a reassurance and a cajoling. Chapter headings are used to signal events:

> What happened to Jack.
> Exciting plans.
> An exciting plan.
> What an excitement!
> A wonderful finish!
> A very exciting finish!

Readers are constantly reminded that events will happen (not that there are too many) so that there is a sense of constant if fairly uniform pace. One incident per chapter is more than enough, but if the pace is uniform, it does not slacken. One form of the overheard remark which gives the clue is the written message. When this is found it gives a time and a place where the villains can be overheard. Invariably the anticipated meeting becomes the subject of the subsequent chapter. Scamper (sic) finds a notebook with a name and a message.

> Meet him at the Post Office seat 8.30pm. 15th.
> That's today!
> Colin's heart began to beat faster – this *was* fun![47]

> Chapter 3. Exciting Plans.
> Gang meet in old workmen's shed. 5pm Wednesday.
> Phew, that's tomorrow. Gosh, we *are* on to something.[48]

This is the moment at which they 'gobble' their food so fast that adults are astonished.

Children have excitements within the framework of a safe world. Part of the frame includes adults. One of their primary functions is to provide meals. These are regular intervals sometimes drawing attention to passing time, sometimes reminding the reader of the 'normal' context and sometimes relished for their own sake. Adults provide the food or provide the 'treats', the rewards. Adults also have a certain authority so that the children's attitude to them is somewhat ambivalent. Adults, especially parents, play a peculiar role in children's lives. They are seen to be moody, having their own eccentric preoccupations, living in a mysterious world of their own.[49] But they also intrude at regular intervals. In these books the status of children living within an adult world, seen but not heard, is reversed. It is the children who are free to make decisions. Only occasionally do adults seriously interfere, although they always have the authority and the potential to do so.

> Blow Miss Fly! ... He kicked his toes against each step as he went upstairs. He didn't dare to slam the door 'though he felt like it ... Miss Fly should *not* stop him from doing what he wanted to do![50]

Part of the pleasure of the adventures is the escape from adult authority and this would be diminished if we were not occasionally reminded of it. At beginnings and endings, especially the latter, adults are brought in, to give approval or hand out tips. They provide food but also tell them to 'tidy their rooms'. The excitement of going out in the dark is strengthened by its clandestine nature, like midnight feasts: adults would not approve, although they would understand and afterwards condone. Adults are peripheral because they live in a world of their own. This is not unlike that of the actual experience of all children, for whom friendship and peer groups are of far higher salience. Adults are closely observed and often found peculiar.

> Julian winked at Dick and Anne kicked George under the table. Would Uncle Quentin explode into a temper, as he sometimes did?
>
> Uncle Quentin lived in a world of his own, a world of theories and figures and diagrams.[51]

Adults provide a support, a firm base, and they also provide the villains. Good people live in pretty cottages and like children. Bad people not only do not have children of their own but dislike them. In many of these stories there are several occasions when the children are shouted at. It might be a safe world but they are not alone in it, and they are hurt by being told off.

> I won't have any cheek from children . . . You clear off now before I tell my husband to chase you.[52]

> 'Now then! What are you doing here? Clear off, you kids, or I'll report you to your parents!'[53]

> A voice called out to him. 'Clear off, you! We Don't want no strangers here!' [sic][54]

The children might be free to roam but they are repeatedly told to 'clear off'. When that happens, of course, it is a clear indication that they are on to something but there is nevertheless a reverberation in the lives of children reading the stories. Being shouted at by an angry adult can be a laughing matter but only if you are in a group and like to provoke it. Otherwise it can be disturbing.

> 'Now, then, what are you doing here, lolling about? Don't you dare take fruit off my barrow! I've caught you boys doing it before and I'll call the police if you do. Clear off!'
>
> . . . Peter was shocked. How dare this man say things like that to him?[55]

The appearance of adults in these stories is significant and however stereotyped is part of the essential appeal. Children both accept and resent the authority of parents. They want their approval even if they cavil against their rules. Part of the reward for their success is this approval.

> He spoke in such a severe voice that the children felt quite alarmed. Then he smiled and they saw that actually he was very pleased with them.[56]

There are times when adults treat them with contempt – 'Don't ask silly questions and waste my time!' Enid Blyton concentrates on children's general reaction to, or relationship with, an adult world. There are no characters as such but a series of fairly anonymous figures with whom or against whom the children carry out their actions. It does not therefore matter that these are stereotypes: 'Mr Holikoff, it's a peculiar name, isn't it?' Could this be the villain? [He is.] The children themselves are not really characters as such but types that carry out actions. In so far as there are many characteristics – and all remember the girl George who wishes to be a boy and whom even her father apparently calls 'he' – they are indistinguishable from the roles they will play, like ranks in the army.

> Anne . . . was the smallest and the only really manageable one.
>
> George *was* difficult, but it didn't make her any less difficult if the fact was pointed out.[57]

Even dogs play their characteristic part:

> 'Woof' said Timmy, wagging his tail politely.[58]

This lack of distraction from description or characterization does not mean that Enid Blyton does not take relationships into account. Others need to be related to, and dealt with, whether child or adult. The children are, in fact, very snappy with each other.

> Peter could be very strict. Jack didn't like being ticked off in front of people . . .
>
> Peter's indignant face looked out. 'Whatever are you shouting for? Do you want everyone in the village to know our password, you fool?'[59]

Just as strangers shout 'clear off!' or 'pestering little varmints!', so their relationships are characterized by phrases like 'Be sensible!', 'Don't interrupt!'. Words like 'sternly' abound. Outsiders are patronized.

> If there was any answering back to be done, Julian could always do it!'[60]

There are, in fact, just enough glimpses of misery for the journey into the freedom and security of adventure to be the more prized. There are not many of these and mostly they are so subtle that they are hardly noticed. But, as with adults, unhappiness is the background that throws into relief the immediacy of the adventures.

> Richard looked quite taken aback. He shrank into a corner and didn't say another word. He was very miserable. Nobody liked him, nobody believed him, nobody trusted him. Richard felt very, very small indeed.[61]

However simply expressed, all children will recognize the trauma of that feeling. But the recurring background for the lovely adventures these children have is that they are both in control of them and wanting something to happen. They are bored. Therefore Enid Blyton suggests they can create events (just as she does for them).

> 'We've been here a week and I've been bored every single minute!', said George.[62]

Being told off, having to write letters, tidy the room, eat healthy food, being shouted at and treated with contempt – these are the conditions of childhood against which the actions are set. Even the act of reading is depicted as drudgery, as if Enid Blyton had ironically transformed it.

Enid Blyton continues to have a huge following. Her remarkable success lies in her instinctive awareness of what appeals to children. Her peculiar 'genius', if that is the right word, is to have found a formula of foreground safety and action that emerges from what is for all children, at least at times, a background of the traumas and disappointments of growing up. No other author of adventure stories creates such a world of safety and security. No other author keeps the real social world so much at bay. But perhaps no other author had such an instinctive belief in suppression. Whatever the reason, her formula works and says something about children's needs, as well as tastes.

There is, however, one character who will always be linked with Enid Blyton: Noddy, that prize possession for the marketing men. I once wrote an ironic piece – not a mistake Enid Blyton would have made – linking Noddy's value system to that of Mrs Thatcher.[63] It appears that some people thought, or chose to think, that this was serious. Whilst it was amusing to explore the strange world of Noddy and Big-Ears in which, as usual, many stereotypes and politically ambiguous as well as incorrect attitudes abound, a more significant theme also emerged. The world that is encapsulated in Noddy does not include the intrusion of adults. It is self-contained. But it also captures the outlook of children on the adult world. They attempt to make sense of so much that engages the attention of adults, from adults' own peculiar preoccupations and arguments to the most powerful medium of transactions: money. Children are rarely told how the economic and social world operates but are left to find out for themselves. This is a difficult process. The result is that their unsuppressed intelligence has to make sense of what is to them a secret and secretive world – 'you're too young to understand' – in their own way.

Enid Blyton, whatever her own financial prowess, which was considerable, captures the outlook of an untutored mind on the visible and complex world of social and monetary interchange. Toyland, as depicted in the *Noddy* books, gives a clear, and unironic, account of a society in which individuals, through their hard work, or through their understanding of the system, or through their ability to undermine the system, succeed and accumulate money. Some are rich and some are poor. There is no such thing as society or community, but individuals seeking to do the best for themselves. The essential theme is of Noddy, once he has been passed by the immigration services, proving he is a valuable and upstanding citizen by earning his keep through running his taxi-service. His ambition is to have the security of owning his own house. He knows he is up against competition, and, with his friend Big Ears, is not afraid of bending the rules, let alone morality, to win.

The contrasts between rich and poor are clear. So is the need to try hard, to make money. Some make more than others, according to their performance. Rewards, in the palpable form of money, are paramount. If one had to give a crude description of capital, market forces and all the essential parameters of a modern economy to someone coming from another planet, it would be something like this, the world described as it is at the essential core of market forces. Enid Blyton would have been taken aback both by the idea that she described the real world, or that she preached a gospel of Thatcherism or the Welfare State. But she wouldn't have laughed. What she managed to do, inadvertently or not, was to reveal the way that children actually see their circumstances, try to come to terms with them, and reconcile themselves to them, as well as hiding from them. No wonder her books appeal.

Notes

1 Westerman, Percy F. *The Isle of Mystery*. London: Blackie and Sons, 1950.
2 Ibid., pp.100–1.
3 Trocadero, buying out Enid Blyton's two daughters to own the world rights.
4 Dixon, B. The tiny world of Enid Blyton. *Children's Literature in Education*. No.15, 1974, pp.43–61.

5 Blyton, E. *Five go to Mystery Moor.* London: Hodder and Stoughton, 1954, p.43.

6 *The Mystery of the Vanished Prince.* London: Methuen, 1951, p.72.

7 McKellar, P. *Imagination and Thinking.* London: Cohen and West, 1957.

8 Stoney, B. *Enid Blyton: A Biography.* London: Hodder and Stoughton, 1974, p.149.

9 Ibid., p.206.

10 This idea of being taken over by an almost unbidden muse has a long history at a rather higher level. Cf. Robert Graves's *The White Goddess.*

11 Stoney, B. Op. cit., p.207.

12 McKellar, P. Op. cit., p.87.

13 In, for example, *The Secret Seven Win Through.* London: Hodder and Stoughton, 1955. The *Famous Five* books are almost as important to the children in their cave as the food.

14 Stoney, B. Op. cit.

15 Ibid., p.7.

16 Ibid., p.19.

17 Ibid., p.35.

18 Ibid., p.101.

19 Ibid., p.66.

20 *The Secret Seven.* London: Hodder and Stoughton, 1949.

21 In *The Secret Seven Win Through.*

22 *Five Get into Trouble.* London: Hodder and Stoughton, 1954.

23 Barker, K. The use of food in Enid Blyton's fiction. *Children's Literature in Education.* Vol.13, No.1, 1982, pp.4–12.

24 *Five Get into Trouble.*

25 *Good Work, Secret Seven.* London: Hodder and Stoughton, 1954.

26 Ibid.

27 *The Secret Seven Win Through.*

28 *Five Get into Trouble.*

29 *Five go Down to the Sea.* London: Hodder and Stoughton, 1953.

30 Fry, D. *Children Talk About Books: Seeing Themselves as Readers.* Milton Keynes: Open University Press, 1985.

31 Sarland, C. The Secret Seven vs the Twits: Cultural clash or cosy combination? *Signal.* Vol.42, 1983, pp.155–71.

32 *Good Work, Secret Seven.*

33 Ibid.
34 Davies, B. *Life in the Classroom and Playground.* London: Routledge, 1982.
35 Hart, R. *Children's Experience of Place.* New York: Levington, 1979. Cullingford, C. *The Inner World of the School.* London: Cassell, 1991.
36 Cullingford, C. Children's attitudes to the environment, in Harris, G. and Blackwell, C. *Environmental Issues in Education.* Aldershot: Arena, 1996, pp.21–36.
37 *Good Work, Secret Seven.*
38 Ibid.
39 *The Secret Seven Win Through.*
40 The books are probably as dependent on this theatrical device as *Much Ado About Nothing.*
41 *Five go Down to the Sea.*
42 *Five go to Demon's Rocks.* London: Hodder and Stoughton, 1961.
43 *The Secret Seven.*
44 Sarland, C. Op. cit.
45 *Good Work, Secret Seven.*
46 *Five Get into Trouble.*
47 *The Secret Seven Win Through.*
48 *Good Work, Secret Seven.*
49 See Chapter Six in Cullingford, C. *Parents, Education and the State.* Aldershot: Arena, 1996.
50 *The Secret Seven.*
51 *Five Get into Trouble.*
52 *The Secret Seven Win Through.*
53 *Good Work, Secret Seven.*
54 *Five Get into Trouble.*
55 *Good Work, Secret Seven.*
56 *The Secret Seven.*
57 *Five Get into Trouble.*
58 *Five go to Mystery Moor.*
59 *Secret Seven.*
60 *Five Get into Trouble.*
61 Ibid.
62 *Mystery Man.*
63 Cullingford, C. Why Toyland is really our land. *Times Educational Supplement.* Nov. 11, 1994.

6

Sense and Sensuality: From Angela Brazil to *Point Romance*

There have recently appeared a number of books which analyse and deconstruct the content of girls' stories. This is an avowed result of the growing interest in the feminist perspective. What marks these books out is their interest in the content, and in their presentation of a woman-centred world.[1] Thus the remembered childhood pleasures of reading Elsie Jeanette Oxenham, Dorita Fairlie Bruce or Elinor Mary Brent-Dyer are reconsidered in the light of the latent messages that they presented.[2] The authors cited here all wrote series – like the *Chalet School* books – with recognizable characters and familiar themes.

In the analysis of such stories it is sometimes hard to catch the right tone. It is easy to mock, and yet these books are taken seriously for depicting a women's world in which they are free of the domination of men. The undercurrent of the arguments about these books is ostensibly concerned with their depiction of women. Are women shown as passive and domestic in contrast to the heroic actions of men?[3] Are women saved by marriage and domestic duties? Are these books depicting a patriarchal society? Or do these books actually explore the realities of life beyond the 'training to be a wife and mother'? These arguments are about content and tone, but they all rest on one major assumption, and that is that what is read somehow will affect, indeed form, the reader. The ostensible concern is about the depiction of women, but the underlying one is about the effects on the readers.

This chapter is not about to enter into the same field. It is not about content and its hidden messages, but the reasons *why* the books appeal and why they are so widely read. It is, of course, impossible entirely to separate content from appeal, what is depicted from what is influential. But the focus is different. There are certain characteristics, in style and tone, in construction as well as in the depiction of attitudes, that provide another example of children's tastes. The authors might have explicit or implicit messages in their stories but their primary motivation is to satisfy their readers. They instinctively know what will appeal and be attractive and they consciously put this into practice.

The most popular of the writers of girls' fiction wrote series, creating familiar territory. The success of one book would reinforce that of another. It became de-rigeur to collect all the books in a series, a phenomenon that has been fast surpassed by more recent marketing when a prolific series like the *Baby-Sitters Club* written by one author is produced almost as fast and easily as books by Barbara Cartland.[4] In one sense all popular children's books are part of a series. There are few genuine 'one-offs', for they tend to follow the same patterns, the similar formulae that are known to appeal. There are certain characteristics which have not changed over the years, just as there are others, like attitudes towards sex, which have. Here we are interested in what is attractive, in structure, style, and tone.

Part, if only part, of the appeal of the books lies in the images of women with which the readers can relate. This might be an image of sturdy self-reliance or of another example of women 'learning their place', or both at the same time, but it is not the stereotypes that are the central secrets of popularity. Whilst certain stereotypical images have an appeal in themselves, provided they are shared by the reader, they appeal more because they depict superiorities over others than because they advertise a particular point of view. There are stereotypes of adventure as well as of people, stereotypical behaviours as well as attitudes. At one level it is apparent that many girls' stories are versions of Herbert Strang or of Westerman, a world full of safe adventure in which there are brave heroes and obvious villains and where the hero or heroes will prevail, giving vent to familiar attitudes. Some books are designed to appeal to girls, but they do so essentially because they have a heroine, not a hero, rather than because the style of action is different.

One such example of writing for girls is Bessie Marchant who wrote many books at about the same time as Herbert Strang. She specialized in 'tales of adventure' set in Uruguay, or Australia, or New Zealand, or Central America, or the Indian Frontier, or Western Canada, or Tierra de Fuego, or Manitoba ... her geographical spread is impressive. But the stories, whilst differing in descriptive detail, all convey familiar attitudes of their time and rely on similar constructions of plot. As in the stories written specifically for boys there is a contrast between the pluck, honesty and the uprightness of the individual hero and the more generalizable and pitiable limitations of the patronized natives.

> because I promised her a red ribbon if she did the work quickly and well she is going ahead as vigorously as a white woman.[5]

> The Indians can't stand overmuch in the way of temptation, neither man nor woman.[6]

There is, however, another dimension to these books which is the raising of the question of role. On the one hand we are offered the homilies that could apply to anyone, the messages that the author wishes to convey –

> of course she succeeded, as people always do if they only try hard enough.[7]

> troubles are not mended by being brooded over.[8]

But these are girls, or women, showing the same independence and the same pluck as the men. To an extent this is taken for granted but the juxtaposition of the heroes with the native points out something of the distinction. Natives, generalized as they are, reveal the standard norms:

> Ignorant she was, and as superstitious and dirty as the rest of her class, but her faithfulness and devotion were not to be excelled, while the maternal instinct in her rose to the height of a passion and she mothered every weakly thing that came within her reach.[9]

Here we have the dominance of the maternal 'instinct' that leads both to estimable qualities or (blind) devotion and to equally instinctive ignorance, superstition and lack of discrimination. But is that typical of the 'woman' or of the 'native'? In contrast, the eponymous heroine is independent and avoids the 'domestic ménage'.

> If anyone had been so bold as to suggest that her time would be more profitably spent in looking after the affairs of home, she would probably have laughed them to scorn, declaring that any stupid could run a house and cook food, but that it took a person with brains to tempt the wily otter to its doom or secure a good hank of halibut and herring.[10]

This is a recognition both of the qualities and the unusual nature of the heroine. Whilst it might not in fact be thought easy to run a house or cook food and it might even require some brains, as well as 'instinct', the heroine is singled out as unusual.

> Never even wishing for luxuries or prettiness, such as the hearts of most girls yearn after.[11]

There is an ambiguity of attitude that belies the notion that these romances are designed to prepare girls for motherhood and for subservience. Motherhood might come to many of them, but these homilies do not suggest that 'luxuries or prettiness' are all that they should yearn for. What is apparent in these stories and in those of Angela Brazil is that there are roles for women that are genuinely independent and which lead to careers. Their worlds are neither self-enclosed into men-free zones nor preaching a simple message.

Whilst Bessie Marchant concentrated on the outposts of Empire, Angela Brazil became famous for her school stories. Her work was characteristically praised as 'so realistic that it should appeal to all girls'.[12] This theme is reiterated about all her stories as if she had a remarkable grasp of reality and as if the real was what should most appeal. Her books, in fact, follow the fantastic formula of many of these adventure stories and in a number of ways they exhibit the same characteristics as Enid Blyton, who could never be called realistic. There are, however, some interesting differences. Perhaps it is these particular differences that were earmarked as 'realistic'.

As in Enid Blyton the adventure takes place after a period of waiting for it to happen. Perhaps this boredom with school or with holidays – nothing to do – could be called realism, but it is in fact a device to engage the reader in the mood that makes her turn to a book looking for contrasting excitement. One story begins with returning to the boredom of school.

> If there's one slack, slow business in this wide world . . . it's coming back to school after the Easter holidays . . . [13]

Another begins with complaints about thirteen weeks of boring lessons.[14] In such circumstances what else could a book provide but alternative excitement, an adventure waiting to be created. But the assumption which is shared is that 'normal' life, from which the book creates relief, is dull, even if necessarily so. In such conditions there will be the desire for excitement, if not in real life, then in the mind. The girls look for 'romance'.

> The idea that Mrs Wilson was concealing the treasure for her own ends was a thrilling one.[15]

This control over adventure leads to several similarities with the techniques of Enid Blyton. There are a number of passages and dark places, caverns, hidden rooms and large medieval trunks.

They present the opportunity to eavesdrop on what is going on. There is the strong corporate life of groups, belonging together, sharing the same mission and identity. This is part of the advantage of the setting, as Angela Brazil explicitly recognizes –

> It is not always easy for a day school to have the same corporate life as a boarding school.[16]

The life on which she focuses, however, is that of the group, normally a central pair at its core, around which others – 'girls, and teachers, and servants, and everyone' – remain in the background and which is defined against the strange and alternative world of adults, at once respected for their power, and despised for their idiosyncrasies.

> Mrs Greenwood . . . insisted upon a certain standard of home politeness being maintained, and would tolerate neither domineering in the elder ones nor whining amongst the younger.[17]

> Mrs Hoffman . . . knew no language but her own, and had no desire to acquire any other, regarding German as the tongue into which her husband relapsed when more than usually annoyed and therefore better to be ignored than understood.[18]

The attitude of Mrs Hoffman to her husband's idiosyncrasies, better ignored than understood, is shared by and encapsulates children's attitude to the arcane mysteries of adulthood. They seem to have their own peculiar agendas. At the same time adults in positions of authority are required to exercise power and judgement, to set fair rules and insist on their effectiveness.

The marking out of the territory of the group, the seeking of adventure against a context of boredom – both on a bedrock of security – is familiar to many writers. But Angela Brazil also differs from Enid Blyton in some respects. The main difference is that there are at least some hints of the real world. Perhaps the blurb writers were correct. There are some insights into issues which unite character and opinion. In many of these books there are many homilies about general behaviour. There are also types who exhibit certain characteristics. But only rarely do we read a summary of a person who could be said to raise questions of moral ambiguity.

> A good landlord and a kind master, he liked to have everybody bright and cheerful around him, but did not care to be distressed by social problems or tales of outside misery . . . he had a vague idea that people's

misfortunes were mostly caused by people's own fault and that lack of success was due to lack of merit.[19]

What is intruding into the text here is an adult tone: a sense that there are questions that should be asked about people's motivation and behaviour. Whilst this is a rare excursion into a 'real' world, from which Enid Blyton's readers are spared, it suggests an alertness to wider issues and a dimension outside the stories that has, or will have, an impact on the protagonists' lives. Whilst there are the usual array of stereotypes based on a very strong sense of class and a respect for clear distinctions between them –

They look a disreputable set. I believe they'd have stolen anything they could lay their hands on if they'd realised I was alone[20]

– there are also glimpses into judgements of people that are more subtle –

Miss Hardy, the mistress of the Lower Fourth, had been strict but scrupulously just: she might be sometimes disliked by her pupils, but she was always respected.[21]

The adult world in Angela Brazil is not only a somewhat more real one but also suggests that the girls will have a future. Some of them even have ambitions. One wishes to be a great artist, 'like Kate Greenaway', another wins a scholarship to a Conservatoire, and Laura wants to go to Girton:

'I'd like to be principal of a college some day or else go in for scientific research work. Don't laugh.'[22]

This sense of context contrasts with the fictional world of Enid Blyton, where adult interests hardly intrude, and aspirations are solely towards the next adventure. But in terms of the relationships between the friends, there are again striking similarities, as well as one difference, for there is in both the security of belonging to a group permanently, and the volatility of argument. Angela Brazil often uses phrases such as 'tempestuous', 'lively', 'decided opinions of their own', 'enterprising'. The heroines are depicted as having a certain amount of mental as well as physical liveliness. But there is no real argument. In the end, they are united in adventure.

Angela Brazil's books are typical of the genre which appeal to children. They are unlike Enid Blyton's in their deeper characterization, their sense of a large world and in their style. Even a few quotations demonstrate that they are far better written. They do not have the simple limitations of Enid Blyton. But it is Enid Blyton who is still massively popular.

Enid Blyton remains undistracted from the task in hand. Angela Brazil's excursions into homily or description mean that her books are far more characteristic of their time, like those of the equivalent writers for boys. Enid Blyton's distinct style applies to her own series of books set in girls' schools, *Malory Towers* and *St Clare's.* She emulates the usual formula, two girls who are dissimilar but who get on, the sense of the group, the constant reminder of the excitement even in unpromising circumstances. But her books are that much simpler. Here are two new girls – 'very English Bill (short for Wilhelmina . . .) and very American Zerelda', for whom the term 'very English and very American' should give adequate clues. 'Bill' is so 'crazy' about horses that she brings her mount to school. Zerelda is extremely glamorous and sophisticated.[23] All live in an untroubled world where minor skirmishes of temperament and major crimes are all treated as one. We are constantly reminded of the excitements; Darrell and her friends move up to the fifth form and it is more exciting than ever. The pace does not slacken.

> Now the days began to slip by more quickly. Two weeks went – three weeks – and then the fourth week turned up and began to slip away, too. Everything was going well.[24]

Enid Blyton's characteristics, including blandness and no sense of particular context, are clearly apparent; but however slack and neutral her style, the artifice of success is such that her readers would neither notice nor care.

School stories are not essentially different from other adventure stories although they are often taken as an almost separate genre. Whilst there is an old tradition of using the school as a distinct background with particular consequences, as explored earlier, there are many more devices in common than differences.[25] The school setting merely intensifies some of the characteristic elements of children's stories: the sense of belonging to the group, the intensity and security of relationships, the role of adults at once controllers and arbiters and an almost separate species. The school is normally a background for some other kind of adventure. The routines of school life are characterized as being boring. It is the extraordinary event that matters. The role of all adults in stories is characteristically that of teachers. They can be friendly or distant, fair or untrustworthy. Their personalities are discussed and measured. Pupils make considerable efforts to work out how to deal with them; how far they can be joked with, the extent to which they can be disobeyed or ignored, and the exact standard of work they will accept or reject.[26] They are important figures but not exactly people. The relationships that matter are between pupils. Teachers play a distinct role, and it is sometimes a shock for a pupil to realize, say on a school camp or any event outside school, that they are also individual human beings with a life of their own.

Clearly teachers have their own personalities, and a great deal of attention is paid to this by pupils. But most important to pupils is the role that teachers play; they have distinct tasks to carry out and these are more important than the relationships with individuals. This essential role of adults, as people on the perimeter, laying down rules, making judgements and providing essentials like food, characterizes both the underlying and shared attitudes that pupils have towards their teachers and the view of adults in these school stories. The essential world of the story is an enclosed one in which it is the pupils, or children outside school, who are the protagonists, the friends, the adventurers and the heroes.

The appeal of girls' stories is wider than the stereotypical messages about gender. In a sense the books of Enid Blyton or Angela Brazil are gender free, even if no boy would dare to be seen reading them.[27] The messages that they give are of people, all girls, who are determined, who are excited by adventure, who are independent and who long for something out of the routine. They also have strong friendships and occasional rivalries, and if the ways in which these rivalries are expressed is different – teasing rather than fisticuffs – the importance of being inside or outside a group, and of being popular, is just as essential as in boys' books. Whilst the literature of girls' stories that discuss latent messages and the characteristics of womanhood is very interesting, it does not capture or deal with the essential appeal of these stories. As in the stereotypical gestures of Enid Blyton, they are not the part of the book which engenders the reader's immediate response.

The books of Angela Brazil and other writers are no longer sold and appear to hold no appeal to readers today. This is partly because many of their details are dated, even if the story lines are not. But it is also because there is now a quite different kind of literature that is marketed for girls. Whilst the girls' stories of the past were often set in schools but were in a sense gender free, today's stories are set in any place but school and gender is the essential ingredient. One can argue that school still has a place; but, as in *Sweet Valley High*, it remains in the background. It is the relationships that count.

The women's writers of the past found it popular and lucrative to write series. This is a ploy which is exploited to a far greater extent today. Whilst there are many individual books the best sellers are those in series like *Sweet Valley High, Sweet Dreams, Heart Break* and *Point Romance.* The books are not only similar to each other but to the various children's television shows, whether emanating from the United Kingdom, the United States or Australia. There is a growing inter-dependence of media, not just in marketing, but in tone. There is also one distinction between the earlier books and the present ones, and that is that the emphasis is placed so firmly on a type of appeal, the tone and the subject matter that almost anyone can write them. *Sweet Valley High,* for example, is 'created' by Francine Pascal but 'written' by others. All the books are still credited on the front cover with 'Francine Pascal's'. It would be impossible to detect individual authors by reading them.

The inter-dependence of media, books, magazines and television, is at one level an established marketing strategy –

> *Starsky and Hutch,* 'created' by William Blinn, 'based on the teleplay', 'adapted' by Max Franklin, 'based on the BBC television series', 'published' by Ballentine Books, New York, 1979.

But at a more profound level it is an inter-dependence and a uniformity of tone and style. The characteristics, from the way that children talk to each other to their clothes and their interests are very similar. Readers know exactly what they are buying. Despite the homogeneity of tone each story is self-contained. There will be a happy ending when the misunderstandings are overcome and she gets her boy. There are no cliff-hangers that lure the viewer to the next half-hour slot. Instead, there are invitations to repeat the same experience.

> Rose Jameson is certain to get into P. Beta. Or is she? Find out in *Sweet Valley,* No. 81, *Rosa's Lie.*[28]

The essential theme of these books is not just sex. They are all about fairness and unfairness, truth and deception, security and insecurity. The core lies in misunderstandings, and the plot is almost invariably either about a girl realizing that a nice 'guy' she is friends with is also quite 'fanciable' or that the boy she is already dating quarrels with her before the misunderstanding is cleared up and they are reconciled. The concern with friendship and its changeability might have been channelled into boys, but it is still the underlying concern. Unlike real life, these books both recognize difficulties but give a reassurance that they can be overcome. Their very titles suggest the recurring pattern: *Double Love, Secrets, Dangerous Love, Deceptions, Promises, Out of Control, On the Edge, Pretences, Cheating to Win.* Each of the books has a different setting but the plot is concerned both with girls talking about boys, and girls talking with boys.

The books, typically, start with the concern of the heroine that she is not the centre of a boy's life.

> Michael probably wouldn't go to the hottest party ever given in Southern California if it was the night before a meet.[29]

The premise is, of course, that all will be well by the end but before that happens there must be difficulties and misunderstandings. The underlying concern which the heroines constantly discuss is their relationship to boys. Which ones fancy them; and which of them do they fancy? What are the rules between friendships and relationships? Most of the books deal with that fine distinction between liking someone and being attracted to them. But everyone is assumed to be obsessed with relationships with the opposite sex.

> 'That's it!' she announced dramatically. 'I've had it with the opposite sex . . .'
>
> 'What's the matter? Weren't there any cute boys at the rally?'
>
> 'I waited all Saturday night and all day yesterday and he never called'.[30]

The books depend heavily on 'scenes' with dialogue. The plot is carried by the conversations, sometimes *about* the boys but usually with them. Whilst there is the assurance of a happy and romantic ending there is also the recognition of intense feelings, of jealousy and anguish, of envy and betrayal, of frustration and loneliness. These books take the centrality of intense relationships to an extreme. Instead of the security of the group as an end in itself, they have the group – a crowd of boys and girls – as a background to the main concern of the books. There are usually two relationships depicted, foreground and background, for the friendship of girls is also considered important. The essential plot lies in the arguments and reconciliations.

> 'If you'll just give me a chance, I can explain everything'.
>
> He grabbed her arm. 'You've already made me look like a fool in front of the entire school'. 'How could you do this to me?' he shouted. 'How could you betray me like this?'[31]

At this point she is miserable and deflated. He walks off.

> 'April', he whispered. 'Please listen to me. This afternoon has made me see how wrong I was'. He swallowed hard. 'Accidents really do happen. I see that now'.
>
> April leaned toward him. 'It's too late to say you're sorry, Michael. And it's way too late to say you were wrong'.
>
> . . . she slipped over him and strode down the hall.[32]

At this point she is happy and triumphant. *She* walks off.

Happy endings like reconciliations would not be the same without the anguish. A lot is made of big moments, when their perspective on the world suddenly changes and when their feelings are both exposed and rewarded.

> 'I was hoping that we could kind of, you know, make it official that we're going out together'.
>
> Jessica felt her heart leap. It wasn't until he had said that that she realized how much she had been waiting for that moment.[33]

The strength of emotions, from triumph to anguish and the difficulties of communicating are constantly alluded to – 'he swallowed hard', 'he grabbed her arm', 'he shouted . . . ' 'suddenly she knew what she was hearing in his voice. It was sadness and loss'.[34]

Whilst the girls in the books are obsessed with boys they are by no means seen as the weaker sex. They are never depicted as demurely waiting for someone's attention. They discriminate between those who are attractive and those who are not, those they like as friends and acquaintances and those they chase. They also discriminate between those boys they lust after at first glance, and those they slowly learn to appreciate.

> Wearing tight pants and a black leather vest with silver-tipped cowboy boots, Buck stood in the spotlight . . . Chills ran down Mandy's spine.
>
> Glancing at his strong profile she imagined for a minute what it would be like to cuddle up to his arm and snuggle against his shoulder.[35]

This refers to a friend's brother who was previously unconsidered but who turns up having taken to contact lenses, wearing his hair longer and 'working out'. All that transforms him.

Whatever the themes of misunderstanding and reconciliation and the emotions that surround them a central obsession is with what people look like. It is only when a boy 'works out' or rejects glasses for contact lenses that he can be deemed attractive. The clothes that people wear are very important – an attitude reinforced by the magazines. Much of the time is spent in choosing and buying clothes. A *Sweet Dreams* book begins:

> School was starting in little over a week and Mindy Hamilton had nothing to wear! At least nothing she liked.[36]

The theme, the name, the tone and the excitement are quickly established. School is first and foremost the social meeting place, as if it were specially set up for girls to meet boys.The author reminds us of a familiar difficulty of choice (from a no doubt burgeoning wardrobe) and reinforces the tone of voice that exaggerates the anguish of choice – 'absolutely nothing to wear!' – and the fact that it is an exaggeration. After some time the heroine does find something.

> It flattered her trim figure and showed off her long, tan legs.

Only then can she 'flop down on the hall floor' and telephone her friend to give us the context of the story, a who's who of boy-friends.

The world of these 'teenage' romances is a consistent one, whatever particular series they appear in or in whatever country they are set in. There are the same themes, like the surprise that someone could be considered attractive –

> She'd known Vik for years; how could someone like him ever be thought of as sexy[37]

– which signals the happy ending, and the instant lust that characterizes them all.

> . . . looked [him] up and down with all the studied appraisal of a pair of pre-pubescents out on a hunk-hunt. They liked what they saw – firm muscles, lithe body, and thick raven locks to run their fingers through . . .[38]

They all deal with the fashionable dialogue or backchat about clothes and people. The series all conform with each other, and suggest codes of what is considered normal behaviour. This rests on an interest in the opposite sex and in designer wear. Whilst there are slight suggestions towards what seems like individuality – the boy you end the book with is pleasant as well as handsome – the major concerns remain the same. Whilst the heroines are able to see through superficiality in their choice of boyfriends, and whilst they are supposed not just to conform to the norm, the essential message is one of standard behaviours and dress:

> By the end of the evening, instead of being in a corner snogging away with some stunner out of town, you're more likely to find him in a corner with a couple of cans of cheap cider, watching the late-night football . . . with a couple of mates.[39]

This is considered abnormal behaviour, and the underlying theme is that this person, unattached and unconsidered, not only turns into an Adonis but more importantly into a lover who will perform the standard tasks like 'snogging away'. Much is made of deep kissing, often accompanied by jokes that rely on the assumption that people can only breathe through their mouths:

> 'I thought you'd never come up for air!' Emma had teased her the following day. 'Who says you need oxygen anyway?'[40]

Conformity does not rest only on behaviour and interests but also on clothes. Designer wear, 'limited edition Swatches', the 'in' pop groups are all used as demarcation lines between those who are trendy and those who are not.

> Jackie looked at herself in the bathroom mirror and nodded approvingly. She was wearing her favourite leather jacket and tight black 501s.[41]

In these books the protagonists are all attractive, not necessarily overwhelmingly pretty, but gaining the attention of others. At the very least they have a 'nice smile'. It is the feelings of being sought after or rejected, of being in a secure as well as a romantic relationship that are suggested, nothing more complex than that. Such feelings – happiness or sadness – are played up, as if nothing could be more intense.

> . . . which had just changed her life for ever. [half-way through the book]

> She turned the corner, and her life changed for ever. [near the end of it]

Whilst the latter change of life comes about because he was wearing a 'Chevignon sweater', there is always the security of the ending which suggests that by the age of sixteen nothing will ever change again.

> ... knowing that whatever happened now they would always be together.[42]

Conformity and security are the essential framework into which a jumble of emotions and arguments are placed. The intention is to capture the immediate and superficial interest of the reader. This is done by offering what is considered a familiar world, expressed in common phrases – cool, fab, wicked – 'I'm totally zonked' – with backchat that is considered smart – 'easy on the calories', 'grown men kicking a piece of pig's bladder around the park' – with a hint of a dream. The romances offer a set of routine excitements, combining a recognition that relationships can be difficult, with easy imaginary solutions. This is familiar territory. There is, however, one aspect to this popular modern fiction that differs markedly from the stories of the past. It stems from the relationship of the stories to other media – the concentration on sex and appearance. A glance at the front cover of any magazine which is aimed at young girls of 10 to 14, like *Bliss* or *Sugar* (no one aged 17 would buy a magazine with such an age as its title, just as '19' is aimed at 15-year-olds), instantly reveals the narrow range of interests. 'Shocking confessions', 'Cringe', 'The hottest lads on screen!', 'I got pregnant the night I lost my virginity', 'My parents caught me naked on the lounge floor', '10 autumn fashion essentials', '100s of beauty goodies to grab', 'Your guide to perfect party hours', etc.

The question remains the extent to which girls are influenced by what they read. The way they read these romances is at such a level that it does not connect to the actual and more complex events in their own lives. But the romances and the magazines have an appeal. The designs on girls to conform and to spend money – certainly on the reading material and perhaps on the goods advertised so that the manufacturers will wish to keep taking display space – might come from those who are in the market to appeal to them. However, it is a mute point, given the similarity of the material on offer, whether they closely mirror the girls' interests. Some commentators see these media, the magazines in particular, as an articulation of the interests of capital and patriarchy,[43] with girls as consumers who are free to choose for themselves, for a while. But the appeal of the books does not lie in an outline of girls' roles. The satisfactions on offer stem from a stimulated interest in sex, and therefore clothes and make-up. But they also arise from the concern with relationships. They might be encouraged to show an early interest in boys, but the anguishes from which these texts offer some respite and even imaginary advice, are real enough. The interest in sex is new but the formula remains the same.

Notes

1 Auchmuty, R. *A World of Girls: The Appeal of the Girls' School Story.* London: Women's Press, 1992.
2 Cadogan, M. and Craig. P. *You're a Brick, Angela! A New Look at Girls' Fiction from 1839 to 1975.* London: Gollancz, 1976. Auchmuty criticizes Cadogan and Craig as 'old-fashioned feminists'.
3 O'Connor, P. Images and motifs in children's fairy tales. *Educational Studies.* Vol.15, No.2, 1989, pp.129–44.
4 Series such as *Sweet Dreams* or *Sweet Valley High* which are delivered by many authors run into the hundreds, but at the latest count Ann Martin has produced around 120 of the *Baby-Sitters Club.*
5 Marchant, B. *A Heroine of the Sea.* London: Blackie, 1915, p.48.
6 Ibid., p.145.
7 Ibid., p.34.
8 Ibid., p.151.
9 Ibid., p.114.
10 Ibid., pp.9–10.
11 Ibid., p.10.
12 Fly leaf advertisement to Angela Brazil *A Pair of School Girls: A Story of School Days.* London: Blackie, 1923.
13 Angela Brazil. *The Girls of St. Cyprians.* London: Blackie, 1927.
14 Angela Brazil. *The Manor House School.* London: Blackie, 1943.
15 Ibid., p.38.
16 *A Pair of School Girls.*
17 *Manor House School,* p.104.
18 *St. Cyprians,* p.78.
19 Ibid., p.147.
20 *A Pair of School Girls,* p.125.

21 Ibid., p.76.
22 *St. Cyprians,* p.269.
23 Enid Blyton. *The Third Year at Malory Towers.* London: Methuen, 1948.
24 Enid Blyton. *The Fifth Year at Malory Towers.* London: Methuen, p.69.
25 As in Chapter Three.
26 Cf. The studies of school life, e.g. Cullingford, C. *The Inner World of the School.* London: Cassell, 1991; or Measor, L. and Woods, P. *Changing Schools, Pupils Perspectives on Transfer to a Comprehensive.* Milton Keynes: Open University Press, 1984.
27 Cf. Attitudes to girls' comics, Chapter 9.
28 The Afterword of No. 80.
29 Francine Pascal's *Sweet Valley High* No. 80. *The Girl They Both Love,* by Kate William. New York: Bantam Books, 1992, p.3.
30 Ibid., p.43.
31 Ibid., p.49.
32 Ibid., p.105.
33 Ibid., p.135.
34 Ibid., p.53.
35 Dale, A. *Sweet Dreams: Three's a Crowd.* New York: Bantam Books, 1989.
36 Ibid.
37 Tanner, R. *Point Romance. Ice Hot!* London: Scholastic, 1996, p.7.
38 Ibid., p.78.
39 Ibid., p.15.
40 Ibid., p.6.
41 Ibid., p.81.
42 Ibid., p.179
43 Tinkler, P. *Constructing Girlhood: Popular Magazines for Girls Growing up in England 1920–1950.* London: Taylor and Francis, 1995.

7
Political Correctness and the Subversive: Judy Blume and the *Baby-Sitters Club*

Memories of reading girls' stories like Elinor Mary Brent-Dyer's *Chalet School* series bring with them a sense of a cosy, enclosed world. But such memories are then joined by a different critical attention that seeks out underlying messages, or an historical stance that encapsulates the beliefs of an age.[1] Whilst there might seem to be either a disjunction or a tension between the two styles of reading: – the purity and immediacy of the pleasure, or the realization of the meaning of some of the latent messages – they are in fact joined by an additional motivation that is a characteristic of a great deal of children's literature. The author justifies the writing not only because it provides entertainment but because it gives advice.

The grand tradition of writing for children stems from the moral motivation of teaching as well as entertaining. Herbert Strang is welcomed as teaching the readers about the glories and the responsibilities of the British peoples; Percy Westerman seeks to outline the desired characteristics of the gentleman. Even Enid Blyton justifies herself as teaching

> a sure knowledge that right is always right and that such things as courage and kindness deserve to be emulated.[2]

There is no doubt that the authors of books for children normally feel a moral duty to present a good example: of kindness to others, of fairness, courtesy and truthfulness. One would not find anything reprehensible in the works of Angela Brazil or her followers.

The motivation to help children is one that has not disappeared but its manifestations and characteristics are very different. The contrast between the ethos of Angela Brazil and Judy Blume could not be greater. And yet the latter has established the 'Kid's Fund' that is designed to help children cope with society and receives thousands of 'agony aunt' letters. She points out:

> I try to be honest in my books. I think all people, young and old, want to know that others share their feelings. That no matter what, they're not alone.[3]

What Judy Blume and Paula Danziger set out to do is to deal, in passing, with various problems and experiences that children and young teenagers might have, like diabetes or divorce, sex or misunderstandings with parents. The phrase 'in passing' is important since they both set out to entertain and rely on a tone of voice that derives from that of their readers. They reflect a certain society and outlook. Their appeal lies not just in the issues but in the style and tone of the books.

Popular writers today capture an outlook and a point of view that is summed up by Paula Danziger.

> My books are often anti-establishment and dumb-joke funny. I've got worse with puns, like the grubs in *This Place has no Atmosphere* being called lunar-ticks.
>
> A book should tell a good story first, but it's a chance to bear witness, too.[4]

The heart of the books' appeal is their entering into the point of view of a certain kind of girl. Some of the titles encapsulate this:

> *Can You Sue Your Parents for Malpractice?*
>
> *Everyone Else's Parents said Yes!*[5]

Whereas parents and other adults were usually marginal figures in earlier literature, they are now becoming both less marginal and less respected. The objective gaze at the oddities of adult behaviour as well as the collective obsessions of childhood and adolescence are to the fore. Nothing is hidden from that gaze.

The appeal as well as the tone of these books can best be captured by a complete short story. What makes this interesting is that it characterizes the themes of the books and their style. There are close friendships and anger, the plot is carried by dialogue and the characters talk directly to the reader. They contain moments that will 'change my life forever'.

Parent's Don't Know Anything!

> Don't you just hate it when parents argue. I certainly do. Mine are arguing now. That's all they ever do and this time it's about something too minor to mention! I'd go downstairs and tell them it's frightening me to make them stop but that wouldn't work and besides I'm too old to do that sort of thing now (I'm 14, nearly 15). Actually I am a little frightened – frightened that my parents will get divorced. I suppose if

they do it would be for the best – after all I lie here in bed every night listening to them arguing.

I woke up the next morning really early.

'I'm really scared Lindy. I heard mummy and daddy arguing real bad!', said my 8 year-old sister, Jenny.
'It's OK, come on, get dressed. We have to go to school. Everything will be OK!'
'OK'.

And Jenny slid off the bed.

Actually I wasn't too sure about what I just said. I didn't think everything would be OK! I got up and got dressed. When I got to school I met up with my best friend, Rosie.

'Hi Rosie. How are you doing?'
'Fine thanks. How about you?'
'Well, actually, not that good. I um . . . my parents, I think they're going to get divorced. I mean, they're always arguing non-stop!'
'Oh come on, everything will be fine. I mean, if they do, it would be for the best', said Rosie with reassurance.
'How would you know. You don't know anything about what I'm going through. How can you say that. You don't know half of it!', I shouted.
'Hey, don't get so stressed out!'
'I can if I want!'

And with that I stomped off. I can't believe I did that. I expect Rosie will never speak to me again. I've just got to get my life together!

'Hey Dave, I don't know why you like Linda!', said Rosie.
'What do you mean?', asked Dave.
'Well, she keeps saying how her parents keep arguing and she thinks they'll get divorced and she just got really stressed because I said everything would be OK. The way she's acting at the moment it really sucks!'
'Are you just saying that because you're jealous of me and Linda?'
'No! You've just got to help her. She's just really weird!
'OK, I'll see what I can do'.
'Thanks!'

To make things worse, when I got home my parents had something to say that would change my life forever and I'll never forget it . . . !

'Jenny, Linda. Your father and I, um, think it would be for the best if we don't live together anymore!'

'What . . . Oh, I knew this would happen. Why can't you think about us kids for a change. It wouldn't be for the best for me and Jenny. How can you say that. You don't know how we feel. It's going to ruin my life!'

And with that I stomped off to my room. Jenny just sat there and cried. There was a knock at the door.

'Linda. Can I come in?'
'If you wish!'

I wasn't exactly going to give my mum a hard time but I was not going to act like a saint.

'Linda, everything will turn out alright in the end you'll see!'

As my mum said that she came in and sat on the end of my bed.

'How would you know?' I shouted.
Mum, trying to keep calm, said 'But wouldn't it be nice if you could go to sleep straight away instead of lying there listening to your father and I arguing.'
'How did you know?' I asked, suddenly becoming interested.
'Well, I don't think anyone could sleep through the racket your father and I make!' she laughed.
'But why do you argue and why didn't you say you were fed up with each other and want someone else.'
'Now hang on a minute. Did I say we both wanted someone else?'
'No.'
'Exactly. Where did you get that idea? Look your father and I find it hard to live with each other and so we get irritable and snap at each other at the slightest thing and so we have an argument,' she replied almost crying.

But it didn't make me feel sorry for her.

'Why do you say "*your father and I*". Why can't you call him by his proper name "Ted", or at least "darling" like you used to. Why can't you actually say his name to talk to or call him. You just shout something like "dinner's ready" and hope he'll come. Why . . . '

I got so angry with her I just burst out crying. My mum just sat there and held me. I felt so childish sitting there like that but I wasn't about to say so.

'How's Jenny?' I blubbered, trying to stop crying.
'I don't know. She's downstairs with your father'.
'Mum, could I be on my own for a while?'

Mum didn't say anything, she just left. Just like that. Without a word. Wow, she's never done that before! I must have really hurt her.

I heard them talking in low voices downstairs. Well that makes a change from the last thousand days! I just lay there. I don't know how long for because I must have fallen asleep because mum was shouting something.

'Linda! Dinner. Can you come downstairs.'

I didn't really want to go but I felt I had to.

'What's for dinner mum?'
'You'll see.'

I sat at the table. Everything was silent. No one spoke. As we ate it was still silent, but I broke it.

'Who's moving out of here then?' I asked trying to sound cheerful.
'Your father is.'
'Stop calling him "your father". He has got a voice of his own or didn't you know!'

I couldn't take it anymore. I felt they had let me down. I pushed back my chair and walked out the room.

'Linda, wait you . . . '

I ignored her.

' . . . haven't finished your dinner yet', finished my mother.
'What are we going to do with her?'
'I don't know. Look she'll come around. She's just finding it hard to come to terms with,' said my father sounding unsure.

It was only 7 o'clock but I got into bed and went to sleep. I heard what they said. I'm not trouble. They're the trouble. I'm their daughter, not someone to call 'her'.

'Linda! You've overslept now. Come on get up or you're going to be late for school!'

I'm on the plane to Florida. I'm crying only a little, but it's still in public. Mum and Jenny were crying. I had massive arguments with Rosie and Dave but all the same they came along but they weren't crying.

When I finally got there it took me a long time to find my dad, but I did in the end. My dad was really happy to see me.

'Hi! Now tell me, why would you want to live with your old dad then?' he said.
'Everything was going wrong.'
'That's all?'
'That's all, yep.'

I didn't expect his house to be heaven but it was a complete and utter hell hole! It was grotty, damp and cold.

'You live in this?'
'Yep! It's not much, but it's home!'
'Come off it dad. It's horrible. It's . . . it's diabolical. You can't possibly like it!'
'I know, but there's no place else!'

It's school today. I don't know anybody. I was too nervous to eat breakfast.

'What's wrong? Nervous?'
'Yeah, very.'
'Oh, don't worry. You'll be fine!'
'Quiet please! Now, this is a new pupil, Linda Smith. I want you to be kind and help her settle in,' said my new form tutor, Miss Dark.

Was I embarrassed when she said that. I sat next to a girl called Nicola.

'Hi', she said kindly.
'Hi', I said nervously.
'Don't worry. I'll show you around. Oh, and most of the teachers are OK, but some can get a bit annoying.'

I soon settled in, and Nicola and I became new best friends. Oh, and there's this boy in my year that I really like. Mum phones once a week now.

'Now you're sure you're OK, Linda.'
'Yes, mum. Goodbye!'
'Linda! Can you come here!'
'Sure dad. What is it?'
'You know you said this place is a dump!'
'Yeah.'

'Well, I've met this really nice lady and she wants us to move in!'
'Yeah, OK.'
'Good.'

I wasn't upset (like usual) about it because I'm much happier now than at mum's.

We've just moved in. She's got a daughter and guess who it is – Nicola! The house is great and I share a room with Nicola. I'm so much happier. I'm seeing mum next week and Jenny. I can't wait.

Rosie and Dave are going out but I'm not upset.

Well, it's been two months now and my dad and I are on the plane to New York to go for the divorce and you know what, I'm not upset. I know it's for the best. I've really changed – mostly because of Nicola because her parents are divorced. Well, I'm dressed all smart. So's dad and I bet mum and Jenny are too. I'm going to stay living with dad. Mum knows but she doesn't mind. She knows I'm happy here. Oh and I'm going out with the boy I fancy in my year!

I thought that my life was over, but now I know I was wrong. I feel on top of the world – well almost.

Well, we've just arrived at court and we're going into the courtroom. Well here it goes . . .

This story was written not by Judy Blume, or Ann Martin or Paula Danziger but by an 11-year-old girl. Perhaps that was obvious. But that should make the point the more strongly. The appeal of such a style of writing, grown-up, gossipy, confessional and exploratory of feelings and attitudes lies in its immediate connection with the everyday worries of children, their relationships with others and the strengths of their emotions. What the 11-year-old writes about is clearly outside her own personal experience. The question remains whether such a tone of voice and such descriptions of emotional weakness and instability are a reflection of the books, indeed fostered by the books, or whether the books have, through experience and imaginative recreation, captured part of the reality of childhood. The themes, like the meaning of the self in relation to the world, and the different contexts of society, the family, the group, the school and society at large, are all ones which are of deep, if not always articulated, concern for children. But they are rarely taken seriously by adults and for the most part are deliberately ignored at school.

These books appeal not just because of the familiarity of their story lines but because of the familiarity of their picture of the world. Wherever they are read there is a recognition of an environment in which relationships, both personal and public, are central. Quarrels with parents, arguments with friends, reconciliations, unfairness; these themes are the narrative glue that holds the books together. At the core is the sense of belonging to a group of friends. Boys are important as we are constantly reminded, but they are not central. Parents are enemies as well as friends. It is relationships with other girls, changeable, fierce, and cruel as well as sentimental and forgiving, that matter. Books such as the series the *Baby-Sitter's Club* both acknowledge the changeable nature of relationships and, as the title indicates, create a sense of belonging, as do the *Famous Five.*

Belonging to a group means being placed in an organization which is outside the control of adults. The baby sitters organize themselves. They make the arrangements and are like a self-contained society, in touch with each other on their parents' 'phones. Their parents might supply them with telephones as well as food but are essentially outsiders. As in Enid Blyton the children go to a different emotional country which although it overlaps with that of their parents, has its own completeness and its own etiquettes. Unlike Enid Blyton, the baby sitters' inner country is placed firmly within their homes, and those of other adults, rather than outside. The landscape is less imaginary.

One secret of writing for children is to take their concerns seriously, but assume that they are out of reach of adults. The result of this is that adults are, yet again, presented as unpredictable and moody, living their own half-secret lives, struggling with their own relationships. Their children look on, amazed, overhearing, complaining – and judging when is the right time to ask for something and when their parents' moods make conversation injudicious. All children are seen as belonging to a different club, not only choosing carefully those who belong to it, but also never deigning to consider the possibility of their parents or other adults being members. They are the outsiders, the aliens, the ones to be blackballed.

The reason that parents feature so much more strongly in these books is their setting within families. These are usually described as chaotic, not so much physically as emotionally. They are sites of conflicts of mood.

> The next morning, everything went wrong. Our house was in chaos. David Michael woke up with a stomach upset. Louie went sneaking through the living room, skidded on a rug and hurt his paw. Mum was grouchy, Charlie couldn't find his football boots, and Sam overslept . . . I myself was doing fine until the 'phone started ringing.[6]

The dog is as much a character as the others, but the only person to whose emotions attention is drawn is the adult. Parents are usually looked on in a knowing kind of way. Whereas in Enid Blyton parents provide food and approval and the occasional sanction, parents here are depicted as unpredictable and moody. They have to be observed and then manipulated.

> When Mum came home a little while later, she had a pizza with her . . . But Sam and Charlie looked sceptical. 'I wonder what she wants', murmured Sam.
> 'Yeah', said Charlie, 'Mum only gets a pizza when she has to ask us a favour'.
> I decided not to beat about the bush. 'How come you bought a pizza, Mum?' I asked. Charlie kicked my ankle, but I ignored him.[7]

They all have opinions about their parents, and of other adults who might encroach on their lives, giving their mother's boy-friends a bad time, calling them 'Goggle-eyes' or worse. They know all the circumstances of divorce.

> It's not her fault that Dad ran off to California and got married again and doesn't send Mum much child support money.

> My father can be a jerk sometimes. He hasn't called us for over a year. And he even forgot my twelfth birthday last month.[8]

One of the advantages of setting these stories in a divorced or dysfunctional family is that it places more responsibility on the survival instincts of the children themselves. It means that the concerns of the children are paramount, even within the home environment. And it throws attention on their rivalries. The tone of the books gives recognition, in a laconic way, to some of the concerns of children and through sarcasm in particular allows different types of concern – divorce, rivalries or school food – to become similar. School food, and what boys do with it, is described in hated detail – except for the ice cream – as if we can immediately understand the point of view. The reader is supposed to know at once and to share the outlook of the 'ordinary' or 'average' heroine.

> A person with an IQ of 160 is considered a genius.
> Janine's IQ is 196.
> Sometimes she makes me want to be sick.
> She almost always makes Claudia want to be sick . . . She thinks she knows everything.
> (Actually, she does).[9]

The assumption is blandly made that all will share the same attitudes. There are some strong conventions, that parents are moody and inconsistent, for example, and that school food is dreadful. The status of boys and of age is also of assumed importance.

> Now here's the interesting part. *Sam is in high school* [her italics]. And Stacey is only twelve. Most high school boys wouldn't be caught dead with a lowly middle school girl – unless the girl was a knockout.[10]

In the *Baby-Sitters Club* boys have not yet become the centre of attention. But their potential importance, like designer wear, is already acknowledged. It is part of the convention that certain attitudes are struck up. There are changing fashions but it is assumed that all people share them. There might be arguments over people but there are no conflicts of opinion, not, that is, about anything which really matters.

Whilst there are a host of peripheral people, the centre is the close relationship of girls and the world they live in. This world gives a sense of being self-enclosed – as if all people shared the same tastes and had the same thoughts. There is a cosiness about the relating of conventional pleasures – like the listing of food in Blyton.

> I thought it was the perfect night to a) curl up with *The Phantom of Pine Hall* – a really spooky Nancy Drew mystery – and the liquorice bootlaces I'd hidden in my desk and b) work on the still life I'd started and daydream about Trevor Sandbourne.[11]

The daydreams are always of the 'most gorgeous boy in school' and having long hair.

The importance of conventional attitudes is underlined by the stress on political correctness. There are certain things you ought to think – although there is no strenuous preaching. The adults are used to make a distinction between the conventional outlook of children – 'she's a witch' – and what they ought to say, publicly – 'an eccentric old lady'. Thus the small world of children is set within a world to which they will later have to adapt, acknowledging that healthy food is good for you even if 'it makes you throw up'. The political correctness of attitudes towards other people means that whilst the club or group are intolerant of others, they cannot be so on the grounds of 'race' or 'gender' or 'age'.

'Political correctness' can be seen as part of the convention, but it can also be acknowledged as part of the mission statement of the books. The devices used to attract and sustain the reader are chosen with commercial exactitude, but are to be justified by the fact that they deal with and teach 'real' problems. However peripheral to the stories, particular problems of domestic life including illness, divorce and death, abound. One of the Baby-Sitters Club has diabetes. We learn about the symptoms – getting thinner, insatiable thirst – and the explanation – the pancreas and insulin.[12] It becomes woven into the story, so that those who read it can cite it as making them more understanding and sympathetic to those who have the illness. But the more interesting and pervasive signs of political correctness are those that become apparent as a result of the diabetes and demonstrate the avowed intent to open everything up to liberal tolerance. The person who helps diagnose Stacey's diabetes has been called a 'quack' by the conventional doctor because he is 'holistic'. It is no surprise that he is successful, sympathetic and black.

The diabetes is not the central theme of the story but the threat of a rival gang of baby-sitters who turn out to do everything wrong – cigarette burns on the carpet, letting their charges into the street and using the telephone to talk to boyfriends whilst watching TV. There is a message in that too. But more important, in the sense of understanding the story's appeal, is the consistent tone, the shared attitudes, the conversations and the opinions: 'All boys are pretty interesting'. Whilst Stacey is having trouble with the diagnosis and arguing with her parents' 'overreactions' –

> On the way I passed Pete Black. I nearly fainted.[13]

Somehow that remains the central reality.

The 'Baby-Sitters' set the tone for whole ranges of books. They demonstrate the importance of having a series, with familiar expectations and familiar satisfactions. Above all, they suggest something so familiar that it is as if they had been written with knowledge from the 'inside'. Those commercial pressures on what to buy and what to do and what to think and how to say it are given a kind of legitimacy by capturing the sense that real everyday life for millions of girls is being captured in all its reality, including the strength of instant judgements and the difficulties of relationships. Judy Blume dedicates a book to Randy and Larry – 'my experts on fifth grade, loose teeth, *The Book of World Records*, stamp collecting and school bus action'.[14]

The sense of insider knowledge depends on the feeling that nothing is hidden, that the assumed personal interests of children are no longer suppressed. I say 'assumed', since it is difficult to make a distinct demarcation line between the excitement of finding out about sex in terms of the politically correct crusade, or in terms of titillation. The books rest on an ambiguity. On the one hand they assume that children are not innocent. They have their interests, in the body, in sex, in cruelty, and emphatically in themselves, and that at last these books will give expression to such concerns. On the other hand they assume that children do not know about such things and need an open-minded agony aunt to tell them all about it. But does that mean that it is from these books that children learn such an interest in the subjects of girls' magazines – boys and what you need to buy to attract them?

The implications of the approach are not thought out, but the style itself is. The basis of the appeal is the liberal acceptance, or creation, of the fact that all children secretly share the same interests:

> For a while I watched Michael and Irwin as they passed a *National Geographic* magazine back and forth. It was open to a page full of naked people.[15]

The books themselves are like the parody quoted earlier. It is difficult to know in such a symbiotic relationship the extent to which the books legitimize or give expression to such an 'adolescent' world. In that they are both like Enid Blyton – the unaffected unselfconscious appeal – and unlike her, in their rootedness in the contemporary world. But are they a passing phenomenon? Will not their appeal remain? Such an approach has been going on for a quarter of a century in the same way.

There are certain characteristics that do seem to emerge from the universally shared experience of 'adolescence'. These have more to do with tone than with the facts or circumstances. The protagonists are very fond of their own cleverness about other people. They are pert, or sarcastic or plain vicious. These books give examples of the snide comments which the reader might wish she had thought of first:

> Dear Superior Stamp Company
> If you got fifty cents allowance a week you'd have trouble ordering a lot of stamps too. Besides, you are not the only stamps company I deal with. You are not even my favorite. Half the stamps you send don't go in my Master Global Album. So you are lucky to get any business from me.
> Unsincerely
> Jill Brenner.[16]

The smart remark and the incisive comment are at the heart of the books, although it must be noted that these are made in the knowledge that such thoughts are hidden from others. You are not supposed actually to *hurt* anyone.

> Most of the time Donna smells like a horse but I wouldn't tell her that because she might think it's a compliment.

> Bruce went to work on his nose. He has a very interesting way of picking it. First he works one nostril and then the other and whatever he gets out he sticks on a piece of yellow paper inside his desk.[17]

At the same time you are not supposed actually to *like* most people. Classmates are fat or stupid or clever or thin or ugly or attractive. Whatever it is there's something *wrong* that can be picked on. The fact that Bruce picks his nose is not in itself significant but it is relished as much as Roald Dahl would have relished it. The fact is accepted. The style is unique. So we have people with heads 'shaped like a potato', meals so awful they do not deserve the descriptions they attract, and criticisms galore.

Criticisms include the behaviour and beliefs of the protagonists. These reveal the juxtaposition of the balance of authority, where it is the children who have the weight of choice placed upon them, and who analyse the aberrant behaviour of adults. Instead of the conventional idea of responsibility being in the hands of the parents, and children coming to terms with this, the children not only make their point of view known, but tell their parents off, as if they were recalcitrant and not respectful enough. Their parents are clearly not even politically correct.

> 'Smoking causes cancer and heart disease', I told her.
> 'Animals are for loving, not wearing', I told her.[18]

The descriptions of home life suggest that the parents have their own idiosyncratic interests. They are viewed as people with moods and needs, desires and habits, like some strange, but necessary presence of a domestic animal. They are far more present than in earlier literature but taken far less seriously.

> My father said he'd had a really rough day and would I mind scratching his back for a little while.

> When Mom had finished showering she came into the living room carrying two Bloody Mary's.
> My mother's not shy about swearing.[19]

The crucial point about the Judy Blume books is the way in which they enter into the tone of thought of an observant, opinionated, pert, conventional girl. It is assumed that all people of that age have the same interests. The heroines are clever but not intellectual. They are leaders in fashion and whilst they share all their (naughty) thoughts with the reader, know how far to go with their friends. It is as if we are being allowed to enter a secret, but very familiar world.

> Sandra changed her clothes in my closet. I think she is getting fatter. But I wouldn't say that to her face. She is very sensitive and would start to cry. She should go on a diet. I can't understand how such a fat person can swim. Why doesn't she sink to the bottom of the pool? Some day I will ask Marty about that.[20]

There is a sense of the acerbic as well as the pert, the snide asides as well as the sudden earnestness of political correctitude. The feelings conflict with judgements; the battle between emotion and reason becomes the ground rule of the tone of the books. Thus Sheila, the eponymous heroine, *hates* dogs as well as spiders – they smell – *hates* boys, *hates* swimming and has tantrums. She is concerned with her own independent status – equal with parents but superior to those younger than her – 'yo-yo's are for kids' – and does not any longer like playing games with her father that remind her of her own youth.

These books are popular because they reflect the perceived aspirations and interests of their readers. But they also show the need for a certain type of entertainment, one which both recognizes some of the worries of childhood and gives comfort and security. The books both mirror anguish and provide an alternative, an escape from them. Enid Blyton praises escapism but these books provide it. Books described here have been produced for a quarter of a century. Some series, like the *Baby-Sitters Club*, keep adding number after number. Does that mean that anything has changed? Only one small detail.

> The author gratefully acknowledges Jahnna Beecham and Malcolm Hillgartner for their help in preparing this manuscript.[21]

As in the case of other 'created' series the burden of constant production becomes more difficult and less necessary. The fact that the reason might be illness is not as significant as the ease with which the standard style and tone can be emulated. The whole world and mental outlook is completely familiar – we are presented with home life.

> Life at my house is usually pretty crazy but today things were totally bonkers.[22]

We are presented with the familiar characters and what marks them out as being distinctive.

> Stacey grew up in New York City and is the most sophisticated member of our group. She wears super-trendy clothes and her long blonde hair is permed . . .
>
> Stacey sounds perfect, doesn't she? But she has a problem which is really serious. Stacey is diabetic.[23]

It is as easy to enter the end of the series as the beginning. It is all familiar territory. Whilst one should not expect development of such a formula, the similarities of all the stories reinforce the nature of their appeal. The outlook on the world, whichever character's 'voice' is heard as the 'I' of the author, is always the same, a balance, resolved in a particular tone of voice, between personal feelings and a concern with more rational things, like clothes.

> I would have died if anyone had seen what I was doing. I mean, it was *so* embarrassing![24]
>
> The funny thing is, her stepdad's extremely rich so she *could* buy the most expensive clothes around.[25]

As far as the politically correct message is concerned the secret of life is that finding 'Mr Perfect' is not the ultimate solution to a 12-year-old's life; that friends matter after all. That, in itself, is a kind of central security throughout the time that Mr Perfect is the theme of the book.

Part of the familiarity and approachability of the books is their consistent tone. Contradictions abound as this analysis makes clear, but these contradictions are far closer to the actual muddled experiences of people than any logical consistency. All the unresolved absurdities are more true to experience than an overall moral truth. But the other part of these books' appeal lies in their use of the familiar devices of plot: of excitement, of conflicts overcome, of the sense of the impending happy ending. Whilst the background to the stories is a mythical but recognizable version of a suburban ideal – houses, gardens, roads and trees – there are a series of small excitements in as regular a sequence as in Enid Blyton. And, as in the case of Blyton, there is in the circumstances an ironic attack on the reading of books:

> One wasn't so bad but the other was so boring I never got past the first chapter.[26]

Perhaps the readers are being warned off other books. But the background of boredom, as in school, is often invoked. Against that are the themes of success: overcoming the fear of dogs or being able to swim. These are, however, the structures or plot that make the books create a sense of an ending. More important is the cohesion of tone and outlook. It should, however, be noted that between the light use of political correctness and the serious use of lightness of tone, certain themes *are* dealt with in terms that suggest real insight. The descriptions of the vicious feelings of the bully are particularly well done.

The appeal of these books lies in their unaffected mixture of security and insecurity. They offer at one level a bland and homogenous world of friends and happenings, of the everyday fantasies of youth. But they also appeal because they are read by girls with real or latent worries. Here are two story ideas, written by the 11-year-old.

Searching . . .
It would be about a girl whose mother died and she had to do an essay for school about someone whom you've never met. So because her mother died two hours after she was born she hadn't really seen her so she decided to do the essay on her mother, but to find out things about her mother, Davey has to go and stay with her uncle in Los Angeles for her mother grew up there. Davey goes on an exciting and treacherous journey to find out things about her

mother with surprising findings about her and an unexpected ending. Davey finds out a lot about her mother . . .

And a sequel to *Parents Don't Know Anything!*

(Blurb)
Must things always get worse? I mean, just as you think you're on top of the world (near enough will do) things start to go wrong. It's typical isn't it. My parents get divorced; I'm unhappy. Things start to get better. I think it will last, but no, no, no, that's just too much to ask for! Why me?

Linda's back with more problems!

When people seek escape in one form or another it draws attention not just to a refusal to face some of the difficulties or anguishes of life, but to their existence. These books are another manifestation of the recognition of a world of childhood that shares adults' difficulties. They might deal with it in a very different way, and they would probably shock previous writers for children, as would the magazines for sale. But they have many things in common below the surfaces. Their approach gives an insight into the gaze of the young mind. The readers of Judy Blume also read Enid Blyton, but as the former would point out and encourage, they would not be *seen* doing so. What the writers of these series of fictions bring as something new to the genre is political correctness, and a complete absence of morality; not in the slightest bit immoral, but amoral.

Notes

1 E.g. Auchmuty, R. *A World of Girls: The Appeal of the Girls' School Story*. London: Women's Press, 1992.
2 Enid Blyton, preface 1951, quoted in *Children's Literature in Education*. No.15, 1974, pp.43–61.
3 Quoted in Nettell, S. *Meet the Authors and Illustrators.* London: Scholastic, 1994, p.27.
4 Ibid., p.54.
5 Danziger, P. *Can You Sue Your Parents for Malpractice?* London: Heinemann, 1986.
Danziger, P. *Everyone Else's Parents Said Yes!* London: Heinemann, 1989.
6 Martin, A. M. *Kristy's Great Idea.* New York: Scholastic, 1986, p.108 (in the 3-in-1 edition).

7 Ibid., pp.13–14.
8 Ibid., p.19.
9 Ibid., p.29.
10 Ibid., p.80.
11 Martin, A. M. *Claudia and the Phantom Phone Calls.* New York: Scholastic, 1986, p.151.
12 Martin, A. M. *The Truth about Stacey.* New York: Scholastic, 1986, p.316.
13 Ibid., p.378.
14 Blume, J. *Blubber.* London: Heinemann. First published 1974.
15 Ibid., p.17.
16 Ibid., p.73.
17 Ibid.
18 Ibid.
19 Ibid.
20 Blume, J. *Otherwise Known as Sheila the Great.* New York: Dutton, 1972 (and London: Bodley, 1979, p.87).
21 Martin, A. M. *Baby-Sitters Club* No. 69. *Get Well Soon, McIlory!* New York: Scholastic, 1993.
22 Ibid., p.2.
23 Ibid., p.17.
24 Martin, A. M. *Claudia and the Perfect Boy* (No. 71). New York: Scholastic, 1994.
25 Martin, A. M. *Stacey and the Cheerleaders* (No. 70). New York: Scholastic, 1993.
26 *Blubber.* Op. cit.

8
The Exuberant Incorrectness of Roald Dahl

The ostensible motivations behind the writings of Judy Blume or Paula Danziger are a far cry from Roald Dahl. He does not try to justify anything. The sheer exuberance of his stories, the uncontrolled relish with which he follows lines of thought or games with words, and the energy of his descriptions of all that is foul and ugly makes political correctness seem absurd. But the appeal of the books is not. By far the most popular author with children (along with Enid Blyton), the marketing of the stories through films is no more than a useful addition to the royalties of at least £4 million a year.[1]

The reason for Dahl's appeal is, at one level, clear. The stories combine some of the essentials of popular children's fiction – narrative drive, excitement held in check by security, and the sense of the world of children being self-contained and self-concerned. They also add some ingredients of their own, like the relish in the discomfort of adults and the pleasure of schoolchild humour. In these books adults are not just observed with bewilderment or disdain but as objects which are absurd and often disgusting. But then Dahl's books are a far cry from the pseudo-realism of the *Baby-Sitters Club*. They are essentially nursery stories, the kind told at bed-time off the top of the imagination. But they add an exuberance of language and description that derives from their being written rather than told.

Let us start with the example of the *Enormous Crocodile.*[2] It has the classic outline of a story for young children, a clear direction so that there is a sense of the ending from the beginning – the crocodile sets out to eat children but is prevented from doing so. It also has a clear pattern of repetitions that are the other secret of such stories, so that a familiarity of narrative structure is set up. The crocodile meets a Hippopotamus, then an Elephant, then a Monkey and finally the Roly Poly bird. To each he does something dastardly. When reaching his goal, he carries out four 'clever tricks' which are numbered, in order to catch and eat some children: pretending to be a palm tree, a swing, a ride on a roundabout and a seat. The pattern dictates that the four animals previously insulted warn the children and prevent the crocodile from having his meal. But this is just the outline. The effect is brought about in the pleasure of the telling. The enormous crocodile announces his intention.

> I'll bet if you saw a fat juicy little child paddling in the water over there at this very moment you'd gulp him up in one gollop.

This vision of doing something enjoyably disgusting is reinforced by constant rhymes, at once trying to shock and, by the language, mitigating any effect of realism.

> I'm off to find a yummy child for lunch.
> Keep listening and you'll hear the bones go crunch.

This is a simple appeal to children's humour. Words like 'yummy' and 'gollop' show how unaffected is the relish with which such ideas are related. And the crocodile naturally gets his 'comeuppance' literally by being spun round by the elephant faster and faster for six pages and seven illustrations until 'at last' [end of page]:

> With the most tremendous BANG
> the Enormous Crocodile crashed head first into the hot hot sun.
> And he was sizzled up like a sausage!

Given that Roald Dahl writes what are essentially nursery stories, without any connection with the realities of the world – unlike other writers of such popularity – his appeal to children of various ages is an interesting one and again gives an insight into the tastes of the readers. That adults should look on the stories with disdain (tempered perhaps by envy) is not surprising. A story like *The Twits* is deliberately disgusting with a series of tricks – a glass eye in beer, frogs in the bed, worms in spaghetti – that show the attempt to go beyond the limits of the comic.[3] It is so exaggerated that it becomes funny. But the descriptions of such foul things as gravy encrusted in a beard have an appeal, whether we like it or not, to all ages. 'That's disgusting!' says the reader, with a certain pleasure. Exaggerations, attempts to think up something even more extreme, are both nauseating and comic.

Roald Dahl brings a consistent style to his stories. But this cannot be easily emulated. The reason for this is that it seems to come to him naturally, without affectation. The style is the personality. Just as Enid Blyton enters into her world without self-consciousness, so Dahl drives through his stories indifferent to any implications or reactions. They are told with all the self-belief of the story teller, with a sense of spontaneity and pleasure in the telling. Take the opening of *The Witches.*[4] The author asserts an opinion as a fact, drawing attention to the idea of a 'story' or fairy tale where the fantastic needs to be treated as real. 'This is what I am telling you' says the author 'listen and believe'.

> In fairy tales, witches always wear silly black hats and black cloaks, and they ride on broomsticks.

Already we know that this is not just an opening statement of fact but a 'straw-man' of an idea to be knocked down. They 'always' wear 'silly' hats. The idea of a 'fairy tale' is dismissed as if the story teller, for the first time, was to reveal the real truth.

> But this is not a fairy tale. This is about REAL WITCHES.

The distinction between fact and fantasy is broken down. The direct and obviously false assertion – 'this is not a fairy tale' – creates a sense of joining the teller of the story. It is not so much self-advertisement as a shared conspiracy.

> The most important thing you should know about REAL WITCHES is this . . .

Real witches turn out to take on the disguise of the kind of women who go to the Institute or RSPCA wearing hats. The basic outline of the story follows the opening premise and the hero manages to get into a good and secret place to overhear the witches plotting. But we have already been made aware of the predilections of real witches, for Roald Dahl cannot resist the pleasure of explaining all about them, with his *own* relish. Naturally enough these witches, like so many creatures in Dahl, love eating children.

> 'Which child' she says to herself all day long. 'Exactly which child shall I choose for my next squelching?'
>
> A REAL WITCH gets the same pleasure from squelching a child as *you* get from eating a plateful of strawberries and thick cream [and Dahl gets from writing about them].

Dahl goes on to describe with deliberate bathos, as if it were the most ordinary thing in the world, that if witches eat less than one child a week they become grumpy, and that means

> 'One child a week is fifty two a year
> Squish them and squiggle them and make them disappear.'
> That is the motto of all witches.

Dahl cannot resist an immediate rhyme, triggered off by a word. Cannot resist? The writing suggests that it is done without thought and without innuendo. There is no subtlety. Once the story line is thought of, the rest follows without design and without constraint. There are no real distinctions between fact and fantasy for Dahl's secret is to mix up the two. The *Twits* hair is an exaggeration. The idea of women being witches in disguise is a point of view. The children who are told about the witches have grandparents who endorse the author's message. It is as if the real world were turned upside down and twisted and turned into a fantasy, and as if there were no limits to the absurd. Some authors have suggested that it is possible to get away with one fantasy but never two. Roald Dahl piles them together. This is partly because he mixes different levels of fantasy. There might be one central premise to each book – a hungry crocodile, real witches, a chocolate factory or a giant. But then there are fantasies of different kinds – a multitude of strange creatures, like the Oompa-Loompas, and a series of caricatures of real adults. The Grand High Witch, for example, is German:

> Vye have you not rrrubbed 'zem all out, these filthy smelly children?

The sense of the one-liner or remark that destroys the opposition, and which children either wish they could think of or wish they had thought of at the time, is also much used.

> The Manager whose name was Mr Stringer, was a bristly man in a black tail-coat. 'I cannot permit mice in my hotel, madam.'
> 'How dare you say that when your rotten hotel is full of rats anyway,' my grandmother cried.
> 'Rats?', cried Mr Stringer, going mauve in the face.

Thus hints of an alternative reality are bound up in the fantasy.

The juxtaposition of fantasy and exaggeration suggests a world which is self-contained. Whilst the style could not be more different, there are some essential similarities to Enid Blyton. There is nothing really complicated, however far-fetched the story, and nothing really considered. The pressure to tell the story seems a natural one, and the exuberance unforced. It is as if the appeal to children's humour is not so much knowing as unaffected. The Grand Witch kicks the mice.

> Her aim was extraordinary. She would have made a great football player.

And the book ends with the advice that children relish since it is so unlikely.

> 'Children should *never* have baths', my grandfather said.
> 'It's a dangerous habit.'

The unmitigated triumph of the child over unpleasant adults is a famously recurring theme in Roald Dahl and part of the appeal. But this is not his invention. Children's stories in their different ways from Herbert Strang to knockabout comics place their heroes in positions of adventure which involve adults playing the part of villains. Roald Dahl therefore takes on the convention and slightly adapts it. His adaptation reveals itself in two ways. Parents are often expunged and their place taken for bad or good by others; in the case of *The Witches* by grandparents. It is as if he, like Enid Blyton, could not bear even to think about his parents. Thus the children are surrounded by lots of *very* old people as well as very weird ones. And, at the same time, the heroes in Dahl's books tend to be by themselves rather than in a pair or a group. Other children do appear, but as we will see, they tend to be caricatures of nasty habits.

The essential appeal of Roald Dahl, if not the explanation of his achievement, is not the exaggerated coarseness of his description but a fundamental simplicity of idea that befits the storyteller. He retains the freshness of the first telling; like Blyton, he gives the sense of surprise and pleasure in what emerges as if it were by chance. Some of his ideas are simplistic but saved by their obviousness and the pleasure taken in them, like the title *Esio Trot*[5] or the story of three window cleaners, the pelican to hold the water, the giraffe because it is tall, and the monkey, because Dahl is fond of monkeys.[6] And another appeal of the books is that the starting point for their creation is a sense of 'us' versus 'them'. Again, this is the age old theme when 'they' are clearly villains or foreigners or both. But Dahl brings a particular strength of hate against his unreal villains. They are typically

> as nasty and mean as any men you could meet[7]

so that they are going to have an unhappy ending. But he also invites the reader in on the conspiracy of power an author has over his victims. The blurb of *The Magic Finger* asks:

> Have you ever thought something was terribly cruel, and wished you could do something to stop it?[8]

The answer is the ability to point at someone you dislike and turn them into a cat, or some such creature according to what is considered appropriate. The reader is invited to think of what creature would be most appropriate to take over his or her own hated teacher. Nor is punishment considered a temporary lesson. It is the ultimate, complete revenge.

> I cannot begin to tell you what happened after that but if any of you are wondering whether Mr Winter is quite all right again now the answer is No. And he never will be.[9]

Simple exaggerations, or deliberate hatred? It is hard to draw a distinction between them since the emotion that informs both is the same. Hatred and anger are one of the strongest forces that drive these books on, and also one of the strongest emotions experienced by their readers. Just as Judy Blume deals with embarrassment and trades on what seem to the protagonists to be life-shattering events in relationships, so Dahl captures some of the anguish and anger of childhood – at unfairness or loneliness, that sense of being utterly isolated and dislocated. This is then turned on its head and an imaginary revenge – 'I will show you one day and then you'll be sorry' – made reality.[10] But whilst the Judy Blume books concentrate on one 'world shattering' relationship which causes anxiety before the happy ending, Roald Dahl spreads his sense of grievance over a range of characters and every day incidents. Again, this is not unlike the habits of childish thought – 'isn't it disgusting, and fun'.

In *Matilda* Roald Dahl lets himself go against different kinds of parents, those who like their children and those who do not.[11] What matters is the tone. He hates sentimentality. He hates people; adults and children. He not only relishes the thought of writing horrible end of term reports for 'the stinkers in my class', but gives examples of them. But he also gives versions of end of term reports about adults, their attitudes to children, and their characteristics.

> It's a funny thing about mothers and fathers. Even when their own child is the most disgusting little blister you could ever imagine, they still think he or she is wonderful.
>
> Well, there is nothing wrong with all this. It's the way of the world. It is only when the parents begin telling *us* about the brilliance of their own revolting offspring that we start shouting 'Bring us a basin! We're going to be sick!'[12]

The assumption is, of course, that all children are disgusting little blisters and that parents' lack of realism is something to be put up with, as the way of the world.

The anger is not just directed against sentimentality but against examples of 'silly little lives':

> Mr Wormwood was a small ratty-looking man whose front teeth stuck out underneath a thin ratty moustache.[13]

The anger is directed against a number of things that Dahl hates: ordinary life, TV dinners, television, car salesmen, American soap operas, and platinum blondes. It is a sign of spleen against objects, people and habits, a pleasure in taking umbrage, a joy in exaggerated and wilful prejudice. People are 'gormless' and 'revolting' and 'disgusting'. Many of the terms are gratuitous and applied even to the 'beastly second-hand car garage'. In one telling remark Dahl suggests that such letting of spleen can be a kind of relief.

> But the new game she had invented of punishing one or both of them each time they were beastly to her made her life more or less bearable.[14]

There are a number of attractions in the book beyond the story and the ultimate revenge. The reader is assumed to be, like Matilda, clever. It is assumed that people like and read Dickens, Shakespeare and Dylan Thomas, and that C. S. Lewis and Tolkein are boring. There is in fact a great deal of snobbery: not just in matters of taste and reading but in the fact that *other* people are either 'beastly' or disgusting.

> He looked like a low-grade bookmaker dressed up for his daughter's wedding.[15]

But this applies to almost everyone; 'Her father said she's a real wart', 'Nasty dirty little things, little girls are'. The language is exaggerated and enjoyed.

> 'This black-head, this foul carbuncle, this poisonous pustule.'

> 'Casting a look of such simpering sloppiness at his wife it would have made a cat sick.'

Children are embarrassed at sentimentality and Dahl plays on this. But he also shares their exaggerated experiences of distaste. The language is exaggerated and so is the action. There is a kind of fascination at the extremes of behaviour. Miss Trunchbull is the big formidable headteacher who gives a performance we are invited to look at, fascinated by cruelty.

> The Trunchbull will throw anything around just to keep her arm in, especially children.
> 'I don't give a tinker's toot what your mummy thinks!'
> . . . and Amanda went sailing like a rocket right over the wire fence of the playground and high into the sky.[16]

Miss Trunchbull did not like Amanda's pigtails. The fantasy is not confined to magic powers but to exaggerations of physical gestures. We do not know where Amanda lands – presumably not in the sun – but the pleasure in imagining it is conceived as a pleasure in a performance. We are invited to be like the children:

> The children sat there hypnotized. None of them had seen anything quite like this before. It was splendid entertainment. It was better than a pantomime.[17]

The everyday terrors of school and its discipline are exaggerated to a manic degree. Cruelty and hatred abound. This all implies that it is based on a sense of reality, however stretched. If Miss Trunchbull did not make any connection with a big formidable woman who enjoyed her power over others there would be no point or humour or attraction in the story. But what makes it interesting is the way that the same violence – verbal rather than physical – applies to a whole range of things. It is as if all people are contemptible (apart from the reader) and either stupid or nasty.

This is the impression given in the relatively subdued autobiography of Roald Dahl's own childhood.[18] There are a number of signs in the feelings expressed that the sense of anger is deep-seated. The 'loathsome' Mrs Pratchett into whose jar of gobstoppers a dead mouse is placed is described as if she were one of the Twits. This is because of Dahl's deep-seated grievance at being spanked.

> The violence was bad enough, and being made to watch it was even worse, but with Mrs Pratchett in the audience the whole thing became a nightmare.[19]

The one real theme of the book, apart from displacement from one country to another, is his horror at institutionalized violence, especially that of Dr Coggan of Repton, the future Archbishop of Canterbury.

> By now I am sure you will be wondering why I lay so much emphasis upon school beatings in these pages. The answer is that I cannot help it . . . I have never got over it.[20]

At first reading, *Boy* seems a relatively calm book, but it is also full of pain, of boils and scalpels, of matrons who are 'merciless' and 'relished the whole business of caning' and who 'didn't like small boys'. There are traumas – 'I'm a murderer' – and the pleasure of seeing others suffer in their turn, especially if they seem to be prigs, like the suitor who has goat-droppings put into his pipe. Naturally the style of Dahl's writing will affect all he touches, but *Boy* is interesting for the hints of future themes and motivations, like connections between flogging and chocolates. It also gives a hint at Dahl's attitude to his own writing. There is a note about the stories at the beginning:

> I didn't have to search for any of them. All I had to do was skim them off the top of my consciousness and write them down.
>
> Some are funny. Some are painful. Some are unpleasant. I suppose that is why I have always remembered them so vividly. All are true.

The ease of writing – skimming them off the top of the consciousness – is like Enid Blyton's approach. But here Dahl suggests that early memories are not suppressed but always remembered. Saying 'all are true' is an odd remark to make. What else should they be in an autobiography? The question is whether Dahl feels he always writes with such ease, or whether he is driven. At the end of the book he writes:

> The life of a writer is absolute hell compared with the life of a businessman. The writer has to force himself to write . . . if he is a writer of fiction he lives in a world of fear. Each new day demands new ideas and he can never be sure whether he is going to come up with them or not.[21]

This seems at first glance disingenuous. Allowing for the exaggeration – absolute hell – one would have thought that Roald Dahl's manic energy and off-the-cuff style, leaps of imagination and the relish in the extreme, would come easily and spontaneously. This is how they read. But perhaps Dahl's particular energy and spleen is the result of suppressed anger at what is 'true'. The strong feelings attract children, not only at an immediate superficial level but because they make connections with their own emotions.

Dahl ends his short biography of childhood by speculating about writing about the rest of his life. I imagine he would have found this impossible beyond his relatively innocent early manhood as described in *Going Solo.* The driving force of his life is placed in his books as if they themselves are a kind of release. They contain not only the classical structures and pace of traditional stories but give more than a hint of his obsessions. *Charlie and the Chocolate Factory*, for example, is not just a fantasy about food:

> Most of us find ourselves . . . beginning to crave rich steaming stews and hot apple pies.[22]

– but a chance to attack certain habits that Dahl dislikes, from watching television to gum-chewing.

> 'She'll be purple!' cried Mr Wonka. 'A fine rich purple from head to toe! But there you are! That's what comes from chewing disgusting gum all day long!'[23]

The greatest relief from pain, as comedians keep reminding us, is from jokes. Roald Dahl likes to share the most outrageous, just the kind that children like. There is a sense of the deliberately stupid to mitigate the maliciousness.

> Square sweets that look round . . . ? . . . when you come in they look round at you . . .

Many of the jokes are deliberately silly, again giving the sense of a lack of constraint. The extremes of fantasy are joined by the extremes of self-indulgence:

> 'Knock knock' said the President.
> 'Whose there?' said the Chief Spy.
> 'Courtenay.'
> 'Courtenay who?'
> 'Courtenay one yet?' said the President.[24]

> The Trunk (and the suitcase) of an elephant.
> The Wart from a wart-hog.
> The horn of a cow (it must be a loud horn).[25]

These are the kind of jokes that are supposed to make the reader cringe – but with a secret pleasure.

> [China]'s so full of Wings and Wongs, everytime you wing you get a wong number.[26]

The pleasure in outrageous puns which Dahl takes every opportunity of employing is part of the technique to surprise, and to shock.

> The President said a very rude word into the microphone and ten million children across the nation began repeating it gleefully and got smacked by their parents.[27]

The ability to appeal so strongly to children is not something that is deliberately acquired. It is something that needs to come naturally, without self-consciousness. Roald Dahl's books are consistent in their attitudes and their tone. They have often been accused of being cruel, but they offer that combination of fantasy and escape together with an acknowledgement of pain that makes the escape the more important. In a sense Dahl's books, like Enid Blyton's, are a form of self-indulgence. Like Enid Blyton, Dahl was an instant success[28] and wrote in a consistent and familiar style for many years. We detect the misanthropic not because we know the disappointments of his poor relationships but because it seeps out of the books. The imagination feeds on itself. Once started, a story has an energy and a conviction that gives a sense of shared relish. The books all offer an alternative and crazy world.

Any author who appeals to children needs to do so from the 'inside'. He or she cannot come across as a teacher, but as someone talking directly to the reader. This is why adults are so often portrayed as either peripheral or as an enemy, or at least as creatures that are difficult to understand. Children's authors instinctively know that relationships between children and their parents are very important and often troubled. All relationships have periods of difficulty, certainly from the child's point of view, even if parents are oblivious to the fact. We know that Enid Blyton experienced great difficulties. But we also know that very often the earlier years contain many traumas, in which parents play their part.

> You will learn as you get older, just as I learned that autumn, that no father is perfect. Grown-ups are complicated creatures, full of quirks and secrets. Some have quirkier quirks and deeper secrets than others but all of them, including one's own parents, have two or three private habits hidden up their sleeves that would probably make you gasp if you knew about them.[29]

Is Dahl trying to make children reassess their own parents? This is what it sounds like, but the fact is that children are doing this already. Their world is surrounded by many unexplained characteristics that they have to interpret in the best way they can. The kind of message that Dahl is conveying is a kind of encouragement for the reader to have fun. It is not meant to be taken earnestly. At the end of *Danny, the Champion of the World*, Dahl returns to this theme. The parent here is depicted as 'sparky'. Danny's father is a crook and a poacher, but fun.

A message
to children who have read this book.
When you grow up
and have children of your own
do please remember something important.
A stodgy parent is *no fun at all*!
What a child wants
and *deserves*
Is a parent who is
SPARKY.

What kind of demons drove Dahl on?

The parents of James (of the Giant Peach) are famously disposed of:

> *Their* [sic] troubles were all over in a jiffy. They were dead and gone in thirty-five seconds flat.[30]

But this is to give free rein to the eponymous hero, so that he can see horrible aunts being got the better of and have his fantastic adventure without constraint. The adventures in Roald Dahl's books are exaggerated but essentially safe and comforting. Much is made of the anger, but the humour and the chattiness are just as important. There is a mixture of terror and absurd jokes. There is an attempt to make the flesh creep but never seriously:

> If you can think of anything more terrifying than that happening to you in the middle of the night, let's hear about it.[31]

Flesh-eating giants are, like children, not supposed to be anything more than fun. There is silly language and absurd puns.

> Some [human beans] is scrumdiddlyumtious and some is ukshush.
> Human beans from Panama is tasting very strong of hats.

There is fascination with bodily functions – 'whizzpopping'. The humour is very obvious and done with unselfconscious conviction.

> Search my cave from frack to bunt ... you can go looking into every crook and nanny. There is no human beans or stringy beans or runner beans or jelly beans or any other beans in there.[32]

Roald Dahl might be a writer driven by some inner turmoil, but the result is a series of books that are easy to read, fantastic and undemanding. What joins the motivation of the writer and the result is the sense of talking directly to the reader, of sharing whatever comes along with jokes and puns, with exaggerations and disgust. The world depicted might be an awful place but it is not serious. It is always funny and the stories essentially safe. For Dahl and for the readers they are a kind of exuberant escape.

Notes

1 Library Association Survey 1995. Lennon, P. Not in Front of the Children. *Guardian*, July 27 1996, pp.16–18.
2 London: Cape, 1978. Illustrated by Quentin Blake.
3 Sarland calls Dahl's skill 'incipient fascism'. Sarland, C. The Secret Seven or the Twits: Cultural clash or cosy combination? *Signal*. Vol.42, 1983, pp.155–71.
4 First published London: Cape, 1983. Illustrated by Quentin Blake.
5 *Esio Trot*. London: Cape, 1990. Illustrated by Quentin Blake.
6 *The Giraffe and the Pelly and Me*. London: Cape, 1988.
7 *Fantastic Mr Fox*. London: George Allen and Unwin, 1970.
8 *The Magic Finger*. London: George Allen and Unwin, 1966.
9 Ibid.
10 Mark Twain captures the depth of self-pity and its imagined consequences in *Huckleberry Finn*.
11 London: Cape, 1988.
12 *Matilda*, p.7.
13 Ibid., p.23.
14 Ibid., p.49.
15 Ibid., p.50.
16 Ibid., pp.110–14.
17 Ibid., pp.150–1.
18 *Boy. Tales of Childhood*. London: Cape, 1984.
19 Ibid., p.47.
20 Ibid., pp.144–5.
21 Ibid., p.171.

22 *Charlie and the Chocolate Factory*. First published New York: Farrar, Strauss and Giroux, 1964. This edition London: Puffin, 1995, p.56.
23 Ibid., p.130.
24 *Charlie and the Great Glass Elevator*. London: George Allen and Unwin, 1973, pp. 38–9.
25 Ibid., p.127.
26 Ibid., p.42.
27 Ibid., p.84.
28 With *Gremlins*. New York: Farrar, Strauss and Giroux, 1942.
29 *Danny the Champion of the World*. London: Cape, 1975, p.37.
30 *James and the Giant Peach*. London: George Allen and Unwin, 1967.
31 *The BFG*. London: Cape, 1982, p.17.
32 Ibid., p.73.

9
The Attractions of Escape: Comics

All literature relies on a tension between fact and fantasy. There may be extremes of 'social realism' or of the completely far-fetched, but neither element can be altogether missing. Even the books placed in ordinary circumstances, like Judy Blume's, create a fantasy world of their own, and Roald Dahl's extremes have their roots in the recognizable however exaggerated. This tension is also in the mind of the reader. There are different levels of response ranging from an almost total immersion in the story to self-consciousness and criticism. Those things being read about have associations in the minds of the reader. The act of reading ranges from serious concentration to a light and superficial glance as at the headlines of a popular newspaper. Children's literature concentrates primarily on what is most immediately attractive and what is easiest to read. Nowhere is this ease of impact, and its consequences on the style of reading, more apparent than in comics.

Comics remain popular. There was a time when it was supposed by many that television would replace them by offering something similar, with even greater ease of access.[1] But comics continue to be bought or supplied as part of the Sunday newspapers and continue to be read. On the face of it such popularity might seem surprising. Comics seem unnatural. They depict an unreal world, drawn in a cartoon style of its own, as if graffiti artists were commissioned to present their version of the real world. They not only use stilted language but use this language for the most part to comment on what is already obvious in the pictures. They are full of predictable and exaggerated, if unserious, violence. They cannot be taken seriously.

Some commentators have, however, taken them seriously. The controversy has centred on the extent to which young children will emulate the actions that they see depicted. There have been those who have feared that comics develop attitudes towards violence and social restraint.[2] Some have deconstructed the content and pointed out what a strange and unpleasant world is presented, full of subliminal anger.[3] Others have taken the opposite view. Using the same analysis of the content and agreeing about the violence, they have suggested that children respond to comics because their basic fantasies are all there – temper tantrums, messy play, oral gratification and frequent violence against property.[4]

There are many levels of response, and there must be a connection with the content that attracts children to comics and cartoons. The question of how children read comics and how they respond to them remains, however, relatively unexplored. It is far easier to look at the content and assert an effect than to explore it in the reader. George Orwell began the interest in the study of popular literature by suggesting that boys' weeklies are the 'best available indication of what the mass of the English people really feels and thinks'.[5] Whether one would nowadays suggest that the Bash Street Kids or Dennis the Menace are useful social indicators is another matter. What is significant is the way that children read comics and the comments they make on their own reading habits.

Instead of analysing the content and style of comics we will here turn directly to the voices of their readers. The quotations that follow are used to illuminate what is typical of a large number of children and are representative of them all, for there is complete agreement about the uses and pleasures of comics. What we discover is an important insight into the reading habits of children, and even if comics are at one extreme in the spectrum of literature, children's attitudes do give a telling account of response that could apply to some degree to their other reading. What we discover is a casualness towards the art of reading, and an interest in superficial and immediate gratification.

Comics are enjoyed but treated with a certain amount of contempt. There is a strong connection between reading comics and having nothing better to do.

> 'I read them when my mum has a lay-in and I'm fed up.' *(boy 7)*
>
> 'I save them for a rainy day or if I ain't got nothing to do.' *(girl 7)*
>
> 'On Sundays when Dad turns the telly off and the music's on.' *(girl 8)*
>
> 'When I'm bored, like when there is nothing to do I go upstairs and read my *Beanos*.' *(boy 8)*

To the driven adult, busy with work, and with many chores waiting to be completed, the idea of having 'nothing to do' might seem strange. But it is a central part of the experience of childhood. Being at a loss about what to do is associated with being 'fed up' and with being 'bored'. It is at these times that children most readily seek the instant pleasures of reading. They do not seek to 'escape' from misery by hiding in a book or comic, but turn to them in a more desultory way, to pass the time when there is nothing better to do.

Comics might look sensational but children do not find them demanding. The stories, the predictable outcomes and the obvious knockabout humour are not designed for close scrutiny and the undivided attention of the reader. The way that children treat comics is, in a sense, how they deserve to be read. Children take them lightly, and use them off-handedly to pass the time. They actually express the fact that there is an element of boredom, of passing the time, in their engagement with them

'I read when I'm bored and when I've got the money.' *(boy 12)*

'You could do something else in your time.' *(girl 12)*

It's not as if children are ashamed of reading comics. They are happy to say they read a lot, but they do not put a high value on this reading. They recognize that when they stop and think about it, comics are quite boring. They pass the time, but they are not 'interesting'

'I only read them if there is nothing else to do.' *(boy 13)*

'I get bored after the first few hours.' *(girl 13)*

The refrain of reading them 'when I've got nothing else to do' keeps re-occurring. This association of comics and passing the time when there is nothing else to do is not an afterthought that occurs out of shame. Of course when children actually *think* about what they are reading they realize it is a waste of time. Comics do not stand up to critical scrutiny. Their absurdities are too apparent. But this could be levelled at any number of popular books. When the mass of adult popular fiction, romances or adventures, is looked at in any detail, the formulae and the falseness stands out. But that is not the way in which such books are read. The readers are not critics. They seek the kinds of gratification that come easily, and would resent making an effort. There might be many times when readers have to concentrate on their reading but they feel it would be inappropriate to do so when reading what is meant to be ephemeral.

Comics might be amusing and they might be liked –

'I like the way it takes the world in an optimistic way.' *(boy 13)*

– but they are also found to be tedious. With that one exception, 'interesting' is not a word used to describe the feeling of reading them.

> 'After a while they get boring. After the first few pictures you know what's going to happen.' *(girl 13)*

Comics appear attractive and offer an easy read which does not engage children's attention for long or very deeply.

> 'I don't read it all. It has lots of adverts and posters and pop groups.' *(girl 11)*

> 'I used to like the *Beano* but now it just seems as if it's the same. I mean all it is is this lot picking on them lot. He's [Dennis the Menace] always causing trouble and it just seems as if it's getting a bit boring.' *(girl 11)*

It is apparent that children grow out of reading comics. They seek more interesting pleasures. But they have all experienced the particular style of reading that comics create. Whilst there might be some who go on reading comics as adults, the significant connection is with a style of reading: separating the approach used to study and understand a text, and that which is elicited by light fiction. The ease of reading comics leads to a particular style of reading. If little attention is demanded, little attention is given. Boredom is a natural concomitant to an activity which is soon repetitive. The longer the time spent doing one simple thing, the less interesting it becomes. Children, therefore, do not engage with comics very deeply, even if they do so often.

One result of this is that children use a kind of 'speed reading' when they look at comics. They pick up the central, structural clues, and anticipate what will happen next. They look for the outlines. They do not pass carefully over each picture and attend to the subtleties of the speeches. The comics are, after all, designed to be read fast:

> 'You can follow the pictures.' *(girl 10)*

This means that children do not recall in any detail what they have read. They do not memorize anything and, when asked to recall a particular story about one character, they can do so only rarely. They can say what happens typically but cannot give an account of a particular story. Naturally, if they are asked to read a story on which they know they will be subsequently tested, they will make the effort to read it in such a way that they can recall it, in detail. But this is not how they usually read. Instead, the level of memory that is used is that of recognition. They know *what* they have read previously when they see it again. They give cursory attention to a pile of comics in order to find one they have not 'read' before. They can tell quickly from the pictures which comics they have already looked at.

> 'I start and then I remember the story so I usually send it to my cousin.' *(girl 11)*

The habit of skimming over the pages of a comic is one shared by all the children. Many children rely purely on the pictorial clues and do not actually 'read' at all. The language employed, after all, comments on what is pictured rather than provides any narrative drive. It is like an afterthought, or an extra. When we observe children going through a comic, it is apparent that they 'read' it in about a tenth of the time it would take a speed reader. They are in fact looking for clues, exploring what there is, in case they want to come back to it later. There are times when some children in the privacy of their own rooms might pore over a familiar and favourite comic, but that is an 'escape' at a different level, an immersion in a fantasy world. The slightest critical awareness would remind them of the absurdity of the world depicted, but that would not in itself stop them returning to the familiarity and the repetition of the fantasy. Readers are happy to accept the absurdity of what they read, and either reduce and simplify it in their own minds or expand and elaborate upon it. But for all children for most of the time the 'escape' that comics offer is not one of fulfilling psychological needs for subliminal fantasies but an instant gratification, a distracting of the mind. It is the very lack of sensible connections that make comics so immediately attractive.

Comics are an ephemeral pleasure that are not designed for anything more than passing time.

> 'I sometimes go to bed and then read for about 5 or 10 minutes. I leave it there for a few days and then get it out again.' *(boy 10)*

It is very easy for children to enter into the style of the comics; to 'tune in' to the particular humour and the curious world that they depict. The comic world is a crude parody of the real one, from arguments with parents to anarchy in the school. The very way that they present this world draws attention to itself with pages of additional verbal markers like 'Clunk!' and 'Crack!' and 'Splash!'

and 'Swoosh!'. One 10-year-old boy entered into the spirit of such a style by writing his own comments on the pictures like 'watch this', 'see', 'what a slurp' and 'gulp'.

Children also reveal how they enter the world of comics in terms of their particular style. When they describe a story they have just read they parody rather than just explain the original. Their very language gives a flavour of the experience:

> 'Spider man goes up against Juggernaut who is unstoppable. He even survives a gas tanker exploding in his face. He *is* unstoppable. In the end, he is encased in 50 tons of cement in a building's foundations.'
>
> *(girl 12)*

> 'He has the speed of a panther, the strength of twenty men and the intelligence of a garden snail. He's a real laugh.' *(boy 10)*

The world that is depicted in comics is a mixture of the humdrum – suburban streets, back gardens, football pitches, schools, playgrounds and domestic interiors – and the bizarre. Either the protagonists do ordinary things in extraordinary circumstances – the Numskulls live inside a head – or extraordinary things in ordinary settings – Dennis the Menace or Minnie the Minx plaguing their parents. The way in which the stories are presented draws attention to their unreality, but there is some connection to the worlds of children, however exaggerated. Children, of course, understand the juxtaposition of the real and the fantastic very well. They realize both that the comics are supposed to depict a mad, fantasy world and that they, as readers, are supposed to make some connections with it.

> 'They make up people who don't exist because it makes it more exciting.' *(boy 10)*

> 'It reminds me of – school. I went over there one day and they were all running riot 'cos it was open day.' *(boy 11)*

The unreality of comics is clear, but it is interesting to note how, on reflection, children acknowledge the fact that like all imaginary endeavours they are at least based on real experience. When they put their mind to it the immediate acknowledgement of the fantasy element is superseded by an interest in the possibilities of what could connect to reality.

> 'Well, they wouldn't dare do most of the things that they do . . . jumping on people's gardens, creeping on people.' *(boy 10)*

After all, the romances which are based on 'photographs of real people with speech bubbles' (*girl* 11) have a superficial layer of reality at one level, but also a connection to a different level of real life that gives them interest.

There is no element of the either/or between fact and fantasy. Children are aware that comics and other books, like television adverts, contain a mixture of both.[6] Of course comics are unreal, with fantasy figures and invented stories. At the same time they do depict a version of reality – with people as agents. When children are asked about the levels of reality in comics they show how readily they accept the conventions of reading. At one level what they read is 'only' a comic. But pressed further, they can see the possible applications to real life. They are, however, ultimately non-plussed by such questions about the content since the genre suggests nothing as serious as real life, even if the style and the story are a parody of real life. Comics, like stories, are 'made up' and it is a fantasy in itself to associate them with reality.

> 'I think it could be [true] but it was not designed to be.' *(boy 8)*

> 'No, this story is not true because it is only a comic.' *(boy 9)*

The comments here are about war comics, which depict the stereotyped heroes fighting hordes of wicked Germans or Japanese. At one level what is depicted is based on the facts and the paraphernalia of the Second World War, with an attention to detail in the equipment and uniforms, if not in the actions, that suggests a basis in actuality. But that is as far as the convention of realism goes. It is clear that anything 'made up' is just that. Comics are 'only fantasy'.

> 'It doesn't matter if it's in a comic. It would matter if it's real.' *(boy 9)*

The problem is that a range of products designed to appeal to children, from toys to advertisements, from comics to cartoons, are both obviously 'unreal' and also, in so far as the productions actually exist and can be bought, clearly real.

> 'I don't think much of the characters. They're just not like real people.' *(girl 10)*

> 'It's all made up and not life-like. It's not real life because they are made up.' *(boy 12)*

The very fact that 'characters', depictions of real people, are 'made up' is one kind of unreality, as 'unreal' as the actors posing for photographs. They are clearly fictions. At the same time there are other kinds of extended unreality – like the most exaggerated actions of Superman. Children do not think that comics are depictions of a real world, or of a completely unreal one. The fantasy worlds presented to them and the way they react to them are more complex than that. The real and the fantastic are constantly juxtaposed.

> 'Some of their stories you can imagine but others you can't imagine being realistic.' *(girl 10)*

> 'In *Power Pack* the children are human and they get powers from an alien. In *Star Wars* they're human but they're on a different planet.' *(boy 11)*

In these strange worlds some things can be depicted as real or else they would be meaningless. There needs to be at least some connection with the possible.

> 'It might be if it's a very naughty school, but it doesn't look like a real school.' *(girl 11)*

> 'When they make up people who don't exist it makes it more exciting. Well, in this story they couldn't really get out of the house in time to do that or something, they couldn't do that.' *(boy 10)*

There are times when children realize that comics can depict certain things that no other medium can.

> 'In the TV you can't imagine the boys doing "breaking" but in comics you can and it seems quite funny at times.' *(girl 10)*

There is enough in comics to bring out at least one strand of reality in children. This is the recognition that most comics are aimed at, and read by, *either* boys *or* girls. Children dislike the thought of reading comics meant for the opposite sex. They see their own tastes as being clearly distinct and would be ashamed to be seen reading certain comics.

> 'It's rubbish. It's all about love and just photographs.' *(boy 11)*

> 'I don't mind this story but it's not for girls really . . . I don't know but it's for boys really.' *(girl 10)*

> 'It's girlish. It's about ponies and not many boys ride ponies, do they?' *(boy 10)*

> 'In these comics it's mostly boys, but in these comics it's all about girls.' *(girl 11)*

Boys, in particular, feel very strongly that they would not want to read comics about what seems to them an exclusive world. They assume that only girls would wish to read about romance and ponies, just as girls see action comics as designed for boys. The only neutral territory is the *Beano* and the *Dandy*.

The one divide between comics for girls and comics for boys is the level of supposed seriousness. Whilst it is apparent that all comics are fantasies there are more connections with the actual world in those designed for girls. Some even suggest that girls' comics serve a useful purpose in showing girls to be 'creatures of sound judgement', presenting

> role models which can more easily fit into real life than the antics of Dennis the Menace.[7]

No one would dream of finding role models in comics for boys, unless they are supposed to emulate the actions of the heroes of war comics, where they have the same success over thousands of foes as Arnold Schwarzenegger in one of his typical movies. The realization that all is essentially a fantasy spreads across all fiction.

> 'Comics are more real than books because the words come out of their mouths.' *(boy 9)*

The illuminative quotations from the children are examples of commonly shared attitudes. There is a generally desultory attitude to comics. They are acknowledged as ephemeral pleasures not to be taken too seriously. The *Beano* and the *Dandy* are examples of this half dismissive attitude, but it is by no means confined to them. Reading comics – and magazines for teenagers – is seen as an undemanding experience and as essentially boring. Comics do present a curious picture of the world but also a very predictable one. It is an idea which has not changed for many years. One could argue that the same story outline appears week after week, the same pictorial style and the same comic characters carrying out the same manic activities. Comics can easily be dismissed as no more than predictable.

Why then do children read them? They find comics just as boring as anyone else does, and yet they still undergo that spurious pleasure. No one is surprised that children should seek easy entertainment, but the fact that they find the very pleasures they seek dull should at least give us pause for thought. One possible reason for this is that children read comics out of habit, without thinking about it. When they do reflect on them they realize how slight the pleasure they give is.

But there is no doubting the consistency of children's reflections on comics or their habits of reading. One explanation of children's reading behaviour lies in the analogy that children often make between reading comics and watching television. Comics promise an easy time, they beckon with available gratification, but they soon pall. Television similarly offers entertainment that is undemanding, but many children associate watching television with having nothing better to do. They also think of television as being a form of entertainment which is even less demanding than reading a comic.

> 'Television thinks for you.' *(boy 10)*

> 'You can follow the pictures.' *(girl 10)*

> 'It's easier to switch on the television than it is to get started in a book.' *(girl 10)*

> 'You're used to watching television. You just don't feel as though you're going to take part because you really seem used to it.' *(girl 11)*

> 'Sometimes I just sit in front of the telly just for the sake of sitting down and watching it.' *(boy 11)*

For some time there has been speculation that comics would be usurped by television. Whilst the amount of time spent in front of the television is far greater than that spent looking at comics, there still seems a place for comics in children's lives. This is because both media offer very similar levels of entertainment; and both are seized on by children because of that. In both media, thinking is done for them. The question remains why children should *like* that? To ask that is not to assume that comics have an 'effect' on children – that they go back to school to behave like the Bash Street Kids, or that they become incapable of any demanding activity. The question asked here is what there is in children's lives that makes them want to cover part of it with a void? To say that children seek entertainment begs a greater one: why should they palpably enjoy what they also find dull, given the natural curiosity of their early childhood?

Comics such as the *Beano* and the *Dandy* are symbolic of a small part of childhood experience – doing nothing in particular. They are more symbolic of this than television because, as several children say, things seem more *real* if they are on television. Certainly, television does provide the viewer with periodic interruptions of a certain kind of reality in the form of the news. And nothing could provide a greater contrast to the news than the peacefulness of doing and thinking nothing.

The psychological state of vegetating, much favoured by those who 'pass the time' by watching television, is not a new phenomenon, but relatively unexplored. The term 'escapism' might seem inappropriate, both too positive a description of the state and perhaps too negative of the rest of their lives. Nevertheless, the style of reading comics and the way children talk about the ephemeral pleasure does indicate a peculiar need in their lives, and one that will not change in the least when the content of the *Beano* is brought 'up-to-date' or made 'politically correct'. The sensational activities presented and the sensation of reading will remain the same.

Notes

1 Schramm, W., Lyle, J. and Parker, E. *Television in the Lives of Our Children.* California: Stanford University Press, 1961.
2 Wertheim, F. *Seduction of the Innocent.* New York: Holt Rinehart, 1954.
3 Dixon, B. *Catching Them Young: Sex, Race and Class in Children's Fiction* (2 vols). London: Routledge and Kegan Paul, 1977.
4 Tucker, N. *The Child and the Book: A psychological and literary exploration.* Cambridge: Cambridge University Press, 1981.
Tucker, N. War! Sport! Adventure! Laughs! A new look at the British Comics. *Where.* No.122, 1976, pp.291–333.
5 Orwell, G. *Boys' Weeklies. Collected Essay Journalism and Letters.* Vol.1, Harmondsworth: Penguin, 1970, p.505.
6 Cullingford, C. Children's response to television advertising: The magic age of eight. *Research In Education.* No.51, 1994, pp.78–84.
7 Daniels. J. Girl talk: The possibilities of popular fiction, in Styles, M., Bearne, E. and Watson V. (eds), *The Prose and the Passion.* London: Cassell, 1994, pp.20–35.

10

Preparation for the Adult World? From *Point Horror* to Stephen King

One of the *Point Horror* series, *Teacher's Pet,* sold more than two million copies between 1991 and 1994.[1] This fascination with the macabre, packaged and marketed for children, might seem like a new phenomenon, like the tone of voice employed by Judy Blume. Up to a point this is true both in the designs on the audience and in the style of writing, but the excitement of horror also has a long history. First we have to acknowledge the connection with adventure, with 'cliff-hangers' and the employment of human agencies and happy endings. We also need to recognize the connection with fairy stories which, like Roald Dahl, have a fierce manic energy that to some reveal the darker side of the human psyche.[2]

But with *Point Horror* stories the psychological excitement is all on the surface. The tricks used to promote fear are mostly obvious, and easy to criticize. But they are successful in gaining the easy attention of readers and in relating horror to the everyday, as if the world of adolescence, one of trust and mistrust, was heightened the more by taking unhealthy or dysfunctional relationships to extremes. The world in which the *Point Horror* books are placed is firmly that of everyday teenage angst. This draws attention to the close links between horror and sex, in the fascination with physical details, in the threats and tribulations of relationships and in the fear of the unknown.

In *Girlfriend,* for example, we find that the story centres on a boy's relationships with two women.[3] He has a girlfriend but lusts after someone else.

> She was wearing a tight wool sweater and a very short green skirt over sheer tights.

The centre of the story is the way the hero cheats on his regular girlfriend for which he makes excuses, and for which there is some kind of punishment. His excuses are weak.

> He had had only one date with Shannon. [Untrue.] He had made no promises to her. [True.] He hadn't misled her in any way [just slept with

> her and misled his 'main date']. What right did she have to pester him?
>
> She had no right. No right at all.

Are these his thoughts or the suggestions of the author? It is clear that we are supposed to sympathize, to enter into the mind of the 'hero' rather than be shocked at his self-deception. For he is the victim of what is here called 'pestering' – by what turns out to be a juvenile delinquent who 'needs treatment', and who tries to kill him.

This essential melodrama, however, is overlaid with a patina of gestures towards 'horror', all placed at the end of chapters with signals as clear as Enid Blyton's chapter headings. Instead of 'What excitement!' to increase expectations, we are given a series of gasps, or thrills that are then turned into bathos. With monotonous regularity chapters end with a bang, before the next one gives a prosaic explanation.

> Lora started to say something – but only managed a choked gasp as a dark figure, arms raised to attack, leaped out at them from behind a tall bush.

This turns out to be their little brother.

> Scotty uttered a low cry and shrank back on the sofa as the three enormous men circled the coach, then closed in on him.

This turns out to be only a dream.

> But before he could say another word, a large, dark figure stepped up from behind and grabbed Scotty by the shoulder.

This turns out to be Lora's father.

The almost mechanical exploitation of the end of chapters says much more about the success of these books than complex psychological theories about adolescents' desire for 'clarity' or their fascination with trust and mistrust.[4] They are cheap devices which work.

The question as to whether folk tales, legends, fairy tales, and myths arise out of deep and immemorial collective memories is as difficult and vexed as the question of how each genre differs from each other. But it is impossible to pretend that the formulaic writing of *Point Horror* arises from anything more than technique. The formula is based on a constant stream of essentially visual thrills – shadows, sudden unexplained appearances. It has more to do with Enid Blyton's essential simplicity than the subconscious. 'How could *I* ever get into trouble?' cries the protagonist, begging for exactly that. And it is a very easy read, except for those who are accustomed to greater demands and for whom the obvious is profoundly dull. There are single line paragraphs, manipulated tensions and, essentially, the use of the misleading.

> Her eyes were closed and she wasn't breathing.
> So clear. So clear.
> He had killed her.

But of course he hasn't. The author, once again, is lying to us.

One needs a certain conviction to write in this way, a conviction in the art of the obvious. When there is an absence of actual events, in terms of artificial scares, there are pieces of 'atmosphere'. *The Silent Scream* starts tamely enough.

> The house mother who found Giselle McKendrick hanging from the brass light fixture in her bedroom didn't scream.[5]

The sense of foreboding – 'Nightmare Hall, where College is a Scream' shouts the subtitle – has constantly to be promoted. The style is deliberately portentous.

> Even the birds had left [why?] taking their songs with them [this is logical enough]. An eerie silence fell [sic] over the hill.
>
> [New paragraph] – Lost in shadow and deepening twilight . . .
> the house . . .
> settled into the hillside to wait
> [like a rabbit?]
>
> [New paragraph] All summer long, it waited.

Again in the *Nightmare Hall* series we are offered a group of young people undergoing 'adolescent' misunderstandings and mistakes, full of feelings of 'no one understands me', a tension heightened by the very occasional murder and the common scare.

These books are produced with fluid haste so that the clichés are easy and unexamined. Once the formula is accepted and placed in a different context certain inevitabilities become apparent but they only seem so after the event. When you *think* about it a book called *Fever* set in a hospital will have a series of familiar happenings – from sexy orderlies to tough matrons, from problems with syringes to difficulties with wheelchairs.[6] But the point is that thinking is treated in these books as a kind of hindsight. Everything is precipitate, and wrapped up in what people used to call 'breathless prose'.[7]

> What ... what is it? Sounds ... noises ... ripped [the wind invariably 'rips'] into her tortured sleep. No ... No ... she doesn't want to wake up ... no ... leave me alone, she thinks ...

Here is the heroine, helpless, and worse: 'Her hair felt like an oil slick and she had no make up on'. So the lift does not work (*almost* killed), the wheelchair plunges out of control towards certain death (*almost* killed), someone attacks her in the shower stall (*almost* killed), her drugs are tampered with (*almost* killed) and she is suffocated by a pillow for 17 minutes after which, being only *almost* killed, she brings a carafe of water down on her attacker's skull – and *still* doesn't see who it is.

The most popular of *Point Horror* stories appears to be *Teacher's Pet.*[8] The reason for this lies partly in the plot and partly in the celebration of itself. The book keeps insisting on the popularity of its own genre. There are remarks such as, 'Oh you young people and your obsession with horror!'. The idea of being horrified is not just condoned but encouraged. There is both the sense that all is safe – it's only a story – and the sense that beyond description, beyond such explanations *could* lie something real. The location, at a summer school creative writing class discussing the merits of *Point Horror,* is perfect both for reminding the reader about the fictionality of the whole experience, and for suggesting that there are also the possibilities for terror in even the most familiar and secure of surroundings. It is also set in an enclosed society which means that there can be *more* suspects from the ensemble than if they had to be picked out by inference (or misinformation) from the many. The sense of enclosure provides therefore both the overall boundaries of excitement and the sense that within such boundaries anything can safely happen.

This does not mean that the usual techniques of creating excitement are eschewed. We have the constant reminders of potential shock, and of sexual undercurrents.

> As her ears strained through the silence, the train whistle suddenly shrieked, and she jumped back, her body slamming into something warm and solid.

> Whirling, Kate scrambled away from the silent stranger who stared down at her. He was tall, with hair and eyes as black as smoke.

Even the most unpromising of circumstances can provide the frisson of possibilities: tall and dark; warm and solid ... There is a deliberate ambiguity between sensual pleasure and threat. Throughout the book there are two undercurrents of thought, both concerned with 'which one is it?' Which man will she fall in love with, and which man is the one who wants to kill her? Can they both be the same person? In *Teacher's Pet* we are offered a string of men who combine sexual attraction and veiled threat. This lubricious combination naturally leads from one incident to another. These men are all gossiped about. We hear their points of view. They call each other a 'zombie', or perhaps worse still appear to be so cultured they could be mistaken for being British.

At the core of *Point Romance* is inevitably the concentration on relationships. Whilst the reader is manipulated in well-worn ways the curiosity about *who* will turn out to be the villain is sustained by the sexual interest. Readers are offered not only that curious combination of fear and safety but the excitements of relationships good and bad; and a heavy emphasis on mistrust. It is not clarity that the readers seek but a mistiness of suspense, of ambiguity, before, inexorably, all will be revealed. There are many points of contact, the genre demanding that these should normally be in the dark. Thus we are presented with the overlapping of sexual gratification and fear.

> Without warning his hand closed around hers, and a strange thrill went through her finger tips, driving all fearful thoughts from her mind. His touch was so strong, yet so gentle, and from time to time she stole a look at his handsome profile when she was sure he wasn't looking. 'I can't believe I'm here'.
>
> But it wasn't the fog that chilled her now, as she stared in disbelief at the murky bank ...
>
> It was the tall, silent [sic] shadow at the water's edge.
> A human shadow.
> Black and stark [sic] against the gathering night, it raised one arm ... slowly ... deliberately ... in her direction.

Strong and gentle, tall but silent, the phrases tumble out of the fear and delight combined in new adventures, in new explorations.

All this ambiguity or overlap of the different types of 'thrill', is, however, presented with all the undeliberate artifice of popular writers. There is no fear of cliché. It is easy to anticipate most of the adjectives. But this is not what the readers notice or care about. Instead, they are cajoled into the gentle excitements by a technique which is not unlike that of Enid Blyton; of signposts of anticipation and reminders of their existence. The reader is being looked after. The writers have clear but undeliberate designs upon them, for the writing is done with unironic conviction. The signals of the excitements to be had are clear and constant.

> 'He's pretty strange', Kate said; 'He warned us not to wander off the trails – made it sound almost scary.'
> Denzil considered this for a moment, then nodded.
> 'Yeah, it *is* scary back in the woods.'

The reader will be left to judge whether any 'incidents' will take place in the woods. Not that that is difficult. For Kate is in Cabin *13*, the last one, nearest to the woods.

The other type of signal which is akin to Blyton is the constant self-referencing that suggests that the books are either popular or important or both. *Teacher's Pet* is set at a conference (an enclosed space) to celebrate the art of writing books like *Teacher's Pet.* It starts with ambition.

> 'I love to be scared,' Kate insisted with a smile. 'I'd love to write a book someday that would really terrify people.'

It continues with instructions as to how one does that – as well as a clear demonstration.

> 'Fear' he began quietly, 'seldom plays fair. Its best weapon is surprise. Often, distortion. Always ... the unknown'. [Kate felt helplessly drawn.]

> Perhaps the unknown we fear most is ourselves – our darker sides.

Here we have the author's justification rather than message, a justification tuned to exactly that signal most related to the readers' response. Surprise, distortion, and the unknown. And the underlying frisson of excitement which suggests that we *need* fear, that there is a psychological justification for reading these books.

The result is a series of dots on the printed page ... signifying untold thoughts ... and unthought ones ... leaving the reader to

... ostensibly ... fill in the gaps. The blurb and the text itself become intertwined.

> Bad surprises.
> I heard you say it, Kate ... back there in the woods.
> You like to be scared.
> But not by bad surprises ...
> So this was only a little bad ...
> Because the worst is yet to come ...
> Teacher's Pet.
> Teacher's Pet.
> You're going to die ...
> But not ... just ... yet.

Kate is the heroine. Clearly she is not going to die. This is just the advertisement of safe excitement. The more suggestions or innuendos the better. The sense of threat is more significant than the actual happenings, which partly explains the ultimate signal, the rows of dots that are there to heighten the awareness of tension:

> It was a cemetery. Spattered with moonlight, the tombstones shone gray ... graves beneath dead leaves ... dead weeds ... everything [sic] ... so dead [sic] ... so final.

This might seem a technique too obvious to employ too often, and yet it is used in the most obvious of sentences.

> His face ... hidden ... in the trees ... staring at the marker ... at the black thing ... hidden there.

The designs on the audience are clearly apparent and, in this book, expressed as part of the text. The desire is to make the reader 'scared'. But this is artificial fear. The manipulations are clear. This is so far from the actual fears that can envelop real life that the reader is at once reminded that he is supposed to be scared, and carefully guided away from the actuality of fear. The style itself, full of dots, is a safeguard against surprise. The irony is that as with Enid Blyton, the constant reminder that what is being read is 'exciting' evokes not just the frisson that should come with the idea, but the underlining of the opposite. All this is safe. There might be a riddle about *who* is the villain and who is the true hero/lover, but the reader knows and accepts the manipulations that arise out of the markers, the reminders that 'something bad [is] going to happen'.

> William ... Rowena ... Gideon ... Pearce ... The Night was full of secrets. And she had an unshakable feeling that something awful was about to happen.

Chapter headings, and chapter endings, the pointing out of what the reader is *supposed* to feel, all add to the superstructures of safety, of terror embedded in the obvious. The whole thing is not deeply serious: that might be apparent in the apparatus of any popular novel. But it is the way it is done, with a relish at and conviction of its own superficiality, that makes the genre remarkably successful. It is as if success were bred out of real limitations.[9]

> Creeping down the stairs.
> Slowly ... in a numbness of sickening horror.
> ... Kate raised her eyes ...

Teacher's Pet exemplifies the way in which all *Point Horrors* books are approached. It relies on certain stylistic tricks which are well known and have often been used in the past. It brings a simple and unironic directness to the task of fulfilling its mission to 'entertain'. And it adds the additional artifice, which makes it even more popular than others in the same series, of being centred not only on a place which is self-enclosed but on a conference which reminds us of the sense of self-enclosure: an advertisement to the significance of crime writing.

It is as if the mission to 'scare' the reader was an end in itself. It is as if entertainment at this level and with such designs was the most comforting and attractive thing in the world. There is certainly little difference between the approach and the design of *Point Horror*, mainly written for the young, and Stephen King, ostensibly written for the old, apart from the length. In surveys of what young people read, his is one name to appear. This is understandable. The connection between *Point Horror's* safe and popular writing for children and about children, ostensibly written from their point of view, and King's safe and popular writing for adults, could not be closer or more similar than in this genre of 'horror'. For a start, the writers have the same designs on their audience. As Stephen King writes:

> The job is still getting to *you* ... by the short hairs and, hopefully, [sic] scaring you so badly you won't be able to go to sleep without leaving the bathroom light on.[10]

The design on the reader is to create a world full of 'weird stuff'; a world where terrible things happen, and in which no one is safe. Again it is a fictional world that juxtaposes a vision of actual horror and the suspension of belief. It is obviously not serious, and yet has a relationship with actuality.

Why should authors wish to 'get to' the reader? Stephen King believes that,

> to understand the juxtaposition [of the fabulous and the humdrum] did as much to illuminate the ordinary aspects of life as it did to illuminate its occasional outbreaks.[11]

Certainly the horror only works well if it is embedded in ordinariness. But why should such untoward happenings be explored?

> I think that myth and imagination are, in fact, nearly interchangeable concepts, and that belief is the well-spring of both. Belief in what? I don't think it matters very much, to tell you the truth.[12]

What marks out successful and popular literature is that it is uncontaminated by anything profound to say. It is as if, as with Enid Blyton, the mission of the writer is simply to write, to give pleasure, to thrill or shock, or to create a world which will distract the readers as easily as possible. This sounds very simple, even simplistic. But it is not as common as it sounds. Belief in writing to please becomes almost an imperative that replaces any message. Most people believe that they have something to say, a point of view they wish to convey. These novels, however, have a kind of belief in themselves that means that they do not eschew the obvious or the manipulation of the reader.

Stephen King's *Carrie*[13] is typical of this. Like Dahl's *Matilda* telekinesis is used as a form of revenge; 'the subconscious level where savage things grow'. The book is written as if it were being reported, with bits of scientific explanation thrown in. Into this 'reality' are embedded the signals of horror and the reminders of horror: the book is full of one-liners and one line paragraphs.

> Her and George and Frieda had less than two hours to live.

or

> They stared at each other in silent tableau. Blood began to ooze from around the handle of the knife and to splash on to the floor.
>
> Then Carrie said softly 'I'm going to give you a present, Momma'.

The 'everyday' consists of the tone, the newspaper-like reportage.

The 'horror' is taken to the absolute. They are connected by real hate, some emotionally crippled people, and worries about menstruation.

One curious result of this genre is that the actual world in which the 'horror' is placed is also an odd one. In the *Point Horror* books, for example, there are always people who take an everyday, often sexual, relationship beyond the limits, as if this were always a possibility. The 'real' world is depicted as bordering on the pathological, with heightened emotions and destructive intensities. Take one routine example, Stephen King's *Popsy*. It ends with a sudden twist in which Popsy turns out to be a large vampire.

> His throat was cut with that nail before he realized what was happening, and the last things he saw before his sight dimmed to black were the kid, cupping his hands to catch the flow the way Sheridan himself had cupped his hands under the backyard faucet for a drink on a hot summer day when he was a kid, and Popsy, stroking the boy's hair gently, with grandfatherly love.

One might think that this is the juxtaposition between horror and normality; the invocation of childhood memories and grandfatherly love. But the real background reality is the world into which this dénouement is placed. This is an everyday story about how a man abducts a 6-year-old boy (his fifth) in order to sell him to a Turk who will send the child overseas for pornographic purposes. The man does this because he owes money and is brutally threatened by gangsters. He abducts children by using a van with a disabled badge – called a 'crip plate'. Is this normal life? Are we supposed to think it is a good thing that he is killed by a vampire?

We are, of course, not supposed to think at all. It is only a story. And yet the normal world in these stories is not a particularly pleasant place. It is not uplifting or cultured. There are no questions or debates about meanings or tastes beyond what is acceptable in terms of designer labels. And yet there is a connection with the real fears and the lack of self-confidence that is part of the human experience. It is as if these are recognized at the same time as they are mitigated. There are distractions, but distractions from a potentially terrifying reality. The readers *might* be frightened but they are also fundamentally consoled by the inevitable consolation of a happy ending.[15]

We need to acknowledge the fact of the delicate balance between the easy escapes provided by these popular novels and the fact that there is something that people wish to escape from. None of these genres would work as well, did they not have in them a genuine alternative, reflecting but not confronting those real issues, of relationships, of meanings, of insecurities and self-consciousness that impinge so heavily in real life. They are an interesting reminder of the intensity of feeling that underlie the reader's need for alternative versions of an inner reality. The following comes from a commentary on Jan Mark's novels, bleak and despairing and, in contrast to the easy popular horror of manipulation and fantasy, actually engaged in addressing the issues.

> The issues raised in these novels are adolescent issues only in the sense that they are perhaps best appreciated by human beings before they have embarked on the long process of compromise that makes most of us accept and profit from the world we find ourselves in. There are no tacked on 'happy endings' because these books do not lie about the nature of any universe that contains human beings. The landscapes are as harsh and inexorable as – perhaps – the human soul.[16]

But here we are dealing with the actual confrontation with the difficulties and misapprehensions of childhood, and are reminded of the way that people deal with them. They learn to compromise, to deaden themselves, to go for a middle way that, through habit, allays threats. There are many coping mechanisms which people learn. The books discussed here, unlike Jan Mark's, become part of the means of compromising, of hiding, of settling into a deep forgetfulness. They turn the reader away from the real by ostensibly dealing with it and heightening it, by taking up the everyday anguish of relationships and then demonstrating that there is always the fantastic possibility of the happy ending.

We need to understand the terms 'escape', or 'escapism'. They are often used as terms of disparagement, Enid Blyton apart. This might be fair, but they come about not only because of the human tendency not to face reality, but because there are many things that people wish to escape from. The device of escape is not just the setting up of an alternative world, but the reflection of an everyday world that can be manipulated and controlled. This manipulation is not just a matter of the security of a happy ending but the familiarity of style. The energy of the writing lies in the lack of any awareness of bathos. The conviction of the obvious means that any device is used to draw the reader into a world of almost his or her own fantasy.

> Joe had no choice as the deadly length of metal swept toward the side of his head. He could only throw himself backward.
>
> Landing flat on the cobblestoned street was a nasty jolt to his body. But it beat having his brains knocked out.[17]

Instant adventures; the good guys, the heroes, always winning; it takes us back to the days of Strang and Westerman. What connects this genre to *Point Horror* and Stephen King is the assumption that the reader is in a wicked world but that he, or she, will, at least whilst reading, always win.

Notes

1 McCarron, K. *Point Horror*: The point of horror, in Broadbent, N., Hogan, A., Inkson, G. and Miller, M. *Research Children's Literature: A Coming of Age?* Southampton: LSV Publication, 1994, pp.28–35.
2 Zipes, J. *Fairy Tales and the Art of Subversion*. London: Heineman, 1983.
3 Stine, R. L. *Girlfriend*. New York: Scholastic, 1993.
4 McCarron, Op. cit.
5 Hoh, D. *The Silent Scream*. New York: Scholastic, 1992.
6 Hoh, D. *Fever*. New York: Scholastic, 1992.
7 Cf. Patience Strong – whose verse some might remember.
8 Cusick, R. T. *Teacher's Pet*. New York: Scholastic, 1990.
9 As a Don once unkindly remarked of an undergraduate about to leave university: 'He has so many limitations he should do well' [he did].
10 King, S. *Nightmares and Dreamscapes*. London: Hodder and Stoughton, 1993, p.6.
11 Ibid., p.5.
12 Ibid.
13 King, S. *Carrie*. New York: Doubleday, 1974.
14 In *Nightmares and Dreamscapes*. Op. cit. pp.110–20.
15 Trousdale, A. Who's afraid of the big bad wolf? *Children's Literature in Education*. Vol.20, No.2, pp.69–80.
16 Sheldon, C. The individual and society: Novels for adolescents, in Pinsent, P. (ed.) *The Power on the Page: Children's Books and their Readers*. London: David Fulton, 1993, p.101.
17 Dixon, F. W. *Hardy Boys Case Files*. New York: Simon and Schuster, 1994.

11
Developing Children's Tastes in Literature

The books that children read and enjoy contrast in the majority of cases with those books that adults would prefer them to read. There is a marked difference between the world of popular fiction and the world of English literature. It is this gap that causes so much concern to those who wish children to be educated. The essential problem is that children recognize the distinction and quickly learn to protect themselves through cultural relativism. They stay with what is familiar and what is popular, what is easy and in fashion. They begin to associate reading in school, or approaching more demanding books, with nothing more than hard work, unnecessary and unrewarding. They place the pleasures of Shakespeare into a separate milieu that belongs to the elite, with whom they would not wish to be associated as they tend to disown them as 'snobs'.

The distinction between the two cultures and children's awareness of it has a number of levels. One is the difference between home and peer group on the one hand and school on the other. This is not a physical but a psychological difference. A school is for many children the most significant social meeting place, except for those who play truant. But even within the school many pupils psychologically exclude themselves.[1] They turn away from the demands of lessons or teachers, and pay attention elsewhere. To many children schools are antipathetic places, associated with waiting for something to happen, with unnecessary demands and restrictions. To all children school includes alienating moments; a sense of boredom, bewilderment or unfairness. In these circumstances the shared tastes of the pupils, be they designer wear, the hit parade or their choice of reading, becomes the more important to them.

The difficulty is that any reading which makes intellectual and emotional demands tends to become associated with school. The distinction between popular and high culture is reinforced. This happens in a variety of ways. Surveys by the Book Marketing Council perennially point out the contrasts in choice of books by adults and children, natural in terms of popular fiction, but not so justifiable in terms of literature, given that so many books aimed ostensibly at children are savoured by adults. Even when choosing children's books, parents choose quite different books from their sons and daughters.[2] There is a tendency for adults to choose safe and familiar texts, the very ones children find less attractive or immediate than the more popular, if ephemeral, novels of the time. Perhaps the task of choosing books for children is driven by the desire to 'uplift' the reader, or to protect him or her from the more vulgar manifestations of popular culture. Many parents trying to choose books that would please both them and their children are aware how difficult this is.

The answer to this dilemma is, however, not to put so much emphasis on the books themselves. Handing over a Jane Austen novel (or a safe children's classic) does not guarantee it being read. The only solution is through paying more attention to the act of reading itself, the style, the approach and the level of expectation, whatever the text. The real difficulty is that alongside the expectation that the 'right' text will automatically work its magic comes the attitude towards reading expressed by so many teachers and librarians as first and foremost a skill, in terms of deciphering the hieroglyphics on the page. When teachers and librarians are asked about the purpose of children's literature they usually infer the very ability to read.[3] The habit of reading is seen as paramount, as if the skill involved in deciphering were an end in itself. All the outcomes of reading, like increased understanding, are not mentioned.

The association of school with the 'skill' of reading is constantly highlighted until children think of reading as two almost separate experiences, the one concerned with pleasure, and fantasy, with communication, and the other with gaining new knowledge, gathering facts, and classifying.[4] This distinction is constantly reinforced. Teachers like to hear children read aloud and assume they like to do so. Children however say they prefer to read silently.[5] Children say they do far more reading at home than at school, partly because reading at school is proving the mastery of a skill, rather than a pleasure. Primary school children consistently discriminate between valuing reading and enjoying it.[6]

Whilst there appears to be a distinction between the tastes of children and the high cultural values of teachers, this is not actually witnessed by the children, and indeed is not necessarily the case. It is recognized that the observation of adult reading habits, in a household where books abound, where they are shared and discussed, is very influential on the children's approach to books. But how often do they see teachers read? How many times do teachers have an opportunity to enthuse about the books they are reading? One difficulty is, of course, that teachers do not read. Given the demands of the National Curriculum this is hardly surprising. Teachers actually read less fiction than their pupils and make less use of public libraries.[7] We will gloss over what they do read, when they do.

The subconscious signals that teachers tend to give about books are not necessarily helpful in developing children's tastes. In a survey of primary teachers asked about what they thought was the value of stories, the answer was that the greatest value lay in improving written and spoken English, again emphasizing the skill rather than the cultural experience (which was also mentioned).[8] But when asked about how they used stories and reading the same teachers said they used reading as a means of keeping children quiet, or calming them down at the end of the school day. Does this lead children to rate reading more highly as an activity, or does it mean they suppose the distinction between reading as work or reading as escape is the more reinforced? From the point of view of the beleaguered teacher the uses of reading as instant calming down in the name of gratification is entirely understandable. But the message given to the pupils reinforces the barrier, between reading as a pleasure and reading as a task.

Children are usually nurtured from an early age into an assumption that reading at school, like any school work, is a separate world from their own and that of their peers. Right from the beginning reading schemes present a hidden message that reading is not particularly pleasurable, with low status, and that it is highly school-based.[9] It is not a surprise if pupils who do read prefer reading at home.[10] They can read by themselves. They can read what they want. They can read without interference. Any pleasures that are given by reading are private ones, not communicated at any intellectual level. The readers do not like writing reviews or explaining the reasons why they prefer certain books, or, indeed, what they derive from reading. It is as if popular literature were a secret world, deliberately hidden from the school.

At another level popular literature is an open secret. It is freely available and bought in huge numbers. But it is rarely studied, either for its own sake, or for the light it sheds on children's tastes. That there is a mass reading public taking the time to be entertained whether through romance or horror, eschewing the more arcane pleasures of 'serious' literature, is clear and gives an indication of one aspect of human nature. To discuss the idea that all types of entertainment are equal, that Beethoven's late string quartets are no 'better' than the top of the pops is not the same as discussing the pleasures that people derive from popular literature and other forms of mass entertainment. One might have serious reservations about the types of easy gratification being offered in terms of sex or violence, but one still needs to respect those people whose reading habits remain locked in the banal or the familiar. When children read for pleasure they opt, naturally enough, for the kind of books that teach them about adult popular taste. There are safe adventure stories, many romances and series of books that start with 'goose-bumps' and then become more and more explicitly horrifying. As Altick notes, it was always thus.[11]

There is a distinction to be made between understanding the tastes of the reader, and analysing the way in which books are designed with those tastes in mind. If we do not understand why children like certain books we will never be able to help them develop their tastes. Banning certain books and thrusting others upon them does not help. It merely reinforces the distinction between pleasure and learning. Nevertheless we take it as read that the aim of the educator is to enhance the intellectual and moral taste of pupils, to enable them to have access to books which have a deeper human and spiritual dimension, to books which help us understand the human condition.

How, then, do we develop children's tastes in reading? I believe there are certain important principles that underpin all kinds of ideas. The first is to concentrate on the reader, rather than what is read. Reading has many different levels of demands, but these levels can be applied to any text. It is possible to 'speed read' Dickens, to follow the outlines of the plot and ignore the symbolism or to 'skip read' Hardy avoiding any response to his use of imagery. At the same time it is possible to analyse the style and structure of any text, however thoughtlessly formulated. Of course there is a relationship between text and response, but what we are concerned with is the development of a reader who is aware and discriminating, who can analyse as well as react to what is being read. Our first concern is to bring out the critical abilities of the reader, without which no demanding text can be enjoyed. The only way to change the style of reading is to apply that discriminatory critical judgement to texts which do not stand up to such reading. That they do not warrant such reading needs to be accepted; but the ability to criticize any text must also be understood.

The second principle is that reading should be associated with pleasure. The teacher should be constantly informing pupils about his or her own reading. Teaching must be charged with stories, with anecdotes, with examples from the teacher's own experience.[12] The more that pupils realize that their teachers read and gain a great deal from doing so, indeed, the more they actually *see* teachers read, the more chance they have of being influenced. Reading needs to be seen as a sensible and normal adult intellectual activity, and something which takes place outside the confines of the school. It is very difficult to teach children to read adult texts if the teachers are not themselves excited and interested by their own reading. Example is essential.

The third principle is to overcome the distinction between reading for pleasure and the demands of school by introducing tasks which are as akin to the real world as possible. Too often pupils are given exercises that are completely artificial, like describing grammar or being told to write a story of a kind that they would never encounter in the real world. Some of the examples that children produce, like a story on one side of paper, are not only alien to their own experience of reading, but very hard to do. No one can produce a convincing short story in the confines of time and space imposed on children. Once an exercise becomes routine, or imposed merely to keep children busy, it is not only a waste of time but an inhibition of talent.

The problem from the point of view of children is that lessons can be very boring, and as meaningless as watching a succession of soap operas on TV, but without the theatrical excitement or substitute intensity. Much time is spent waiting. Given all the demands on teachers and the teacher–pupil ratio such vast tracts of empty time are not surprising. Pupils wait their turn, and rarely have direct contact with the teacher themselves. One way of overcoming this is to make sure that whenever children are not doing something else they are reading. There should not be any time, from waiting for the registration to going home, when children are doing nothing. Reading should be developed as a habit when script attracts and gives information or satisfies curiosity. What is more, reading provides something individual to talk about, with answers to open questions rather than the repetition of a succession of answers which are either right or wrong. Just as so much time is spent working so is time taken up with a constant series of examinations. 'What is the right answer to this question?' 'I'm testing you' is a type of dialogue confined almost entirely to schools (or sometimes to police stations). Normal conversation is open and exploratory, where people are allowed to give their opinions. Books provide the material for something 'real', the usual conversations that mark out social relationships. Schools with their imposed emphasis on assessment deal with a dialogue that closes rather than opens ideas.

Books, including popular books with mass appeal, are part of the normal 'real' world of society beyond school. It is possible to turn this to our advantage by recognizing its existence, and by connecting with the other personal interests of children. When we point out that what is read is not as significant for the teacher as how it is read this is because all literature conveys meaning, however banal its level might be. It creates a response and makes some kind of demand on the reader. The reader can therefore be encouraged to have a personal opinion, increasingly sophisticated, on anything. The difference between such an opinion and the answer to closed questions is that even if the opinion, like the text, is banal, it can also be respected. It is not wrong in itself. Only when the opinion is recognized as the often unthought out feelings of an individual and accepted as such can one help develop the depth, or evidence, or sensitivity of that response. What must be avoided is defensiveness or assertion: 'I know what I like and I know you don't like it.' Differences of opinion can be accepted but only if one has a starting point that accepts the right to an opinion. Only then can one ask why? The critic F. R. Leavis talked of the ideal dialogue where the essential connection was 'Yes, but'. This suggested disagreement but accepted the validity of the argument before being allowed the privilege of an alternative. Such argumentary openness did not apply to him or his disciples but the point is still a telling one, to use his phrase.

The teacher is constantly trying to balance a respect for the potential worth of each pupil, and a belief in the possibility of learning. This is essentially what is meant by charisma, a tension between erudition, knowledge and firmness of purpose which lead to respect, and openness and approachability, the possibility of sharing a joke. The means of developing this kind of role model depend on a number of factors. One is the ability to reveal a personal intellectual life, to be engaged in curiosity, to share interests. Another is to accept that pupils also bring with them a whole range of personal interests and emotional ties. But the most important, which binds all together, and combines the person and the role, is a sense of purpose. Everything that is taught, like everything that is learned, should be directed towards the end of enabling each individual to fulfil him or herself as a sensitive and thoughtful human being. Taking that as a starting point – 'what is it that I need to know?' – transforms subjects from history to science.[13]

That might seem to be a long way from what is learned from Enid Blyton or Judy Blume. But the same approach can be applied to them. Why are these books being read? What is it about them that provides the gratification? Are they to remain almost an alternative world to that of the school? How can we enhance the intellectual capacities of children? We certainly cannot do it by ignoring their interests, and tastes, and nor can we do it by making the school and the curriculum like an alien world. The underlying purpose of education, often deuced clearer to teachers, is not league tables or the success rate or the competition to separate the good, the bad, and the indifferent, but to elevate the capacities of human beings towards the intellectual understanding and compassion of which they are capable. Whatever the sense of irony, realism, or humour, it is possible to be sustained by an ideal. The essential reason it is so rarely mentioned is because it is so easy to be disappointed, in the circumstances imposed by the government, until teachers protect themselves by submitting to circumstances, and giving up.

The teacher, and the example he or she sets, is central. The influence he or she has on the pupil is far more subtle and more hidden than either will admit. It is not something that can be measured in carefully defined competencies. Nor is it something that is acknowledged or recognized by pupils. They might detect the relief of a teacher when a difficult boy is playing truant. They might detect the exasperation that leads to a teacher 'picking on' people unfairly. They might closely observe the private weaknesses or worries that teachers bring with them to the classroom and find them irresistible as areas to be probed. But even if they start to respect or admire the aims and concerns of a teacher, they will prefer to keep silent about it. Even those who would wish to be educated do not really like being taught.

There are moments when pupils are startled to discover the person behind the role of the teacher. This can happen on field trips or excursions and such incidents are long remembered.

Indeed, pupils consistently wish they had more personal, individual dialogue with teachers outside the confines of the official curriculum. Any opportunity for a genuine conversation should be used; it does not need to be forced upon pupils for this will seem like yet another series of closed questions, even if it is nothing more threatening than 'how are you?' (Why is she asking me this?), but should arise naturally from mutual interests. The obvious and useful starting point is reading, because even those who do not make a habit of undergoing a series of popular books will read around their own personal interests or hobbies. And teachers will have their own interests and concerns which must include the reading of literature.

Whilst there is a distinction to be made between the role and the personality of the teacher, which is highlighted at times when it has broken down, the teacher is constantly being scrutinized as a personality, with moods and habits. The example that is set in terms of reading is crucial. Teachers should be seen to read, and to talk about their reading outside the set curriculum. The problem with a literary syllabus, however carefully chosen, is that it is approached as work rather than pleasure, as something to be undergone for the sake of a test, rather than something to be enjoyed for the sake of learning. Thus the distinction in styles of reading can be reinforced.

There are a number of ways in which the barriers can be overcome. The central aim is to apply the rigours of critical reading to popular literature and the pleasures of gratification to literary masterpieces. Encouraging children to read for pleasure, whatever they read, is important. Readathons not only raise money, with pupils being sponsored to read so many books, but recognize and encourage the habit of reading. There can be prizes for the best book review of books that the teacher chooses, with plenty of comparisons of style and approach, demonstrating different reactions to the same text. A questionnaire can be constructed with the pupils that tries to elicit why someone likes a particular book. This draws attention to the kind of questions that need to be asked and, subtly, to the nature and construction of books themselves. It is a stage in making children aware of their own reading. Children should be encouraged to share their reading interests with others, and compare them. A story-board can be constructed which communicates which books every pupil is reading, or has just read, why they chose them and what they thought of them. This should include everyone and be constantly updated.

Children find writing book reviews difficult when it becomes a task for its own sake rather than a means of communication. They often say they dislike writing about a book after they have read it, as if the pleasure were an inward and private one, not worth contemplating since it is so ephemeral.[14] There need to be reasons for reviewing books, means of making it interesting. We are aiming to develop critical readers out of those who are reluctant to be critical and self-aware. Reviews therefore should seek to communicate, and have a real audience in mind. Comparisons can be made between their *own* assessment of a book and those which appear in the newspapers. They can also be directed to look at a particular aspect of a book.

Those children who come from homes which are filled with books look upon the act of reading quite differently from those whose lives have been devoid of them. Within a school, therefore, books should not be confined to a library but also be a natural part of classrooms. There are some teachers who bring their own books with them, for reference or interest, turning the classroom into a kind of study. Anyone who has witnessed this will remember the impression it makes. One way of extending the reading habit is to have a class library which gives easy access to the books that are being recommended. It would then be an easy and interesting matter to see which books turned out to be the favourites, and why. The sharing and discussion of books should not, however, be confined to the reinforcing of the favourites but to extending the range. 'It's great' is a perfectly respectable response but not very illuminating. We wish pupils to be able to convey information and not just an instant feeling. One way of doing this is to encourage or arrange the swapping of books. This can be interesting if the individual tastes obviously differ. The gender divide in reading is very strong. Boys tend to reject anything that girls read. But rather than instance stereotypical dismissal it is worth seeing if pupils can give reasons for it, reasons based on actual experience rather than bias. Swapping books between boys and girls can at least enlighten them about the different pleasures gained from books and enable them perhaps to be more self-critical of their own habits.

We have already suggested some principles on which to base the development of the reading habit and its elevation towards more demanding literature. There are a number of techniques that can be used to enhance reading, to foster intelligent response. Again, these techniques share a number of underlying principles, including dealing with real tasks that are associated with reading rather than artificial ones. The first is the recognition of the use of parody. Children do not find it easy to criticise or deconstruct a text. But they do find it easy to imitate, and to make their own version of what they read. Parody is the essential insight into style, the recognition of how people communicate.[15] Almost anything can be parodied, from what is seen to what is heard. When applied to texts parody demonstrates the understanding of style, and focuses attention on real texts and how they are constructed. For we must remember the second important principle, the concentration on style.

For some the recognition of different styles of writing might appear to be very demanding, and beyond the capacities of children. However, not only do children understand style but they cannot do without this understanding. It is part of their everyday experience even if it is not often articulated. The presentation of shop windows, let alone clothes, the decorations of a house and its furniture, and the whole world of entertainment are presented through particular styles. Children cannot fail to see and hear all the differences. Whilst they do not often analyse it, they recognize the distinctions of style. They might not develop great sophistication of taste, but they have their own tastes nevertheless. When children parody they parody style.

The third principle that underlies the development of reading is the importance of vocabulary. It is possible to survive and negotiate with the use of a limited number of words; but this is a restriction of thought and communication. Difficulties that people have in reading are often centred on their unawareness of certain words. In order to help and to extend the range of their thinking the teacher needs to make a conscious effort to introduce new words. These are not mere similes but carry distinct meanings and resources. Young children learn new words rapidly and cleverly by understanding their use in context.[16] This ability, however, tends to atrophy. It needs encouraging, by deliberately fostering the use of an extended vocabulary.

All these principles can best be illustrated by one example. We have all witnessed children being given the task of 'writing a story'. The results, as we have noted, are artificial and quite unlike the pupils' real experience of reading. Where else but in school would one come across a 1000 word story? A real task would be to write a 40,000 word novel; but that would not be feasible, or necessary. The answer lies in approaching the understanding of writing differently.

Many books have illustrations, whether on the front cover, or – as was true of books in the past – interspersed in the text. They depend on particular moments in the plot. The pupils are given or choose a particular postcard or picture and are asked to write the page that would appear next to it, taking just one moment in a whole novel.[17] They would be discouraged from merely describing what happened in the picture. They could even concentrate on its tone, or the suggestive power of the picture. They could start, as any page of a book would do, in the middle of a sentence. But what they would need to do is to have a sense of a particular moment in a plot, with characters, atmosphere, description and action. They could write a page that gave little away. But the result should be what would actually be attributable to a real book. It should be intriguing, especially if we are left guessing at the end of that page. In thinking about what they write the pupils will be thinking about the construction of a text, the sense of a direction in a plot, and the realistic pace of a book rather than the knockabout series of violent incidents that is so easily the response to 'write a story'. And it is a task they find interesting to do, as well as instructive. Different pictures should elicit different approaches and a wide range of tone and mood.

An alternative to writing one page of a novel is to write out an end to a chapter. Writers from Enid Blyton to the contributors to *Point Horror* make blatant use of cliff-hangers; what will happen next? The pupils can create their own versions of these devices, including the start of the next chapter. Is it a genuine surprise or is it mere bathos? How is the atmosphere created? Do we have the sense of a real person? Again, the idea is to create a scene as close as possible to the kind of material they read.

There will always be some pupils who find it easier to be far-fetched, to exaggerate their writing, rather than to be true to the genre they are parodying. They can be helped by reflecting on the stories they have read. How realistic are they? How close to their own experience? Ultimately stories that have very little connection to the actual world and to human feelings become dull. Pupils need to be encouraged to develop their taste for books that reflect on experience, that raise issues, and that delineate realistic human responses to different circumstances.

One task that draws attention to the realism, or lack of it, in a story is to summarize the plot as simply as possible. Would other pupils recognize or recall it, if they have read that book? Writing an outline, knowing how to adjudicate between what is significant and what is not, can be quite a sophisticated task. Pupils can also invent a plausible outline of a plot, including particular characters as well as events. Alternatively they can write their own 'blurbs'. How do you make a book sound attractive? What would engage the attention of the potential reader? When they compare their own blurbs to other peoples which are the ones that elicit the most interest? In understanding the structure and content of books pupils can also analyse the chapter headings of a particular text, and then produce a list of their own. What do chapter headings convey? Are they invitations to read on, or descriptive? They can also analyse the last lines and not only the last page of chapters.

In looking at the techniques of writers and concentrating on the structure of chapters, especially their ending with an incident that is supposed to excite, pupils can see whether enough suggestions have been given about what would happen next. They can compare the original to their own guesses. Again, they can compare each others'. Which is the most plausible continuation? Which is closest to the spirit of the original? And are their versions any better or worse than the author's? It is not difficult to summarize a typical plot of a popular novel, but to work out its actual structure, the build-up of excitement and the denouement is more difficult. Pupils should become sophisticated in their understanding of stylistic devices.

One of the important ingredients in books is their setting. Pupils can reconstruct the place, the atmosphere and the circumstances of books they have read. Why was such a place chosen? They can invent a place of their own, and justify their choice. They can also analyse the relationship between the setting and the plot. What does a sea coast or an island suggest? Or the basing of a story in a summer camp or in a school? And what is the relationship between the cover (or the blurbs) and the story? Does it accurately suggest the kinds of events that will take place? They could also make classifications of stories they have read: are they familiar with all the characteristics of particular genres? How many distinctly different types of popular book are there? To what extent are the *Baby-sitters Club* different from Judy Blume, or *Goosebumps* from *Point Horror*? Pupils can also carry out surveys within and outside school of people's favourite reading.

In popular stories there are bound to be certain events in daily life which are described, like meetings and journeys, getting up and meal times. It is worth focusing on a particular theme in books – like food – and comparing their treatment. The pupils would seek out examples as part of their normal reading until they have a collection. These could be analysed to see what they reveal about changing tastes or attitudes. How are families described? How are the old treated? What is conveyed in these books about schools? There are many set themes that provide a simple basis of comparison and analysis and which relate the experience of reading to that of thinking about it.

Comparisons, like parody, are a useful means of understanding literature. There could be comparisons of different approaches to similar themes, or comparisons of very similar books. What, if anything, makes one more successful than another? And what are the differences between books written in the United States and in Great Britain? Are there differences in vocabulary and tone? Do people behave differently, or express different kinds of opinion in different styles or language? It is best to focus attention on particular passages which are either chosen by the teacher or extracted from the books by the pupils themselves. Similarly comparisons could be made between a page or two of an earlier writer like Strang or Brazil and a contemporary one. What are the differences in approach and attitude? Comparisons could also be made of particular themes, like the perennial one of finding someone of the opposite sex attractive, from the popular texts like *Sweet Valley High*, to *Tess of the D'Urbevilles.*

Once one looks at thematic material there are many comparisons which could be made, between different levels of prose, or between prose and poetry. It is also possible to see the difference between the kind of material pupils are reading at the moment and those that they were reading when they were younger. What exactly *are* the differences in outlook and attitude as well as vocabulary? And what exactly do they find difficult when confronted by advanced and complex stories – like Lawrence, rather than Joyce. Is it the level of thought or the complex language, its theme or the approach? Do they miss the speed or plot or the sense of the obvious? Do they realize what might attract other, older readers to that kind of text? Again the stress is on looking in detail at a page; an opening or an incident, rather than the whole book. That will come later, fostered by this kind of awareness.

The opening of a Dickens novel or a particular scene in it can be looked at with the ostensible design of plundering new vocabulary.

But such texts draw attention to what can be made of style; the relish of language and the pleasure in explanation. Ostensibly the pupils are finding out what they don't know on a simple level, possibly using a dictionary, but at the same time they are being made aware of the range of possibilities that books present. These differences are both of level and of time. It is also possible to compare passages of Swift or Defoe and later depictions of similar events (if there is anything similar to Gulliver). In comparing histories and historical novels the pupils could devise how they would re-write an historical event in fiction, and how the hero or heroine would be part of significant public events. All these ideas derive from a combination of two things: the enthusiasm of the teacher and access to text from which passages are taken. It does demand time and curiosity but it also wins the interest and co-operation of the pupils.

We have considered the openings of books, and themes and pages from the middle of books. But what of the endings? Do they indicate what might have happened before? Do they hint at the resolution of a real problem or an obvious one which has no resonance outside the purpose of the story? And what happens next? Is there a sense of more than an ending? It would be interesting to compare the 'closure', the finality of the popular novel with its happy ending to the more suggestive endings of novels where although there is a resolution there is also the possibility of a continuation, as in real life. In carrying out comparisons it does not matter that much if the pupils find some of the things they look at somewhat silly or dated. This is in itself a sign of criticism. It is better that they find them amusing; as long as they see what it is that makes what they read characteristic. They are, after all, not being forced to dwell on them at length.

Another comparative exercise, which some pupils will at some stage be undertaking themselves, is between novels written for children and adolescents and novels on the same theme written for adults. When passages are compared are they in fact very different? Are the gratifications the same? On this basis it is also possible to compare the treatment of a theme in a book with one seen on television. A comparison between the ways that films and books operate is also an insight into style, and a reminder of the way in which there are certain themes which always interest people. Are these really the central concerns of life? The fact that people are attracted to particular forms of excitement or stimulation is itself a source for discussion. But there are other types of theme as well, concerning subjects for stories, like using talking animals. Can pupils remember different types of story from their childhood? What did they all mean? What made some of them so memorable? Reading, and hearing stories, is not just an extra to the human experience but part of it. Its importance needs recognition. Recalling the effect of stories on early childhood or revisiting some of the books long stored away, is a reminder of this fact.

Making comparisons between passages within texts, whatever the basis, serves to remind readers of the text itself, the way it is put together. It is only really possible to gain a full appreciation of the pleasures of reading if the style, as well as the theme, is conveyed as an integral part, if the words are chosen carefully enough to enable the reader to appreciate this when made aware of it. One could say that good style does not draw attention to itself, but it should also stand up to scrutiny. The analysis of texts which are shown to have clear limitations reveals both levels of taste and a developing awareness of more demanding material and more solid satisfaction. The road from the habit of the ephemeral to the more challenging is never easy but it is one that emerges from the application of intelligence to the act of reading, whatever that reading might be. As an example there are two types of newspapers. For those who read tabloids the broadsheets seem very demanding. But once people read broadsheets the tabloids are no longer readable. They become absurd, a curiosity, a quarry of vulgarity rather than pleasure.

Close encounters with texts help demonstrate their techniques and their limitations. Without using the word 'style' or the word 'criticism' there are all kinds of ways in which passages can easily be analysed. How many clichés are there to a page, and what is a cliché? To what extent do some books rely upon them? Is that the easiest way to communicate to people: 'know what I mean?' Are there certain phrases that are used on several occasions, or certain words which become favourites? When reading their novels can pupils count those words which are repeated most often, like Enid Blyton's 'exciting'? What are the adjectives used in a page of text? Are they the most obvious or are they unusual? Are they apt, when you think about them?

For an easy analysis of the way that a passage is written it is useful to use 'close procedure', when certain words are blanked out and need to be filled in. These could be adverbs or adjectives, any word about which there needs to be a conscious choice, given the rest, and about which there could be alternatives. In this close procedure there are no 'right or wrong' answers but a comparison between an intelligent reading and the original. Can pupils improve on the original, come up with words far more apt? To what extent can they guess what the author would have written? The pupils can both analyse the adjectives the author uses and guess what they would subsequently be. After all the books that are most popular are written very fast. Style might be the result of great thought and craft, but it can also be the result of hurry. Can the readers detect the difference?

Close procedure is usually confined to single words. But every phrase, and every conversation is in context. Given all the passion surrounding an exchange what can the readers detect if a dialogue is blanked out? Can they work out from the description what might have been said, or what is likely to have been said? Are the new inventions actually any worse than the originals? Are they indeed a plausible alternative that would convincingly carry the plot in a new and more exciting, less predictable direction? The study of particular aspects of text, not in the spirit of direct criticism or exegesis, but in the curiosity of exploration, reveals the distinction between the obvious and the unusual; between style as meaning and style as cliché. Pupils can be made aware of the uses of cliché, the verbal 'ticks' that sustain everyday dialogue – 'let's face it' – and the invocation of the most immediate phrase in the texture or prose.

All books are full of action whether they take place in the mind or in the adventure of war and exploration. Things happen and have significance in a way that is far more obvious in reading than in the diurnal struggle of real life. Of course the latter is more dramatic when one thinks about it; but it is so immediate that we rarely do. Books offer insights that connect with the lives of other people and with our own. We are not always aware of this, but need to be. But the connections that can be made with a true reading of literature are very different. Popular literature reflects taste and gratifies it. Books which attempt to explore might not make such an easy connection, but offer something more. Some actions reflect on real decisions. Others are an escape from them. Enabling readers to look at what they are reading leads to far deeper exploration of what action, and decisions, mean. The understanding of text, like the comparison of a page of Judy Blume or Jane Austen, the application of close procedures to both, reveal the possibilities as well as the limitations of reading. It opens up the potential of people as opposed to their gratifications and gives readers the chance to relish the challenging and the unexpected that they will never forget.

It is impossible to know what strikes the individual reader as significant in the text in terms of personal understanding. Associations are varied. But it is clear that those books which to some extent challenge, which present their own point of view rather than seek that of their readers, or the lowest common denominator, have at least the potential to make a difference to the growth of understanding in readers. This implies a level of consciousness, of awareness of what is being written on the page, and how it is being written. This awareness deserves to be heightened. Readers should not have to put up with the obvious or the bland. Enabling them to detect the obvious, like the familiar similes 'cold as ice' 'black as thunder', both helps them to recognize the techniques used and the awareness of language which is necessary in sensitive reading and, indeed, the knowledge of the structures of language.

There are many ways to look at a text which makes the activity interesting and the understanding deeper. If different passages are compared, what can one say about the intended audience? For what kind of response is it directed? If one takes a familiar folk take, can one re-write it? There are many parodies of familiar stories in existence, like 'politically correct bed-time stories',[18] – that could help pupils understand their alternative interpretations. Could they write their own with different characters or endings, different interventions and different settings? There are, after all, so many different things one can *do* with texts.

We are aiming at creating educated readers who love books and who are aware of technique, the combination of which evolves into learning by reading. We are trying to make them aware of how books are written without being put off by this knowledge. At one level or another they are clearly aware of technique. The blurb, the introductory page and the opening of the story are all clearly designed to draw them in and they cannot be unaware of this. They might be so absorbed in the designs that the author has on them that they do not pause to consider how it is done, but they still react, consciously if spontaneously, to the signals and messages given out.

Readers sometimes forget how much they actually bring to the text. They will read a page and have a clear visual account of it in their heads; with blurred edges, and fuzzy concepts, but a picture nevertheless. If you ask pupils to write down how they visualize the text, including the positioning of left and right, it will make clear how different are the perspectives. 'She entered the small terraced house and went immediately up the stairs to the landing.' Does the staircase have a wall to the right and a hand-rail to the left or the other way round? Whatever the Proustian detail of the description each reader will have a distinct and unique impression. Novels have a readership of which every one is different. Interpretations vary. Styles of reading differ. This can also be brought out by putting pupils into the position of critics, not by asking for another review but by designing a page of a newspaper in which reviews are an integral part – together with the advertisements and the editorial. Around the writing and reading of books lies a whole world of secondary activity, production and publishing, distribution and marketing, and pupils also need to be aware of this, and how the whole process works. Readers are, after all, as affected by the secondary processes of promotion and selling, by the choice of publishers as to which authors to favour, as they are by the originality or the erudition of the text itself.

We have mentioned the uses of advertising and the blurbs. There are all kinds of oblique angles into understanding books themselves and the ways in which they are marketed. Parody, or the readers' own version of what takes place, can extend to a number of aspects. The contents of a real book, however lightweight and ephemeral, are, in terms of time, hard or demanding to emulate. But the way they are described, or illustrated on the cover as well as the sample page, are a feasible undertaking, and connect to the original in a way that demands some kind of insight. Popular literature depends not only on judging and meeting the taste of the audience, rather than, as Coleridge suggested, 'creating' it, but on marketing and publicity.

This suggests that there is more attention paid to plot and excitement than to any subtle delineations of character. To most readers this does not matter but they should nevertheless be aware of it. Suppose the hero of one book were transposed into the circumstances of another. Are there enough clues to be able to tell how he or she would behave? Or suppose that the relationships presented in a book were changed; would the characters still be defined as individual people rather than mechanical parts of the plot? The intention is to teach the readers to discriminate, not by undergoing long exercises but by taking new, fresh or oblique looks at material with which they are familiar. All books contain not only heroes but 'baddies'. But what makes them bad, apart from the need for the plot? Are there any psychological descriptions? Or are they merely depicted as wicked or foreign or ugly? All children develop a theory of mind and a moral understanding very young, and this includes their own theories of psychology within social environments. Can they apply this to the characters in the books, or is there simply not enough there to grasp? In which case we hope they move on to books which are more interesting.

Demanding books have a vibrant relationship to the inner life of the reader. However varied the readers' response there will be images and associations that connect with personal experience. Popular books tend to be more disconnected, creating a patchwork of effects and a pattern of dialogue. Pupils can be encouraged to discriminate through comparisons. They can also look in detail at particular events or scenes to seek out those that seem to them the most realistic or the closest to their own experiences. They can make connections with events that have happened to them. On the other hand the books they consider might turn out to be so unrealistic or undelineated that it is impossible to tell. Again, it is interesting to compare visualization of particular scenes and characters. What do they look like? Are they described in any detail?

Another way of visualizing a scene in a book is to translate it into a scene in a play or a film. A screenplay could be produced of an act within the confines of a stage. This would mean having to create dramatic effects, of concentrating on particularly significant moments. How would a film script convey pace and interest? What kind of camera angles would be deployed? The emphasis is on a task that demonstrates analysis of the text, and perhaps shows up its limitations. But the outcomes should also reveal an understanding of dramatic technique and the ways in which films are planned. Translating from one genre to another is another form of comparison. It is also possible to turn stories into other forms of writing, like a newspaper report. What kinds of style would then be employed? What would be the most significant or the most dramatic events? What kind of editorial interpretation would be given? Would one pupil's report be very different from another's, just as they vary from newspaper to newspaper?

All these suggestions depend upon respecting the pupils' abilities and enabling them to develop their critical thinking. They must be free to have and argue for opinions of their own, to engage in sensible dialogue with each other. The aim is to 'unfreeze' the curriculum, to disengage it from the tyranny of fact and assessment. Pupils should be expected to behave as critical readers, engaging in real activities of the kind that are stimulating, attractive and sensible. Through this kind of analysis of text they will also become much more aware of points of grammar, style and structure that more traditional exercises aim for but fail to deliver. One ground rule is to try to take all the pupils *beyond* the stage they are supposed to be at, so that, as in all our experiences of learning, one finds out that what we found difficult looks in retrospect simple.

Our aim as educators is to develop not just the critical skills involved in reading but to foster reading for pleasure, ultimately of those books which engage the reader's attention in understanding human behaviour, and the development of discrimination. In order to achieve this we do not feel it helps the pupils to be prevented from reading what they prefer, any more than it helps them to read from hated texts around the class. To reiterate the salient fact, it is not so important at first *what* they read but *how* they read it. Once they are able to understand the way that popular literature works they will seek out more interesting challenges.

Notes

1 Cullingford, C. and Morrison, J. Who excludes whom? The personal experience of exclusion, in Blyth, E. and Milner, J. (eds), *Exclusion from School.* London: Routledge, 1996.
2 Book Marketing Council Survey. *Children's Choices,* 1985.
3 Ibid.
4 Cf. Nelson, K. Structure and strategy in learning to talk. *Child Development Monographs.* Vol.36, No.1. Serial No.149, 1973, and the distinction between the referential and the expressive.
5 Southgate, V., Arnold, H. and Johnson, S. *Extending Beginning Reading.* London: Heinemann, 1981.
6 Lewis, R. and Teale, W. Primary school student's attitudes towards reading. *Journal of Research in Reading.* Vol.5, No.2, 1982, pp.113–22.
7 Bibby, B. Teachers and their books. *English in Education.* Vol.17, No.2, 1983.
8 Poole, R. Teaching fiction in the classroom: What teachers do. *Research in Education.* No.37, 1987, pp.61–98.

9 Hall, N. The status of 'reading' in reading schemes. *Education 3–13*. Vol.11, No.2, 1983, pp.27–32.
10 Gorman, T., White, J., Orchard, L. and Tate, A. *Language Performance in Schools*. London: HMSO, 1981.
11 Altick, R. *The English Common Reader*. Chicago: University of Chicago Press, 1957.
12 Egan, K. *Teaching as Story Telling*. London: Routledge, 1988.
13 Cullingford, C. *The Effective Teacher*. London: Cassell, 1995.
14 Gorman *et al.* Op. cit.
15 Cf. the advice of W. H. Auden, to imitate other people's styles before becoming original.
16 Miller, G. *Spontaneous Apprentices: Children and Language*. New York: Seabury Press, 1977.
17 This technique has been very successfully used by Jan Mark.
18 Which, as the preface makes clear, could not be called 'Fairy Stories'.

12

Conclusion

Popular literature might seem to deal with simplicities but the reader's response to it is nevertheless complicated. Each text and each reader is sufficiently different for it to be impossible to summarize the nature of the relationship in a few sentences. There is, nevertheless, within the act of reading some essential matters, such as the taste for gratification, and the aim of the author is to provide this. Just as there are favourite authors and favourite texts so there are reasons for this. We gain an insight into one part of the human experience in the kinds of pleasure the majority gain from the experience of reading.

Between text and reader there are many ambiguities. There are also some clear similarities in the popular texts. They share a simplicity of characters and pace, of dialogue and action rather than description and explanation. They also advertise as well as take relish in their own techniques, unselfconscious in their manipulation of the reader. Under the surface excitements they also offer a sense of constant safety. All will be well in the end.

For all the commonalities of approach there are also some marked contrasts as well as ambiguities. There are distinctions between the tone and attitude of books written until the 1960s and those written since. There are different juxtapositions between technique and content. There are clashes between the devices used to make the text interesting and the hidden or overt messages. And there is a curious tension between the inner world of children and the emptiness of the text. Perhaps the best way to illustrate some of these ambiguities and differences is to concentrate on one single theme, but a theme that nevertheless pervades both children's literature and popular adult fiction: food.

In Enid Blyton, and in series like the *Baby-Sitters Club*, food symbolizes the contact point with adults. It is around the dinner table that they meet, and when adult behaviour is closely observed. At these occasions the food is often submitted to, either because the children are in a hurry to go away, or because they do not think much of it: 'only spaghetti and ice-cream'. The food is not as important as the glimpses of adult behaviour – behaviour which provokes the children to kick each other under the table or to speculate about what motivation an adult has in providing a particular dish. Meal times create a framework within which the children construct their lives; they are the reminder of the surrounding adult world, the points of contact. The adult presence is then accepted and observed and the boundaries that adults set up, like having to be there to eat, accepted before the children escape.

In Enid Blyton food is a reward as well as a point of contact. It is also relished. Food is never mentioned with any hint of disgust. On the contrary, picnics or midnight feasts full of those items most popular with children, are lovingly re-created in lists. Food is, after all, one of the most gratifying pleasures for children. They have very clear tastes and know exactly what they enjoy and what are treats. But Enid Blyton's relish contrasts with the approach to food in more modern books. When food is described in the latter it is usually disgusting:

> The Friday lunch at Stoneybrook Middle School is always the same: mince, cold lumpy mashed potatoes, a dinky cup of coleslaw, milk and an ice cream.
> I truly hate it, except for the ice cream.[1]

> How they could eat with boys was beyond me. The boys are always doing awful things like mashing up peas and ravioli in their milk cartons to see what colours they can make.[2]

It is as if the modern relish about food was an attempt to shock or make people queasy.

Some might suggest that these contrasting views of food reflect their times, from one of shortage to one of plenty. At a time of abundance food is no longer valued. But if we study the perceptions of children toward food we see that the shift of attitude and approach goes deeper than this.[3] It is like the shift in moral outlook from stated virtuousness, however chauvinistic, to political correctness within accepted selfish behaviour. It is like the shift from a respect for the examples set by adults to a perception of adults as strange and moody, as utterly self-absorbed. Food is but another sign of a change of tone.

Children know a great deal about food and have a great interest in it. Their range of knowledge is wide and includes awareness of international issues. They have experience of Chinese and Indian food, Italian and American. This availability of cuisines is certainly a new development. But children's awareness of food is usually expressed in terms of bewilderment at other people's tastes. Recognizing the wide range of eating habits tends to confirm them in their own. There is a tendency not to try strange foods but to look on it with distaste.

> 'I know they eat snails which is absolutely disgusting.' *(girl 7)*

Just as certain vegetables, like brussel sprouts, are regarded as uneatable, so are other people's eating habits viewed as beyond the pale. Knowledge of what happens in other traditions appears to strengthen the belief in their own. As one said, describing a holiday in Spain.

> I don't know because we never ate any of their food. We took our own.' *(girl 9)*

The knowledge that children acquire, about food as about everything else that is common or unusual in human behaviour, is almost limitless because of modern mass media. Given what is seen on the news, even if taken in only peripherally, it is no surprise that modern children's literature reflects both an opening up of knowledge, with no holds barred, and a laconic style. Anything goes. Some food is good, and lots of it dreadful. Which does one relish more, the pleasure of taste or the joy of drawing attention to the disgusting? Many books encourage the exploration of things other than the safe and solid middle grounds.

> I guessed I kissed her okay because later on she pushed me for Seven in Heaven. [ie snogging in a cupboard.]

> The teenagers were making out on an escalator. His mouth covered nearly her whole face. Anymore and she might've been swallowed. She pulled her face out of his mouth ... and blew a bubble. Unbelievable. She could chew gum at the same time.[4]

Chewing on bubble gum does not make an appearance in Enid Blyton. But nor does sex. Books such as this are produced for 11–13-year-olds, and are written under the assumption that any gratification of taste is fine, provided you take precautions. Chewing gum is a food, and a habit. But it is symbolic of food as indulgence rather than necessity. It is the taste itself that matters, the discrimination between things that give pleasure and those that don't.

There are two ways of pleasing children: giving them the food they want, as Enid Blyton tries to do, and joining with them in the pleasure of finding certain foods disgusting. Roald Dahl is also obsessed with food. Up to a point he recognized the importance of food:

> [In cold weather] most of us find ourselves beginning to crave rich steaming stews and hot apple pie.[5]

But for the most part he enjoys attacking the nasty habits of those who like the character in *Charlie and the Chocolate Factory* chews gum. There are some terrible habits that Dahl relishes writing about. He describes the Twits in all their venomous detail. He positively relishes worms in spaghetti, entrails caught in beards, and other disgusting imaginings. Nor are these purely imaginary. In his autobiography he connects dead mice, gobstoppers and canings, floggings and chocolates. But the motivation is to unbar that sense of disgust and enjoy it. He explores how far down the road of exaggeration he can go.

Roald Dahl captures a modern pleasure in relishing what is bad. The world seems to be turned upside down. In this he is like all the romantic and horror fiction that is now so popular. The implication is that the upstanding hero can only be a hypocrite, as if only now can one write about real feelings as experienced by children. But Roald Dahl also goes one step further. Earlier books describe what children eat. Roald Dahl describes all the creatures that eat children. In this he touches that exciting, mythical world of fairy story in which people *like* to be frightened, up to a point, frightened for pleasure, for fear of reality. Eating is both a motif and a device. James's parents, he of the constantly edible Giant Peach,[6] are famously devoured by a rhinoceros.

> *Their* troubles were all over in a jiffy. They were dead and gone in thirty-five seconds flat.

That might be them disposed of, but the real food is children. The relish Dahl has in direct communication with the reader, as if she or he were very young, in bed, and fascinated with the telling, reveals itself in books like the *Witches* and the *Enormous Crocodile*:

> A REAL WITCH gets the same pleasure from squelching a child as you get from eating a plateful of strawberries and cream.

The effect is a mix of 'careful, I'm going to get you' and the appeal of strawberries and cream. For the more he goes on, the more he takes pleasure in the exaggeration of effect, the less serious it becomes. When popular novelists talk about 'disgusting' food, especially in school, they know they are making an obvious appeal to the readers. They are desperately trying to be on their side. Enid Blyton innocently shares her thoughts with the readers. Ann Martin deliberately appeals to what she assumes are their interests. Roald Dahl relishes the sense of his own disgust. For the first few pages of *The Enormous Crocodile* he goes on and on about how children are 'juicy and yummy, luscious and muschious'.

> The sort of things that I'm going to eat
> have fingers, toe nails, arms and legs and feet.

And the more he goes on, the more secure is the reader's sense that it's just a story.

The theme of food is a proper symbol for the different uses and gratifications made of children's literature. It is something shared – both as a straight pleasure and as a point of view. We enter into the relishing of sensuous pleasure in the imagination or the excitement of intellectual distaste. There are different ways to appeal to children, and all rest on certain common assumptions: that we know what their generalized tastes are, that we do not dwell too much on the complex difficulties of childhood, whilst instinctively recognizing that they are there, and that there are deep reasons both for readers seeking out the easiest, most gratifying of books, and their underlying search for something better.

The intelligence of children is very powerful and observes and absorbs constantly. The capacity to understand much more than they reveal is rarely acknowledged, any more than their ability to analyse and explain is accepted. Popular literature is an important part of their lives: either temporarily or permanently. It connects with their lives and we must recognize this. The most important thing we can do is accept its existence and to hope to make its pleasure temporary. We do this by both believing in children's capacity and making them aware of it.

Notes

1 Martin, Ann A. *Baby-Sitters Club. Kirsty's Big Idea.* New York: Scholastic, 1986, pp.39–40.
2 Ibid.
3 Cullingford, C. Children's attitudes to food. *Primary Life.* Vol. 3, No. 2, 1994, pp.10–14.

4 Vail, R. *Point Romance. Do Over.* London: Heinemann, 1993.
5 Dahl, R. *Charlie and the Chocolate Factory.* London: George Allen and Unwin, 1964.
6 Dahl, R. *James and the Giant Peach.* London: George Allen and Unwin, 1967.

Index